Tough Girls

Feminist Cultural Studies, the Media, and Political Culture

Series Editors
Mary Ellen Brown
Andrea Press

A complete list of books in the series is available from the publisher.

Tough Girls

Women Warriors and Wonder Women in Popular Culture

Sherrie A. Inness

PENN

University of Pennsylvania Press

Philadelphia

Printed in the United States of America on acid-free paper

10 9 8 7 6 5 4 3 2 1

Published by
University of Pennsylvania Press
Philadelphia, Pennsylvania 19104–4011

Library of Congress Cataloging-in-Publication Data
Inness, Sherrie A.
Tough girls : women warriors and wonder women in popular culture / Sherrie A. Inness.
p. cm. — (Feminist cultural studies, the media, and political culture)
Includes bibliographical references and index.
ISBN 0-8122-3466-9 (cloth : alk. paper). — ISBN 0-8122-1673-3 (pbk. : alk. paper)
1. Women in mass media. 2. Toughness (Personality trait) 3. Femininity (Psychology)
I. Title. II. Series.
P94.5.W65I56 1998
302.23′082—dc21 98-20218
CIP

To my friends Faye Parker Flavin, Alice Adams,
Kate Johnson, Michele Lloyd, Amy Mason,
Gillian O'Driscoll, and Wendy W. Walters

Contents

Introduction

Tough is a word with many nuances. What does it make you think of: Sylvester Stallone as Rocky Balboa? In film after film, he managed to slug his way to the top. If Rocky does not come to mind, maybe you picture Arnold Schwarzenegger in one of his many action films, especially as the unstoppable Terminator. Perhaps you think of the old Superman comic books in which Superman was as tough as steel, and Lois Lane was about as tough as a piece of wet tissue. Or maybe you recall Clint Eastwood's many films. As Dirty Harry, he always ended up saving half of San Francisco and blowing away the other half, rescuing a bevy of screaming women in the process. Rocky, the Terminator, Superman, and Dirty Harry all have something in common: they are tough guys. They are four members of a much larger universe of tough guys from the American cultural past and present, including both real and imaginary figures—Humphrey Bogart, James Dean, Batman, Ernest Hemingway, James Bond, John Wayne, the Six Million Dollar Man, Marlon Brando, Bruce Lee, Chuck Norris, and Rambo. For decades the tough guy has played a special role in the United States, embodying some of our most deeply ingrained beliefs about what it means to be a man. Given American society's fascination with the tough guy, it is hardly surprising that he has become a media staple. It is far more difficult, however, to find examples of tough women.

If you doubt that an overwhelming number of tough men appear in the popular media, stake your claim to a seat in front of the television set and watch the Saturday morning cartoons. You will be deluged with action-adventure cartoons that feature tough men—what critic Tom Engelhardt refers to as "superweapon-wielding specialists in aggression" (94). Even the titles of the shows—*G.I. Joe Extreme, Action Man, He-Man and the Masters of the Universe,* and *Teknoman*—exemplify the connection our culture makes between men and toughness. Most of the central male characters in these shows have a female sidekick, but it is always obvious that she is less important than the hero. Although she may get in an occasional karate chop, or blast a bad guy with her laser pistol, her male cohorts are at the center of the action and engage in all the heavy fighting. The sidekick also may tote a gun, but her primary mission is to parade around in a skimpy outfit (typically pink, pale yellow, or another pastel color), revealing her shapely form. Women are a minority in the Saturday morning cartoons, and those who do appear are sexualized and marginalized; viewing action-adventure cartoons, you would never deduce that women make up over half the world's population.

For another example of the overwhelming presence of tough men in popular culture, visit a toy store, as I did, and stroll down the aisle devoted to action figures. You will discover a strange world that appears to be inhabited entirely by six-inch-tall bare-chested guys on steroids. My trip to the toy store seemed to confirm feminist theorist Susan Willis's belief that "in today's toy market there is a much greater sexual division of toys defined by very particular gender traits than has ever existed before" (24). I first encountered Tarzan: Lord of the Jungle and G.I. Joe, before being overwhelmed by a veritable army of Batman figures: Jungle Tracker Batman, Hydro-Charge Batman, Viking Batman, Desert Knight Batman, Samurai Batman, Manta Ray Batman, Deluxe Attack Wing Batman, and Blast Cape Batman. Robin was not far away—a considerably more butch Robin than the star of the television series that aired in my childhood. Since then, he has been transformed into Street Biker Robin, who rides his Robin Cycle with Ripcord Racing Power—an urban version of the Road Warrior.

Very often male characters such as Batman, Superman, Spiderman, and G.I. Joe have the prestige of being the "star" characters of a complete miniature universe. Although female characters do crop up fairly frequently in groups of superheroes or supervillains, the female group members are always vastly outnumbered by their male counterparts. The only lone female action figure I discovered was Spider Woman with "psionic web hurling action," but she was outnumbered by a whole host of Spider Man figures. Among groups of action figures, Ultraforce had seven men and one woman, and Exosquad Jumptroop had three men and one woman. Only Spiral with "arm-spinning action" from the X-Men is female; the other X-Men characters, including Avalanche, Gladiator, Black Tom, Corsair, Gambit, and Magneto, are male. The Fantastic Four had seven action figures, all male except for Invisible Woman, who indeed proved to be invisible at the toy store, because she was not on the shelves. In fact, none of the female action figures were available. G.I. Joe's Ninja Force had seven figures, all male except for one female, Scarlett, who was not on display. Similarly, the Mortal Kombat team of eight action figures had one female figure, Sonya Blade—also missing. The fifteen figures who composed the Gargoyles included one female, Demona, who was also nowhere to be found—not a big surprise.

Because tough women were in the minority in the action figures aisle, I thought I might have more luck finding them in the two aisles crammed with girls' dolls and other toys. I recognized that I was entering an entirely different world when the color scheme of the aisle's contents changed. I went from a land of khaki, black, and other somber shades to a predominantly pink universe, sprinkled with pastel lavenders and blues. Already, I felt dubious about my prospects of encountering any tough women. I doubted that Ripley from *Aliens* would be caught dead in this pink powder-puff world. My suspicions were confirmed as I ventured further down an aisle that was primarily inhabited by dolls of all descriptions. I encountered Bride Surprise, Makeup Beauty, Katie Kiss 'n' Giggles, Twist 'n Style Tiffany, Pretty Sparkle Dancer, Baby Wiggles 'n Giggles, Baby Go Bye Bye, My Newborn Nancy, Princess Wishing Star, and the Magic Nursery Fuss 'n Giggle Triplets. None of these dolls would stand a chance in the world of Jungle Tracker Batman or Street Biker Robin. Bride Surprise, Makeup Beauty, Pretty Sparkle Dancer, and their friends would never consider giving a man a swift karate chop because they would be preoccupied with babies, fashion, and their future as brides—apparently the three chief concerns in the lives of girls' dolls.

As I continued down the aisles, I recognized that my search for a tough girl or woman might prove futile. The Barbie section offered little hope. Although a full aisle was devoted to Barbie, her pals, and enough booty to fill a dozen Malibu beach houses, tough Barbies were nonexistent. I found Sunflower Barbie, Sparkle Beach Barbie, Twirling Ballerina Barbie, and Songbird Barbie, but there was no Rambo Barbie or G.I. Barbie. The closest I could come to a tough Barbie was Dr. Barbie, but, with her stiletto heels and pink stethoscope, I was skeptical that Dr. Barbie fit anyone's criteria for toughness. Imani the African American Princess, in her pink tights and low-cut aerobics outfit, was no tougher than Barbie, and I had no better luck finding tough women when I moved on to the section reserved for a whole squadron of Tiny Sky Dancers, with names like Misty Moon, Tinybelle, Crystal Shell, Daystar, Star Dazzle, Cotton Cloud, Rose Blossom, and Star Shimmer. These Tiny Sky Dancers were even less tough than Barbie and her buddies. I realized that the one place in the toy store to find tough characters was in the boys' aisle, where G.I. Joe and his pals hung out.[1]

Hollywood is doing better, but not by much. Head for the nearest video store, as I recently did, and scan the shelves of movies under the section labeled "adventure."[2] This section of my local Blockbuster Video store was chock-full of little plastic boxes from which a crowd of men glared at me:[3] Charles Bronson (*Cold Sweat* and *Death Wish: The Face of Death*), Sean Connery (*From Russia with Love* and *Goldfinger*), Clint Eastwood (*Dirty Harry, Sudden Impact, The Enforcer, Heartbreak Ridge, In the Line of Fire, Magnum Force,* and *Pale Rider*), Mel Gibson (*Lethal Weapon*), Bruce Lee (*Return of the Dragon*), Arnold Schwarzenegger (*Terminator, Commando, Conan the Barbarian,* and *Conan the Destroyer*), Sylvester Stallone (*Rocky, Rambo III, Cliffhanger,* and *Demolition Man*), Jean-Claude Van Damme (*Hard Target*), John Wayne (*Hellfighters*), and many others.[4] In the adventure section women were conspicuously absent from most of the video cartridge boxes, although they were sometimes pictured as curvaceous bimbos clinging to male heroes, or as fearful victims who needed rescuing by men. Tough women appeared to be almost nonexistent.

This apparent lack of tough women (a term I use interchangeably with "tough girls") in the popular media is one reason I became interested in researching their depiction; I wondered whether they were as rare as the aisles of the local toy store or the shelves of the video store led me to believe. I discovered more tough women out there than I had imagined, but I found that their representation, for the most part, was lacking in one way or another. Tough women are still commonly portrayed as less strong and less effectual than tough men. I do not wish to suggest that it would be a positive step for woman to display the same kind of toughness that men do in the Saturday morning cartoons or action-adventure movies, but I believe the relative absence of tough women shapes how women construct themselves as gendered subjects. Whether in films, books, television cartoon shows, advertisements, or toys, the paucity of tough women and how the few tough women who do appear are represented makes a difference—a big one.

How tough women are depicted in the media has become an important issue in recent years because they are being depicted more frequently than in past decades. Whether it is Xena giving one of her deadly high-flying kicks, Elektra quickly dispatching a gang of Ninja warriors, Dana Scully handling a gun just as effectively as her male partner, or Captain Janeway piloting the starship *Voyager,* tough women are becoming more prevalent. Even the *Los Angeles Times* has noted this phenomenon and commented on the growing prevalence of "tough-gal films" in 1990s Hollywood (Jordan D1).[5] Similarly, an article from *USA Today* mentions the growing numbers of women in the male-dominated realm of action/adventure films (Thomas D1). A critic for the *Los Angeles Times* discusses the "stampede of movies placing women in traditional tough-guy roles" (Jordan D1), including *Thelma & Louise, Bad Girls, The Quick and the Dead, The River Wild,* and numerous others. Film theorist Patricia Mellencamp describes the change in Hollywood: "The heterosexual dream girl is shaping up—building muscles and getting physical. When male directors wanted to represent strong women in Hollywood films in the late 1980s and 1990s, they looked to working-class or tough women and gave them a gun, a drink, a swagger, a limited vocabulary, and savvy but unschooled minds" (*Fine* 115). There are also more tough women on television, in books, and in advertisements than ever before. Police shows today would look hopelessly behind the times if they did not include at least one woman who was as tough as her male comrades. At the bookstore, it is relatively easy to find detective novels that feature tough women. And it is difficult to flip through *Vanity Fair, Vogue, Glamour, Cosmopolitan,* or other similar fashion magazines without encountering at least one picture of a "tough" girl, usually clad in leather and staring coolly at her audience. Yet the popular media are still deeply ambivalent about how to depict tough women so that they do not challenge gender conventions too dramatically.[6]

This book examines the increasing prevalence of tough girls in the popular media over the past three decades. The tough girl plays numerous roles. Her tougher and more masculine image suggests that a greater variety of gender roles are open to women; at the same time, however, her toughness is often mitigated by her femininity, which American culture commonly associates with weakness. The tough girl's paradoxical role is typical of the contradictions inherent in popular culture; as Tania Modleski writes, "Mass art not only contains contradictions, it also *functions* in a highly contradictory manner: while appearing to be merely escapist, such art simultaneously challenges and reaffirms traditional values, behavior, and attitudes" (112). Tough women can offer women new role models, but their toughness may also bind women more tightly to traditional feminine roles—especially when the tough woman is portrayed as a pretender to male power and authority, and someone who is not tough enough to escape being punished by society for her gender-bending behavior. We shall find that when the media *do* depict tough women, it is often to show that they are exceptions to the rule that women are not tough. However, the media are changing as gender roles change and society changes; thus, as this book suggests, there are new roles in the media for tough girls, particularly in recent years.

Another reason the tough girl deserves attention is that the depiction of tough women in contemporary American society has been analyzed far less than the representation of tough men.[7] Numerous books and articles over the past thirty years have focused almost exclusively on men, with merely a few passing comments about women.[8] As we can deduce from the title of his essay "The Tough Guy Intellectual" (1966), Peter Shaw discusses only men. Similarly, David Madden's study *Tough Guy Writers of the Thirties* (1968) focuses solely on male authors writing about tough men. Harry Hossent in *Gangster Movies: Gangsters, Hoodlums and*

Tough Guys of the Screen (1974) gives fleeting attention to women, as does Joan Mellen in *Big Bad Wolves: Masculinity in the American Film* (1977). In *Tough Guy: The American Movie Macho* (1989), James L. Neibaur discusses only tough men in films. In *What a Man's Gotta Do* (1990), Antony Easthope provides a broader discussion of how men have been represented as tough and masculine in popular culture, but he gives no consideration to women. In a slightly later work, *Hard Bodies: Hollywood Masculinity in the Reagan Era* (1994), Susan Jeffords writes almost entirely about tough men in films. Yvonne Tasker does discuss women action heroes in *Spectacular Bodies: Gender, Genre and the Action Cinema* (1993) — one of the more extensive discussions of tough women available — but men still have a dominant role in her book.[9] The large number of studies that focus on tough guys, giving little or no attention to women, is one sign that American society stereotypes men as tough and in control and women as soft and ineffectual. For much of the twentieth century, the tough male hero has been a staple in films and books, but the tough woman has been far less common because she challenges societal assumptions about innate differences between men and women in regard to toughness. John Wayne is supposed to go riding out on the range and capture the bad guys; his girl is supposed to wait at home, minding ma and pa, until her man returns.

But in the past few decades, as real women, influenced by ideas of feminism, step into ever tougher roles, the media also change. No longer is the little lady content to stay at home and knit socks; now, she is apt to carry a submachine gun and be trained in the martial arts.

Tough girls are in with a vengeance, and they have proven to be quite a lucrative commodity as the latest media sensation. Tough girls are one example of the tendency of media moguls to push the limits of what is acceptable to represent, especially if they think that pushing the limits might help, and not hurt, profits.[10] As we see more intensity and violence in the media, we become desensitized; consequently, media producers have to keep coming up with new, more thrilling and more shocking images. Earlier, we were shocked by killer children; now it is tough women. The appearance of the tough girl is in many ways a response to market forces, but it is essential not to oversimplify her by thinking she is *only* the result of market trends. The tough girl also represents a culture in which real women are re-evaluating what it means to be tough.

One reason it is crucial to study the representation of tough women is the tremendous influence popular culture has upon American society. With the postmodern blurring of boundaries between high and low culture, greater numbers of scholars have recognized the importance of studying popular culture in order to better comprehend our society.[11] Popular sources are invaluable when exploring the changing image of women in our society.[12] Popular culture does not simply reflect women's lives; it helps to create them and so demands critical scrutiny. Throughout my academic career, I have been interested in mapping the many ways that popular culture—including comic books, popular school novels, girls' series books, television shows, films, and a host of other forms—helps to shape and change how our culture views women.[13] This book continues my research into the roles the popular media create for women.

I rely on numerous sources, including comic books, films, books, and television shows, in order to explore the role of women's toughness in popular culture.[14] I have tried to cover different genres as thoroughly as possible in one book, recognizing that I am leaving out far more than I am including. Although this approach makes it impossible to study any particular genre, such as television, in as much depth as I would wish, the mixed genre approach I adopt enables me to show the pervasive nature of the tough girl in the popular media in general, not only in an isolated medium.[15]

Studying toughness is particularly important because, as Rupert Wilkinson observes, everyone in the United States (and much of the world) must address the American fascination with toughness (5). Additionally, toughness has been used to control women throughout America's history, especially in the twentieth century. Wilkinson points out that "by using femininity as a defining opposite, the tough-guy tradition puts pressure on women to be wholesome, sweet, and ultimately submissive, whether as Victorian wives and mothers or as cute majorettes" (8). If one concurs with Wilkinson, as I do, toughness is a necessary topic of study because not only is it nearly impossible to escape, but it also exerts a powerful influence on how both men and women constitute their gendered identities. Traditionally, men have learned that they should be the stoic, brave heroes, capable of overcoming any obstacles that stand in their way. Women have learned that toughness has little to do with them; they should be the ones being rescued, not the ones doing the rescuing. The media have helped perpetuate such ideas; the media also can play an equally important role in tearing down such stereotypes by depicting men and women in nontraditional ways.

The growing number of tough girls in the media also suggests a great deal about the changing roles available to women in our society. Gradually, the tolerance for women adopting nontraditional roles is rising. Whether they are busting broncos at a rodeo, pounding a beat as a police officer, driving a long-haul truck, or engaging in some other pursuit that until now has been considered the province of men, women are pursuing professions and duties that in the past have been considered decidedly "unladylike." Because real women's roles are changing, it has become possible for the media to represent women's roles in new ways. But the media do not simply mirror social change; by showing nontraditional tough women, the media are helping to change how society conceptualizes what it means to be a woman. While expanding the horizons for women, the media conversely serve to limit them as well, suggesting new varieties of toughness that few real women can obtain. Not everyone can be a Ripley. We need to examine with greater care the depiction of the tough woman in the 1980s and 1990s, and explore why she is appearing with greater frequency and what her appearance suggests about changing gender roles in the media.

I am also interested in tough women in the media because of their strong allure to women viewers. Almost every woman dreams at one point or another about having the super powers or toughness of character that will make her invincible. Most of us have longed to be able to run sixty miles an hour like the Bionic Woman. Who has not wished to have the tough, no-nonsense air and the pumped-up pecs of Sarah Connor in the Terminator films? I have seen my most ardently pacifist women friends applaud as Ripley arms herself to do battle (*Alien*), Clarice Starling pursues and kills a serial murderer (*The Silence of the Lambs*), or Xena gives her battle cry right before demolishing an army of foes. One reason for our collective fascination with the Bionic Woman, Connor, Ripley, Starling, and other similar figures is that men traditionally have been the heroes. When we as women see and read about heroic women, we cheer. The tough woman hero is so scarce in American culture that we take notice of her and recognize that her portrayal suggests that women are not as excluded from the heroic as Western history has traditionally taught us. We are fascinated by the female hero (or anti-hero) because she presents a myth of invincibility. Like her male cohorts, the tough woman is portrayed as impossible or nearly impossible to defeat. No matter what perils might confront the Bionic Woman or Xena, we know she will survive. In a society where women are warned that they should not walk alone after dark and should never visit a deserted area by themselves, the tough women who appear in the media offer a reassuring fantasy. Xena would not be fearful of walking in a park after dusk. The Bionic Woman would not be nervous walking into even the seediest of biker bars. In a culture where women are often considered the "natural" victims of men, tough women rewrite the script. Time after time, they are shown defeating the men who attack them—an alluring fantasy in a society where women are too commonly raped, assaulted, and murdered. It is this very real fascination with the depiction of the tough woman that has led me to undertake this study, which explores the reasons for the appeal of the tough girl and examines whether her portrayal marks a change in how the media formulate gender roles or whether it actually has more socially conservative purposes than first appear to be the case.

I am not arguing that the tough girl, as she shoots, kick-boxes, and karate-chops the bad guys, should be a role model emulated by women and girls. Training a generation of girls to grow up as an army of Ninja warriors is not the only way to achieve social change. However, anyone interested in gender roles in the United States needs to reflect on the construction of the tough girl because she suggests a great deal about changing gender identities.

* * *

Despite the variety of sources studied in this work, any single book is not able to do full justice to a topic such as the representation of tough women, which pervades American society and societies around the globe. Omissions are bound to exist; for example, while I am well aware that the representation of the tough woman crops up in a variety of cultures (the many tough women portrayed in Japanese comics come to mind), such images do not have the identical cultural resonance that they have in the United States and deserve another complete study that would be able to examine them in sufficient depth.

Also this book does not explore how audience members (both male and female) perceive the tough women they see—obviously an important concern. Audience members might carry away very different messages from the ones suggested by the media images. Although it is beyond the scope of this volume, scholars in the future need to spend more time exploring the reception of tough women in the media and how such representations might be perceived in different fashions by different groups. Only with such work will we begin to understand how people both resist and accept the images of tough women that the media create.

The book also repeatedly addresses issues of race, ethnicity, class, and sexual orientation, but not as comprehensively as one could with a more limited focus. I have included Hispanic, African-American, and Asian tough women and women from working-class or poor backgrounds. I have also discussed how homosexuality is often attached to displays of toughness in women. Opportunities to explore these topics are limited, however, because tough women in the popular media typically are white, heterosexual, and middle class, reflecting a culture in which these are the norms.

Of course, the *absence* of women from varied backgrounds speaks as loudly as their presence. Alexander Doty's thoughts about queerness in the mainstream media help to explain the importance of such textual absences. He observes that queerness in a text often depends not on explicit displays of queerness, but on the reception of viewers or readers who discern it. Doty argues, "This does not mean the queerness one attributes to mass culture texts is any less real than the straightness others would claim for these same texts" (xi). Although he is discussing queers, Doty's words can also refer to any other group missing from the mainstream media. This book is only a beginning to the work that needs to be done to understand the silences and absences in how tough women are depicted today.

Finally, I cover only some of the many popular sources that include tough women. For instance, tough women are a staple of fantasy novels, where women can wield a sword as easily as a fork. Tough girls are starting to make a small but noticeable appearance in video games, and tough women in the military are a recurring motif in our society. Tough women in the music industry (Sinead O'Connor, k. d. lang, and others) deserve attention. Tough women in detective novels are also common. All of these topics, and many others, deserve a chapter (if not a book) of their own, but they are beyond the scope of this study. I do believe, however, that my thoughts about toughness in popular culture are applicable to many of the sources that I have not covered.

I hope that *Tough Girls* causes its readers to think more critically about how toughness is constituted in both the popular media and real life. We need to reflect on the many ways that toughness is used in politics, athletics, business, and the military (as well as other places) to maintain the gender status quo by suggesting the essential toughness of men and the essential lack of toughness of women. The ways we think of toughness and how it is portrayed in the media need to be considered because toughness and issues concerning toughness are a part of our daily lives and continually shape our ideas about appropriate gender roles for women and men.

Chapter 1
Beyond Muscles

What Does It Mean to Be Tough?

Without even pausing for reflection, we find it easy to identify many men as either tough or not tough. Reagan was; Bush was not (although he wanted to be).[1] Batman was; Robin was not. The Fonz was; Richie Cunningham was not. Oscar Madison was; Felix Unger was not. Although toughness is not always easy to spot, we have some common ideas about what toughness entails. Think about James Dean, the cool, aloof rebel. Actor Sean Connery as James Bond, Agent 007, was also cool and aloof, but he was far more polished and debonair than Dean. Consider the Six Million Dollar Man, tough enough to overcome any bad guys who confronted him and capable of running sixty miles an hour. Then remember Clint Eastwood in the Dirty Harry films. Wearing a sneer pasted permanently on his face and lugging a huge gun, he was the quintessential tough guy who would blow away armies of drug dealers, murderers, pimps, and rapists. All four of these men have similarities but notable differences, too, showing how difficult it is to come up with a narrow definition of what toughness entails.

When women are added to the picture, even more variations exist. In movie after movie, Ripley in the *Aliens* films is the only person tough enough to destroy the deadly creatures threatening humanity. With a rock-hard body, Martha Washington of comic-book fame is tough enough to endure the physical hardships of a soldier's life. In Sue Grafton's detective novels, Kinsey Milhone is a private detective who tackles cases that have been shunned by even the police. Although she is shot at, beaten up, and intimidated, she does not back down from a case before she solves it. Obviously, if we are to arrive at a definition of "tough" that allows for *all* these very different men and women, it will need to be malleable, flexible enough to define the broad range of characteristics and behaviors that are considered tough. This chapter examines the many nuances of toughness, exploring why toughness is associated primarily with men and why tough women still make mainstream society uneasy.

A Tough Definition

Being tough is not a matter of merely having a muscular physique, a fact brought home to me while I was watching the Miss Fitness America contest on television. The contestants, who appeared as if they spent the majority of their lives in the gym, were not as pumped up as Rambo, but they were extremely muscular, far more so than contestants for the Miss America pageant. If being tough were a matter of muscle alone, these women would be considered tough by anyone's standards. However, as I watched the contestants strut through their routines—which invariably included a few back flips, lots of flexing, and a number of contortionist activities that my body cringed at the thought of attempting—I recognized that I did not think of them as tough, because, despite their bulging muscles and buns of steel, they looked stereotypically feminine in all other respects. All had long hair, usually permed, and all were wearing skimpy outfits that barely covered bosom and bottom. All had broad smiles plastered on their faces throughout their gymnastic dance performances. No doubt these women were outstanding athletes, but they did not strike me as *tough* because of their apparent acceptance of dominant norms of femininity in a culture where toughness is perceived as the antithesis of femininity. A super-fit physique is a common attribute of toughness, but there is much more involved, including self-presentation, attire, setting, and attitude. All these attributes go into making someone "tough." Toughness, in many ways, is a performance of a certain demeanor and image, an act that might be more or less successful according to how many tough signifiers are adopted and how convincingly they are presented as "real."

"Toughness" becomes even trickier to define when one is considering women, who are more difficult to identify as tough than are men. Discussing this issue with friends, I began to recognize what little agreement existed about what constitutes the tough woman. Some people identified Katharine Hepburn as tough, others disagreed. Some categorized Jodie Foster as tough; others were just as adamant that she was no such thing. Iditarod champion Susan Butcher, Hillary Clinton, Jamie Lee Curtis, Jane Fonda, k. d. lang, Bette Midler, Sinead O'Connor, and even Barbara Bush were mentioned as being tough but not everyone agreed about any one of these women. Obviously, toughness is difficult to define.

In her essay "Compulsory Heterosexuality and Lesbian Existence," Adrienne Rich discusses a one-to-ten scale for lesbianism, on which women are ranked to define how strongly they identify and are identified by others with lesbianism. One can imagine a similar one-to-ten scale for rating women's toughness, with very tough women being rated a seven or nine and women who are less tough being accorded only a two or three. Thinking about toughness in such a fashion allows the flexibility necessary for acknowledging that toughness is not always constituted in the same manner or to the same degree in different individuals. Still, there are key aspects of toughness that are shared by many.

To gain a better understanding of what was apparently a slippery and elusive term, I turned to the *Oxford English Dictionary* (1989), which provided nearly two densely packed pages of definitions of "tough." Some of them were useful. One was "Capable of great physical endurance; strongly resisting force, injury, fatigue, etc.; not easily overcome, tired, or impaired; hardy, stout, sturdy" (302). Another definition read, "Having great intellectual or moral endurance; difficult to influence, affect, or impress; steadfast, firm, persistent; also stubborn, obstinate, hardened" (302). Both definitions point out some of the important features of being tough that I will discuss. Often, these women possess great powers of physical endurance, sometimes even superhuman powers, as is the case with the female heroes depicted in comic books. Tough women have the stamina to endure when physically weaker women might fail. As Rupert Wilkinson comments, "The tough guy can take it. He can cope with many kinds of stress. In physically demanding conditions his equipment includes willpower as well as muscle tone. Indeed, in some romantic versions, the will takes over from physique, driving a sick or exhausted body to the limits of endurance" (7). These words apply to the tough girl, too. She can endure tremendous physical and emotional suffering and still emerge the victor. She has the tight emotional and physical control that has been traditionally associated with men, not women.

The *OED* also offers negative connotations of tough, such as a "person given to rough or violent behaviour" (303) or a "person of uncompromising or aggressive views" (303). This darker side of toughness is constantly lurking, always ready to spring to the fore, and complicates our society's uneasy relationship with toughness. We idolize it in movie stars such as Bruce Lee or John Wayne. We respect it in military leaders, politicians, and athletes. We admire men and women who run ultramarathons or participate in such ultimately tough sports as the Ironman or the Iditarod. We find tough women (and men) sexy and "hot." But many people are also dismayed and disturbed by toughness and its implicit or explicit connection to violence. Rambo and the Terminator seem barbaric, their use of brute force unnecessary. Often individuals are uneasy about the excessive forms that toughness takes, whether in the media or real life. Toughness always carries the threat of chaos, the breakdown of "civilized" society into a dog-eat-dog world where only the tough can survive.

Whatever our reservations about toughness may be, we worship it because of its association with success and strength. As long as men are the primary people associated with toughness, they will continue to be the ones associated with success and power. This is why it is necessary to study how toughness is constituted in our culture and analyze what the changing representation of tough women in recent years suggests. As we shall discover, depicting women as not tough or as "pseudo-tough" is one of the ways that the media perpetuate the myth that women are less capable and competent than men. Even more insidious are the books, films, television shows, and magazines that depict women as tough, but simultaneously show that a woman's toughness is still not the equal of a man's.

Although the depiction of male toughness offers real social power to men, we also need to recognize the essentially mythical nature of toughness. The toughness we find in films, television shows, or books is frequently exaggerated. Whether we are watching Batman slug out two dozen bad guys or John Wayne shooting and defeating ten tribes of Indians, we are viewing a mythic enactment of toughness. No real person can perform the feats of Batman or John Wayne. No real person is a Rocky Balboa. Toughness is mythologized in the media, creating heroes with far greater abilities than those of mere mortals. Yet these mythic heroes help support the notion that only men are tough and heroic.

The connection between men and toughness assures that men, not women, will be the only "real" heroes in a culture where toughness is frequently associated with power and typically only men are allowed to display it. The ability of such heroes as Hercules, John Wayne, Rocky, and Rambo to endure great physical challenges suggests their tough and heroic character. Being able to overcome great hardships is one of the defining features of a hero. For example, in *On Deadly Ground* (1994), the movie's hero (played by Steven Seagal) confronts both hired mercenaries and the FBI but still manages to blow up a huge oil refinery by himself. In the movie *Bloodsport* (1987), the hero, played by Jean-Claude Van Damme, enters a contest in Hong Kong against the world's greatest fighters. He emerges as the winner, even after he has been temporarily blinded by the champion he fights. Their physical stamina and other tough characteristics make it possible for Seagal and Van Damme to rise to the level of heroes. We must remember, however, that the success of such characters is often dependent on their ability to subdue opponents of other races, demonstrating the superiority of white masculinity.[2] It is important to recognize that the creation of tough white heroes simultaneously implies the nonheroic qualities of men from other races. Similarly, the tough white female hero helps affirm the superiority of white women.

The kind of heroic toughness associated with the characters played by Seagal and Van Damme is ascribed more commonly to men than to women. It is also more typically associated with masculinity (whether in men or women) than femininity (in men or women). Femininity and masculinity are defined as opposites in our culture. Because they adopt some characteristics that are coded as masculine in our culture, tough women challenge this division, which is central to how members of society think about gender and the differences, whether real or imaginary, between men and women. The association of toughness, men, and masculinity is so much a part of our society's ideological framework that we accept it as the status quo. When we watch Clint Eastwood make his day by gunning down a particularly odious gangster or we see Mel Gibson overcome an army of evil desert mutants, we regard it as entirely "normal." Their masculinity and maleness make it "natural" for them to be adopting these tough roles. However, a group of people watching a feminine woman—say, Vanna White—gun down a drug dealer would likely become uneasy, or even angry, having assumed that masculinity is a necessary ingredient of toughness.

The relationship between gender, sex, and toughness is so complex that more time needs to be spent exploring how toughness is connected to both men and women and why toughness is typically linked to masculinity. This is an important concern because the connection between masculinity and toughness helps to support the stereotypical idea that men are the only truly capable leaders. As writer Bruce Curtis comments in his essay on the association between toughness and political leadership, "Concern about the toughness and masculinity of our leaders remain[s] at the center of American politics" (50). This is a concern that is central far beyond the realms of politics.

Tough Boys

As I have mentioned, society rarely questions the belief that toughness is primarily an attribute of men, causing the tough male to be an omnipresent image in our culture. Toughness is associated with a whole school of "tough guy" writers, including James M. Cain, Raymond Chandler, Dashiell Hammett, Ernest Hemingway, Jack London, and Norman Mailer. Tough men and boys fill literature, both popular and canonical.[3] For example Rudyard Kipling's *Captains Courageous: A Story of the Grand Banks* (1897) features Disko Troop, captain of the fishing boat *We're Here*. The epitome of the gruff seafaring captain, Troop is tough enough to keep his crew in line and to make a man out of the spoiled rich boy, Harvey, who falls under the captain's care. With his great physical strength, athletic prowess, and intelligence, Tarzan in Edgar Burroughs's *Tarzan of the Apes* (1914) is tough enough to survive living in an African jungle, where few men or beasts dare challenge his rule. In Burroughs's novel *The Gods of Mars* (1912) and the other volumes of the Mars chronicles, John Carter is a "straight, clean-limbed fighting-man of thirty" who dispatches his enemies, including great white apes, hideous plant men, evil bantha, and black pirates, with ease (viii).

Owen Wister's novel *The Virginian* (1902) features a man who moves "with the undulations of a tiger, smooth and easy, as if his muscles flowed beneath his skin" (2). The Virginian, a man no one wishes to tangle with, is an early precursor to the countless tough cowboys who have filled the twentieth-century media. Another novel featuring a tough hero is Rex E. Beach's *The Spoilers* (1906), which explores the lives of hard-bitten gold prospectors in the Alaskan Klondike.[4] Toughest of the Alaskan men is Glenister, with his "heavy shoulders and ease of bearing, an ease and looseness begotten of perfect muscular control" (10). Like Tarzan, part of Glenister's toughness lies in his muscular strength, but there is far more to the two men. Both are lords of their respective jungles; Tarzan controls the animals inhabiting his domain while Glenister controls the minds of lesser men.

Captain James T. Kirk, Dick Tracy, Dirty Harry, Doc Savage, Popeye, Rocky, Shaft, Superman, Batman, Mike Hammer—tough men appear everywhere in the popular media. It is difficult to escape the influence of tough guy actors, including Humphrey Bogart, Marlon Brando, James Cagney, Clint Eastwood, Edward G. Robinson, Arnold Schwarzenegger, Steven Seagal, Sylvester Stallone, Jean-Claude Van Damme, and John Wayne. In the past three decades, it has been nearly impossible to turn on the television without finding a tough guy character squinting from the screen: Sonny Crockett and Ricardo Tubbs on *Miami Vice;* Mr. T on *The A-Team;* detectives Dave Starsky and Ken Hutchinson on *Starsky and Hutch;* detective Tony Baretta on *Baretta;* Lieutenant Theo Kojak on *Kojak;* Joe Friday on *Dragnet;* Duncan MacLeod on *Highlander;* Hercules on *Hercules: The Legendary Journeys;* John Lawless on *Lawless;* and Walker on *Walker, Texas Ranger,* among others.[5] Whether in television shows, films, comic books, magazines, or a variety of other forms, the media are inundated with tough guys.

This long list of examples provides evidence of the overwhelming presence of the tough guy in our culture and reveals how much we accept his presence and his gender without question. It is difficult to go to a mainstream movie theater without encountering a feature film starring Clint Eastwood, Chuck Norris, Bruce Lee, or other action-adventure stars; similarly, one cannot visit a comic-book store without seeing the scores of cover illustrations featuring Superman, Batman, Thor, Captain Marvel, Daredevil, and other tough male superheroes. The majority of Westerns have a hard-bitten male hero, and imagine flipping through a popular magazine and not coming across the lean, mysterious man who peers out of many advertisements, such as those for Marlboro cigarettes. The tough male figure is so engrained in our culture that we hardly notice him. Yet the tough guy and the fact that he is a male makes a difference in our society.

The connection we make between maleness and toughness works effectively to ensure male privilege and authority. By this, I mean that because being tough is understood as a requirement for all sorts of roles in our culture—including football coach, CEO of a major corporation, and president of the United States—the association between men and toughness, which the media help to perpetuate, serves to keep women second-class citizens. It is too often assumed that women are not "tough enough" for many leadership roles. One area in which this gendered equation about toughness affects women today is the workplace. Toughness is closely associated with certain professions and not others. "Tough jobs" include being a cowboy, athlete (especially a boxer, football player, or wrestler), truck driver, coal miner, oil well driller, soldier, sports coach, police officer, firefighter, big-game hunter, or deep-sea diver. "Non-tough jobs" include being a beautician, home economist, cake decorator, waitress, florist, clothing designer, secretary, dancer, interior decorator, hair stylist, teacher, accountant, or insurance salesperson.[6] What is evident from these two lists is how many of the "tough" jobs are those that have long been considered men's and how many of the "non-tough" jobs are ones assumed to be women's. It comes as little surprise that the tough jobs are typically granted more prestige than the non-tough jobs. It is regarded as more desirable to be a deep-sea diver than a cake decorator. Similarly, it is considered more challenging to be a firefighter than a teacher. The strong association we make between toughness and many male-dominated fields is one way that men's work is privileged and esteemed over women's.

Because the association between men and "tough" jobs—and toughness in general—brings them social power, it is important to study toughness, analyzing how women's relationship to toughness is created, at least partially, through how women are represented in the popular media. We need to understand how representing women as not tough—whether this occurs in something as fleeting as a television commercial or in something as long as a feature film—is a way of keeping them away from the mechanisms of power. Thus, the idea that women are not tough, so much a part of the culture's ideology, is an effective way of controlling women.

Tough Girls

We have been told a lie. The media have supported the myth that men are tough heroes—or predators—and women are frail victims—or prey. Despite what the media might suggest, women have *always* been tough, both in literature[7] and in real life. Some fictional women are tough because of the economic hardships they endure. In Rebecca Harding Davis's novella *Life in the Iron Mills* (1861), Deborah endures atrocious living conditions. A worker in a nineteenth-century cotton mill, she lives a life of "incessant labor, sleeping in kennel-like rooms, eating rank pork and molasses" (15). A similar character is the heroine of Anzia Yezierska's story "Soap and Water" (1920). The working-class woman toils for years in a laundry to afford an education and bursts into irate speech when the dean of the college berates the student for her slovenly appearance: "I felt the suppressed wrath of all the unwashed of the earth break loose within me. My eyes blazed fire. I didn't care for myself, nor the dean, nor the whole laundered world" (72).[8] Despite the tremendous obstacles that stand in her way, she fights to better herself and gain an education. In Edith Summers Kelley's novel, *Weeds* (1923), Judith endures the hardships of being the wife of a poor tobacco farmer in rural Appalachia. She must strip tobacco and raise a family with little money. Similar to Judith is Marie, a character in Agnes Smedley's semi-autobiographical novel *Daughter of Earth* (1929). Marie grows up poverty-stricken in a log cabin, learning the hard way that women and girls have few rights and receive little respect from most men. She is so destitute that all she can depend on are "poverty and uncertainty" (41). To survive, Marie must learn how to be tough; she recalls: "I took my place as one of the leaders of the 'toughest kids beyond the tracks.' In school I let nothing hurt me—no reprimand of my teacher, no look or word. . . . I fought boys and girls alike in the alleys beyond the tracks" (83). These women are a few examples of the long tradition of the tough working-class woman in fiction.[9]

Other fictional women are considered tough because they adopt roles and behaviors associated with men. A few such women appear in nineteenth-century dime novels, particularly those describing life in the Wild West, although male desperadoes, sheriffs, and highwaymen are always far more prevalent. Calamity Jane, for example, in "Deadwood Dick on Deck; or Calamity Jane, the Heroine of Whoop-Up" (1885) is depicted as "wear[ing] the breeches herself" (Wheeler 2). She explains her unusual attire at one point: "I don't allow ye ken beat men's togs much for handy locomotion an' so forth, an' then, ye see, I'm as big a gun among the men as any of 'em" (24). She drinks whiskey, shoots guns, and plays cards. Even killing a huge, ornery bear does not slow down "the noted young female dare-devil" (12). A similar character appears in Charles Portis's novel *True Grit* (1968), fourteen-year-old Mattie Ross, who leaves home to "avenge her father's blood" (13). Following in the footsteps of other Western heroines like Annie Oakley, Mattie faces great odds as she tracks her father's killer and extracts her revenge. Another woman who adopts tough attributes is Idgie Threadgoode in Fannie Flagg's novel *Fried Green Tomatoes at the Whistle Stop Cafe* (1987). As a young girl, Idgie is different from other girls. She hunts, fishes, and shoots "as good as any of the boys" (34). As an adult, she plays a championship game of poker, keeps a gun by her bedside, and is described by one admirer as being "tough as pig iron" (330). Another such character is Aunt Raylene in Dorothy Allison's novel *Bastard Out of Carolina* (1992). Aunt Raylene is a tough, ornery woman who lives alone "with her dogs and fishing lines" (178). At one time, she cut her hair short and dressed in pants to work as a man at a local carnival. She laughs loudly, spits, and makes "the second-best home brew" in the state (180). Calamity Jane, Mattie Ross, Idgie Threadgoode, and Aunt Raylene are all tough characters because they adopt characteristics stereotypically associated with men. By doing so, they place themselves as outsiders in relation to a culture that assumes that women should strive to act and appear feminine.

Fiction is not the only place to find tough women. There are countless women alive today or from earlier epochs who could be described as tough. In her essay on cowgirls in the West, historian Shelley Armitage describes women who are tough according to any standards. Lizzie Williams drove her own herd up the Chisholm Trail in the late 1800s. Mrs. William Mannix drove a stage for fifteen years in order to support her family (169). Sally Skull was a horse trader and sharpshooter (170). Annie McDoulet, known as "Cattle Annie," rode with a bunch of rustlers at the turn of the century (170). Williams, Mannix, Skull, and McDoulet were a few of the many tough women who had to fight to survive the rough conditions of frontier life. Such women, of course, were not limited to the nineteenth century.

Today, tough women exist in all professions. Women who are often identified as tough are those who join the largely male bastions of politics or business. For instance, writer Richette Haywood refers to former U.S. Secretary of Energy Hazel O'Leary as "bright, charming, [and] tough" (94). In another article, Senator Dianne Feinstein is described as "tough enough to win the West" (McGrath 12). In a similar fashion, an article by

Fred Bruning about Hillary Clinton is titled "Tough, Smart and a Presidential Bedmate" (9), while journalist Lewis Grizzard refers to Hillary Clinton as "first tough cookie" (C1). Along with women in politics, successful professional women are apt to be categorized as tough. In an article about Robin Burns, the president and CEO of Estée Lauder who earns one of the highest salaries of any woman executive in the United States, she is called "an inspired leader and a tough negotiator" and labeled "very tough indeed" (Martha Duffy 70). Dr. Frances Krauskopf Conley, one of the few female neurosurgeons in the United States and the first woman resident in neurosurgery at Stanford University, has also been referred to as tough. In one article, a writer describes her as "a woman who has a kernel of toughness à la Hepburn" (Constigan 68).

Yet toughness still must be carefully negotiated for many career women. The husband of Ann Dore McLaughlin, former Secretary of Labor, is quick to declare that his wife is not too tough: "She's almost a paradoxical combination of femininity and toughness in her professional life. . . . She's every inch the executive, but she has not lost her femininity" (qtd. in Polsgrove 34). This curious description makes it clear that for many people toughness and femininity are antithetical. Our society is uneasy about tough women. Whether it is O'Leary, Clinton, Burns, or McLaughlin, tough women are forced to walk a tightrope because they are impinging on male spheres of power. They must be perceived as neither too tough nor too weak and achieve what is an impossible balance: "If gentle, they are womanish; if tough, they are not womanly. By tradition a female cannot be a courageous, charismatic, wise, effective leader as a woman" (Curtis 50). Women's toughness disturbs society, perhaps reinforcing the stereotypical assumption that men are the only ones who are "naturally" tough. For instance, both men and women feel uneasy with Hillary Clinton. Because she is intelligent, powerful, and does not feel obligated to bake cookies, she is clearly not a traditional feminine woman. Her often tough image results in numerous jokes about Hillary as the real power behind the throne, casting aspersions on both her femininity and her husband's masculinity. The reactions to the First Lady are indicative of a culture that still assumes that toughness is for men; thus, our society exerts subtle and not so subtle pressure on women not to be tough. Yet, at the same time, society admires women (like Hillary) who are tough.

The women I just described are notably different from the women I study in this book. They are often tough only in order to protect their children and families, a form of toughness that our society assumes is "natural" for women; thus, their toughness does not call into question gender roles. Also, many of the women I described from fiction adopt tough roles entirely because of necessity; when a man appears to rescue her, the tough woman often returns to a more feminine prototype. Although I recognize the significant role such women played in helping to change, question, and subvert notions about what it means to be a woman, the tough women I am chiefly concerned with are those who openly challenge the dominance of the male tough hero. The women who are the focus of this book question and undermine gender stereotypes by adopting behaviors that are considered to be characteristic of men. The tough women I study shoot guns, become police officers, or act in other ways that, even today, are still strongly coded as male in our society. Many of these tough women openly show that they are more than capable of taking over men's roles, even the toughest of them.

Another feature that sets apart the women I study is that most (although not all) adopt physical characteristics or attitudes that are considered masculine in our society. A number of the women are very muscular and aggressive, both attributes associated with masculinity. As I shall argue throughout the book, her association with masculinity is one reason the tough woman is disturbing to society, because, as I have already stated, she challenges the notion that there is a "natural" connection between women and femininity and between masculinity and men. As theorist Susan Bordo comments:

> "Masculinity" and "femininity," at least since the nineteenth century and arguably before, have been constructed through a process of mutual exclusion. One cannot simply add the historically feminine virtues to the historically masculine ones to yield a New Woman, a New Man, a new ethics, or a new culture. Even on the screen or on television, embodied in created characters like the *Aliens* heroine, the result is a parody. (174)

In other words, American culture has become so accustomed to the notion of male/masculinity and female/femininity, that anything else looks like a travesty, something that fails to conform to cultural notions about what is "normal." The more a woman adopts signifiers of masculinity, the more she disturbs mainstream society. Our culture likes its girls to be girls and its boys to be boys, except in the choreographed routine of a drag show or other carefully staged performances.[10]

One reason the tough woman who adopts a persona that is strongly coded as masculine is disturbing to many is that she reveals the artificiality of femininity as the "normal" state of women. The masculine tough woman reveals that femininity is a carefully crafted social construct that requires effort to maintain and perpetuate. As Myra Macdonald writes in her study *Representing Women: Myths of Femininity in the Popular Media* (1995): "The body's traditional centrality to feminine identity can be sub-divided into a variety of codes of appearance. . . . It is not the body, but the codifying of the body into structures of appearance, that culturally shapes and molds what it means to be 'feminine' " (193–94). The body needs to be carefully regulated and controlled to achieve the appearance of femininity, and the pursuit of femininity is never-ending: "Through the pursuit of an ever-changing, homogenizing, elusive ideal of femininity . . . female bodies become docile bodies—bodies whose forces and energies are habituated to external regulation, subjection, transformation, 'improvement' " (Bordo 166). One reason that a tough woman like comic-book hero Martha Washington is disturbing is because she adopts a masculine persona and shows no interest in the endless quest for femininity. The tough woman calls into question how women should be women and whether femininity has anything to do with being a woman.

Judith Butler's words about the separation between sex and gender clarify the nonbiological nature of femininity: "When the constructed status of gender is theorized as radically independent of sex, gender itself becomes a free-floating artifice, with the consequence that *man* and *masculine* might just as easily signify a female body as a male one, and *woman* and *feminine* a male body as easily as a female one" (6). Toughness thus becomes something attached not to sex but to gender, an association that leaves toughness open to the regulation and control of the social body:

> To what extent do *regulatory practices* of gender formation and division constitute identity, the internal coherence of the subject, indeed, the self-identical status of the person? To what extent is "identity" a normative ideal rather than a descriptive feature of experience? And how do the regulatory practices that govern gender also govern culturally intelligible notions of identity? In other words, the "coherence" and "continuity" of "the person" are not logical or analytic features of personhood, but, rather, socially instituted and maintained norms of intelligibility. (Butler 16–17)

The regulatory practices that govern gender work to govern toughness, ascribing it to certain bodies and not to others. According to Butler, gender becomes a performance that must be endlessly performed in order to exist. Toughness becomes one display of many that is associated with "man" and "masculine"; those words, however, might have little to do with the physical male body. Associating toughness with gender rather than sex is threatening to the social order because it breaks down the essentialist argument that gender and sex are indissolubly linked. Instead, any subject who presents an effective performance of toughness can be tough, despite the body's sex.

Although Butler's words point out the cultural codes and restrictions that lie behind toughness or any act of gender, the larger culture still views toughness as a "natural" attribute of men, making toughness in women disturbing to both men and women. Women are often uneasy about being tough because they have been socialized to believe that they should not be tough but yielding.[11] Feminist philosopher Iris Young writes:

> The norms of femininity suppress the body potential of women. We grow up learning that the feminine body is soft, not muscular, passive, incapable, vulnerable. Our parents, teachers and friends suppress our natural urges to run, jump, risk, by cries that we should not act so boldly and move so daringly. . . . Developing a sense of our bodies as beautiful objects to be gazed at and decorated requires suppressing a sense of our bodies as strong, active subjects moving out to meet the world's risks and confront the resistances of matter and motion. (qtd. in Bartky 35)

Women are led to believe that physical (and emotional) toughness belongs to men. The connection between toughness and male / masculinity is so strong in our society even today that many women are uneasy about appearing *too* tough. Driving a motorcycle, getting a buzz cut, or wearing men's clothing — these are examples of acts that are problematic for women to perform; women fear that such behavior might make them appear too tough — too masculine.

Of course, such displays of toughness are also closely linked in our society to being a lesbian, an image that many heterosexual women seek to avoid at all cost. Lesbianism is always a "ghost in the closet" when women act or appear tough, and a label that society uses to police such behavior; in order not to appear as lesbians, women are expected to shun tough actions that might make them appear too masculine. Queer studies scholars, most notably Judith Butler, Sue-Ellen Case, and Judith Halberstam, have done a tremendous amount of important work on the connections between masculinity in women and real or imagined lesbianism.[12] Butler, Case, and Halberstam have demonstrated the importance of recognizing that displays of masculinity in women are always haunted by lesbianism and lesbian desire. As we explore the depiction of tough women, we shall find repeatedly that lesbianism is an issue that needs to be negotiated in complex and varied ways because of its taboo nature.

Despite their fears, women are often fascinated by toughness when it is displayed by other women, finding it sexy and alluring. Women cheer when Susan Sarandon and Geena Davis blow up an obnoxious truck driver's rig in *Thelma & Louise.* When Alex, in the science-fiction film *Nemesis 2,* overpowers a much larger man who is coercing her to have sex, women applaud. In many ways, the tough woman embodies women's fantasies of empowerment — the dream that the lone woman can take on the massed powers of our collective society. It is clear that toughness in women has a highly ambiguous place in our society. We are fascinated by it, yet we are horrified by it. We admire it, yet we fear it.

This ambivalent relationship to toughness in women is embodied in the character Jael from Joanna Russ's novel *The Female Man* (1975). Jael is a caricature of absolute toughness; she is reminiscent of a female James Bond, calculating and in control. She represents everything American culture dreads about tough women. She lacks stereotypical feminine emotions and acts out her violent thoughts, such as when she kills a man and remarks, "I always carry firearms" (182). Muscular and aggressive, Jael is all that women traditionally have been told that they should not be. Russ gives her readers a complex image of Jael. Despicable, she is also curiously appealing, because she is so obviously able to take care of herself. There are two sides to Jael and other tough women. The tough woman is disturbing to her audience because she often acts or shows the potential to act on her aggressive emotions. She is also alluring, however, because she embodies women's desire for power, self-sufficiency, and autonomy. Her contradictions are what make her a fascinating character to study in contemporary mainstream media.

What exactly comprises the New Tough Woman, as I call her, referring to the many tough women who have appeared during the past three decades in the popular media—women who, like Ripley or Xena, openly claim men's roles and power as their own? I have pointed out how difficult it is to arrive at a single, narrow definition of toughness, but there are some characteristics that are shared by many New Tough Women—women who seem as capable of presenting a convincing performance of toughness as their male counterparts. These traits can be broken down into four groups: body, attitude, action, and authority. Body refers to how a woman presents a physical body that signifies toughness in our culture. For both men and women, the physical nature of the body is commonly a visible sign of their toughness, a fact that Yvonne Tasker notes in *Spectacular Bodies: Gender, Genre and the Action Cinema:* "Action heroes and heroines are cinematically constructed almost exclusively through their physicality, and the display of the body forms a key part of the visual excess that is offered in the muscular action cinema" (35). Tasker's words also apply to tough girls in genres other than film. As I have mentioned, the tough girl often displays well-defined or even unusually heavy musculature because American society perceives large muscles as one attribute of toughness. One extreme example of such a woman is Alex, the main character in the film *Nemesis 2,* which will be discussed in greater depth later. Her body bulges with muscles, serving as a visible signal of her ability to overcome even the most overwhelming odds. The muscles are also a sign of the physical and mental discipline that she possesses in order to craft such a physique. As we shall find time after time, muscles are one of the most visible signs of toughness in both women and men.

The body also signifies toughness in other ways. A tough body is typically an athletic, fit body.[13] For example, in Elizabeth A. Lynn's fantasy novel *The Northern Girl* (1980), Paxe, the leader of the guards, is quite capable of taking care of herself: "She was tall, as broad-shouldered as any of her guards, a stern and striking figure" (10). In the fantasy movie *Red Sonja* (1985, director Richard Fleischer), the heroic star is a woman who has enormous physical strength, which helps to make her one of the best swordswomen (or men) in the land. Another woman who is exceptionally physically fit is Sharrow in Iain M. Banks's science-fiction novel *Against a Dark Background* (1993). Sharrow is physically strong enough to punch out a man who dares to slap her. Like well-developed muscles, a high level of physical fitness shows the ability of a tough woman to endure great hardships. Moreover, the physical strength and athletic prowess of the tough woman are often raised to a mythic level—as is true with Xena—one that no real woman could ever hope to achieve. In this fashion, the tough woman becomes a superhuman hero, someone whose supreme physical fitness serves as a physical sign of her heroic nature.

The body is also made to appear tough through style, which has a profound effect on whether or not a woman is read as tough.[14] Styles that suggest toughness are almost inevitably ones that suggest masculinity and maleness because femininity is perceived as antithetical to toughness. A pair of khakis has a higher tough quotient than a pink tutu. A plain white t-shirt ranks higher on the scale of toughness than a bright orange angora sweater. A black leather biker's jacket is tougher than a white suede jacket with a decorative fringe. Clothing is an important element in the performance of toughness because it serves as a visual reminder that a woman has distanced herself from femininity. Masculine clothing also suggests a woman's capacity for action and leadership.

Another defining feature of toughness is attitude. No matter how a woman's pecs might bulge or how strongly her clothing might be coded as tough, she will not be considered tough unless she has the right attitude. Generally, she must display little or no fear, even in the most dangerous circumstances; if she does show fear, it must not stop her from acting. For example, Ripley reveals little fear even when confronted by alien monsters that would like nothing better than to have her for breakfast. Red Sonja rarely displays fear, even when being attacked by hordes of sword-wielding soldiers or hideous creatures. Xena also never shows fear. The lack of visible fear shown by Ripley, Sonja, and Xena is something that they share with many tough women. Along with showing little fear, the tough woman must appear competent and in control, even under the most threatening circumstances, when everyone else falls apart. Often her cool nature will be evident in her relative lack of affect; we know that she is feeling a tremendous amount of emotion, but she does not always show it because such a display would interfere with her performance.

The tough woman, however, is not *always* emotionless. Sometimes she shows her anger, but her rage does not interfere with the performance of her duties. When she must, she acts. Others hesitate. The tough woman acts because she recognizes that people depend on her and that she needs to take a leadership role in times of adversity. When she acts, the tough woman's actions are often excessive. She dispatches not one man who menaces her but six. We recognize that the tough woman acts in a way few (if any) real women could act. Her actions are larger than real life, showing not reality but a myth and a parody at the same time, as do the actions of male action heroes such as Schwarzenegger and Stallone. Just like Hercules performing his twelve heroic labors, the tough woman's actions reveal her ability to endure and triumph where all others would fail.

Along with her stamina and strength, the tough woman's actions reveal her intelligence. Typically, she does not act without carefully thinking through the results of her actions. While others might want to spring into battle, the tough woman hero or anti-hero often pauses for reflection before acting. The comic-book character Elektra, for example, is unsurpassed as an assassin because she waits to attack her victim, carefully calculating the best time for an attack. The tough woman must consider when she should act, and sometimes being a tough hero means that she needs not to act but to wait. When the time comes to act, however, the tough woman is ready.

Even with her physical prowess, her "bad" attitude, and ability to act when necessary, the tough woman must project authority if she is to be heeded. Writer Richard Sennett provides a concise definition of authority: "Assurance, superior judgment, the ability to impose discipline, the capacity to inspire fear: these are the qualities of an authority" (17–18). He writes, "authority is not a thing. It is an interpretative process which seeks for itself the solidity of a thing" (19). In other words, authority is an intangible and elusive trait that has to do with many characteristics, including a person's cool and collected bearing and ability to discipline others when necessary. Certain jobs—particularly ones that demand leadership skills—are apt to imbue one with an aura of authority; a captain of a ship or the CEO of a large corporation would typically have more authority than a dishwasher or a short-order cook. The tough woman must have authority because she often acts as a leader, and a leader with no authority is not capable of leading, especially in times of great stress.

Tough Thoughts

How body, attitude, action, and authority come together to create a tough woman varies a great deal; thus, different tough women have different images and styles. Elektra, a hired killer, is different than Captain Janeway, a starship captain. Xena, a warrior from a mythological past, is different from Martha Washington, a soldier from the distant future. Even though these characters and others have diverse ways of bringing together body, attitude, action, and authority, they are all nontraditional tough women whose depiction challenges the bipolar systems of femininity/masculinity and male/female. The collective appearance of these women and others in popular culture suggests a great deal about how gender roles are being reimagined in the media today.

By exploring and analyzing the changing depiction of the tough woman in the popular media, we shall discover her paradoxical position: she both contests gender norms and reaffirms them. For more than thirty years, the tough woman has become increasingly tougher and (seemingly) more of a challenge to traditional male gender roles. We need to examine whether the tough woman in the popular media has actively undermined stereotypes about men and women and masculinity and femininity *or* whether she has helped to support such stereotypes. I hope that after exploring tough women in the media we will have a better understanding of how the depiction of women's toughness often helps affirm that men are the only people tough enough to be leaders and heroes.

Our exploration of how the representation of the tough woman has changed begins with some of the first television shows—*The Avengers, Charlie's Angels,* and *The Bionic Woman*—to portray pseudo-tough women. Such characters played an important part in allowing women to adopt roles that were tougher than roles formerly played by women on television, such as Beaver's mother. But even these early tough roles, we will discover, ultimately were not as tough as they might have first appeared, and they served in many ways to reassure the audience about what was presumed to be the essential femininity of women. An examination of these pseudo-tough women and others will help show how the ever-changing depiction of the tough girl has offered women an illusion of freedom and power but has, simultaneously, operated to support the gender status quo.

Part I
Pseudo-Tough

Chapter 2
Semi-Tough

Emma Peel, Charlie's Angels, the Bionic Woman, and Other Wanna-Bes

If you grew up in America in the 1970s and were not a hermit, Charlie's Angels, with their long manes of hair and designer wardrobes, were impossible to miss.[1] Farrah Fawcett was particularly hard to avoid; one popular poster of her sold a staggering eight million copies (Durkee 113). *People Magazine* once referred to *Charlie's Angels* as "the jiggle heard round the world" (Durkee 113). I recall visiting numerous friends' homes where the ubiquitous Farrah poster hung on the wall, and I remember many of my prepubescent girlfriends blow-drying their hair in a vain attempt to imitate her. For girls who found the cheesecake style of the Angels too much to stomach or who despaired of ever achieving the famous Fawcett look, there was *The Bionic Woman,* a show that premiered the same year as the Angels. The Bionic Woman was far tougher than Fawcett and her gang. She could outrun Olympic athletes, rip sheets of steel with her bare hands, and kick holes in cement walls—all without messing up her hairdo. Intelligent and independent, she participated in all kinds of intriguing missions as a secret agent, and spent far less time in the beauty salon than did the Angels.

Charlie's Angels and *The Bionic Woman* were not the first television shows to demonstrate that women could shoot guns or capture bad guys. In the 1960s, the British import *The Avengers* featured Honor Blackman as Mrs. Catherine Gale, "a cool blonde" who knew judo, was an expert mechanic, could shoot any firearm, drove a fast car, and had a penchant for leather clothing (Rogers, *The Avengers* 29).[2] When Blackman left the show, Gale was replaced by Emma Peel (played by Diana Rigg), a secret agent skilled at karate and kung-fu and even tougher than her predecessor.

This chapter analyzes how Emma Peel, the Angels, and the Bionic Woman served as precursors to the tough women of the 1980s and

1990s.[3] The programs that featured these early heroines had a dual purpose: they offered women viewers potentially powerful role models, but the shows simultaneously helped to reaffirm that women, while more capable than generally given credit for, were still less competent than men. The representation of feminine toughness was in part a response to the very real feminist activism of the 1960s and 1970s and women's demands for personal and political power. During this time of profound social upheaval, television shows such as *The Avengers, The Bionic Woman,* and *Charlie's Angels* presented women as far more tough than did shows of the past. Yet, these new programs also emphasized the importance of femininity and sex appeal for women, thus diffusing the threat posed by Second Wave feminism.

Although these programs helped to reaffirm women's traditional roles, I do not wish to suggest that they failed to depict alternatives to the status quo. Like most popular culture texts, the shows have many meanings. As popular culture theorist John Fiske writes:

> Television, books, newspapers, records, and films are popular partly because their nature as media enable them to be used in ways in which the people wish to use them. As they cannot impose their meanings on people, neither can they impose the way they are received into everyday life. Popular discrimination extends beyond the choice of the texts and the points of pertinence within them, to cover the choice of medium that delivers the text and the mode of consumption that best fits the "consumer's" sociocultural position and requirements.[4] (*Understanding* 158)

As Fiske points out, a wide range of factors, including social class, ethnicity, race, age, and sexual orientation, influence how people consume and interpret popular culture. Because of the tremendous variability of the audience for popular culture, room always exists for resistant readings, ones that go against what appears to be the dominant reading of a film, television show, or other popular culture text—the reading that is favored by many, although certainly not all, viewers. For instance, one common way to interpret *Charlie's Angels* is as a show that focuses on beautiful women who are more interested in wearing designer clothes than in solving crimes. But it is possible to view this program from many perspectives. It is too simplistic to categorize the shows as entirely good or bad. Instead, it is more appropriate to view them as multivalent texts, which, paradoxically, encourage women to adhere to traditional roles and also to challenge them. As cultural critic Patricia Mellencamp observes, "Television embodies contradictions—rather than an 'either/or' logic, one of 'both/and' . . ." (*High Anxiety* 5). This chapter will uncover the mixed messages about toughness conveyed by these television programs. Despite the ways they adhered to traditional gender ideology, they were influential in the late 1960s and mid-1970s in demonstrating that a woman *could* be tough, a message that had significance both in the popular media and the real world.[5]

"Constantly Kinky": Diana Rigg and *The Avengers*

A "leather-suited, judo-kicking vision of ice-cool beauty" was one description of Cathy Gale, the original heroine of *The Avengers* (Unsworth 41). The woman who later replaced Gale, Emma Peel, "wasn't just gorgeous, she had a withering intellect and could kick a baddy's ass to the other side of Kingdom Come" (Unsworth 41). These descriptions of Gale and Peel help to explain the fascination with the characters of *The Avengers,* a 1960s British television program that was a hit in both the United States and Great Britain. *The Avengers* presented some of the toughest women to appear on television in the 1960s. Neither Cathy Gale nor Emma Peel was the Beaver's mom. This section explores how *The Avengers* played an important role in demonstrating that women could be just as tough as men yet also helped support stereotypes about women.

The Avengers aired from 28 March 1966 to 15 September 1969 in the United States, after being imported from England where it had been one of the top television programs since 1961. The highly successful show had a total of 161 episodes, which ran from 7 January 1961 to 14 September 1969. By 1967 it was playing in over seventy countries, and Diana Rigg was even nominated for an Emmy (Rogers, *The Avengers* 131). Today the show continues to air as reruns, and fans write books and maintain internet web sites that focus solely on *The Avengers.* Some of the show's long-lasting popularity is due to what Steve Chibnall calls its "self-conscious sense of absurdity and its fascination with genres" (476). Although *The Avengers* is a James Bond-style secret agent show, it is far more adventuresome than the Bond films, and it self-consciously combines realism and fantasy with a sense of wry humor. The appeal of Rigg's partner John Steed (Patrick Macnee), a dry, dapper Englishman who serves as the perfect foil for Mrs. Peel, also adds to the program's interest.

Another reason for the popularity of *The Avengers* is its female stars. When the show began, Patrick Macnee's partner was Dr. David Keel (Ian Hendry). Hendry dropped out before the end of the first season, to be replaced by the first of Macnee's female partners, Honor Blackman. She played Mrs. Catherine Gale, "a cool blonde with a Ph.D. in anthropology" who was "an expert mechanic and photographer [and] skilled in firearms and judo" (Buxton 100). Gale was an interesting character for many reasons. As Blackman commented, Gale was "the first woman to fight back" (qtd. in Rogers, *The Avengers* 29). When Blackman originally appeared on the series in 1962, she remarked, "I'm a first for television.

The first feminist to come into a television serial. . . . [W]hat she doesn't have in the way of brawn, she makes up for in motorbikes, black boots, leather combat suits and judo. We had enormous problems with re-writes at the beginning. Cathy was so wet I had to say 'Look, write my part as if I were a man and I'll turn it into a woman's part' " (qtd. in Rogers, *The Avengers* 29). Blackman describes some of the reasons Cathy Gale is a notable figure in the development of tough women in the media. She showed that women could be as tough as male action-adventure heroes—a startling notion in the early 1960s, when the conservatism of the 1950s was still very much an influence.

But this chapter is primarily concerned with Emma Peel, who replaced Gale when Blackman decided to leave the series. Mrs. Peel was "the beautiful young widow of test pilot Peter Peel and the daughter of a wealthy ship owner. A woman of independent means, she was the complete one-jump-ahead jet-set female" (Rogers, *The Avengers* 75). The "lithe jumpsuited" Diana Rigg was the female member of the Avengers with whom Americans were most familiar, since she was featured on the show when it moved to the United States (Brooks and Marsh 53). Without a doubt, she was one of the toughest women to appear on American television in the 1950s or 1960s. She was, however, also a feminine woman in many ways. As one writer described her, she was an "intellectual versed in the martial arts," and she delivered "her karate blows in the latest John Bates fashion. Above all, she [was] capable, and tough without ever appearing unfeminine" (Chibnall 477). This description of Mrs. Peel aptly describes her often paradoxical personality. She was tough, but the show also stressed her femininity and sexuality. She was untraditional in her toughness and her choice of profession, but she could not break free of certain gender stereotypes. Namely, she still adhered to the notion that women must be sexually attractive to men, and she maintained a socially acceptable feminine appearance.

Because Rigg wanted to leave *The Avengers* to pursue other career possibilities, Mrs. Peel appeared for the last time on 20 March 1968, when she was reunited with her long-lost husband, who had been presumed dead. This episode showed Mrs. Peel reverting to a more acceptable role as wife; she had been a secret agent only until her husband returned. This conclusion to Mrs. Peel's career suggests that being a secret agent (or other adventurer) might be tolerated for a single woman but not for a married one. Thus, even a program that seemed intent on challenging stereotypical women's roles worked to support them, too. After Mrs. Peel's exodus, the female characters changed dramatically. Diana Rigg was replaced by Linda Thorson as Tara King, who was only slightly more threatening than the Avon lady. While her predecessors appeared cool and distant toward Steed, King was infatuated with him and often gazed at him with admiration. Her fighting skills were not on a par with those of Gale or Peel. "There was . . . no new fighting technique for Tara. No judo, karate or kung fu. Instead, she would rely more on feminine guile than muscular skill. Tara would hit her opponents with a straight right-hander, her handbag, or whatever was at hand that might be used as a weapon. She would even give the occasional scream for help!" (Rogers, *The Avengers* 131). One clothing designer for the show described Tara as "curvy, pretty and feminine" (qtd. in Rogers, *The Avengers* 133). Patrick Macnee's sidekick certainly had changed. She changed even more notably when *The New Avengers* appeared in 1976, featuring Joanna Lumley as the lead female character, Purdey, who was more closely aligned with King than Gale or Peel. Lumley herself said about her depiction of Purdey, "It will be lovely to play a feminine lady. There have been far too many butch-looking girls in TV recently" (qtd. in Rogers, *The Avengers* 172). Although she was an expert marksman and an excellent driver, Purdey never had the panache of Gale or Peel. By the time King and Purdey appeared, the series presented a more traditional vision of women and femininity than it originally had, which is why this chapter is primarily concerned with Diana Rigg's character.

Despite Mrs. Peel's tough image, her toughness was undermined in a variety of ways, such as through her repeated use of masquerade and disguise. In the episode "Honey for the Prince," Peel masquerades as a dancing girl and joins the harem of a Middle Eastern prince. In "The Gravediggers," she pretends to be a nurse to infiltrate a hospital. In "The Master Minds," she again disguises herself as a nurse, and in "Death at Bargain Prices" she pretends to be a salesgirl in the lingerie department of Pinter's department store. To understand the function of Mrs. Peel's disguises, it helps to refer to Terry Castle's book *Masquerade and Civilization: The Carnivalesque in Eighteenth-Century English Culture and Fiction* (1986), in which she writes about disguise and masquerade. "Fashion is endlessly separable from truth. Despite the existence of what one could call a sartorial social contract—an implicit agreement that individuals in society will wear revelatory, 'communicative' garments—one is always free to wear misleading dress, dress that is either playfully or criminally inappropriate. Just as one may lie, so may one go 'in disguise' " (56). She continues, "Disguise, when unveiled, is perceived as profoundly anti-social; witness the persistent association between the mask and criminality, travesty and treachery" (57). Castle's words indicate the threat of disguise. Because disguise is perceived as potentially deceitful, Mrs. Peel's reliance on disguise shows her to be someone whose subjectivity is amorphous. Thus, her toughness can be seen as only another example of her play with disguises; we need not fear her if we can believe that underneath the tough exterior a "true" woman resides. As we shall find in

Charlie's Angels and *The Bionic Woman,* masquerade is often used to reveal that a woman's attitude is only skin-deep.

Mrs. Peel's tough image was also undermined by an emphasis on her sexuality. She frequently wore clothing that revealed her every curve. Certain outfits were referred to by the show's fashion designer as her "Emmapeelers" (Rogers, *The Avengers* 103): "Emma's fighting suits . . . were in stretch crimplene and jersey, with a recurring motif of buckles, links and braiding, but they differed from previous fighting suits by having bootees of the same material to give an all-in-one effect from throat to toe" (Rogers, *The Avengers* 103). These suits were custom-designed to reveal a great deal of Mrs. Peel, and often the program went overboard to make sure that she appeared as sexually desirable as possible. An associate producer of the British show commented, "We're constantly kinky. . . . If there's a choice between Emma Peel fighting in a wet dress or a dry one, we choose wet" (qtd. in " 'Good-Chap' " 94). Emphasizing the sexual side of Emma—she was called by one critic "the kinkiest thing about 'Avengers' "—was something that the show did frequently, even if it entailed having her nearly tortured while wearing a very revealing outfit, as in the episode "Escape in Time" (" 'Good-Chap' " 94). Another way the program emphasized women's sexuality was to have Emma expose her curvaceous form. Nowhere was this done more vividly than in the episode "A Touch of Brimstone," which presented Emma dressed as the "Queen of Sin," complete with a corset, high leather boots, and an iron collar with three-inch spikes—transforming her into an object of male sadomasochistic sexual fantasy. Emphasizing Mrs. Peel's sexuality was one way that *The Avengers* reduced her tough image and showed viewers that, despite her karate abilities, she was still all woman.

Yet another way that Emma's toughness was reduced was by having her repeatedly rescued by Steed—far more often than he was rescued by her. In "The Joker," she could not defeat the madman who confronted her; she was saved only when Steed appeared on the scene. In "Return of the Cybernauts," he rescued her when she was mesmerized by the watch she wore. In "How to Succeed . . . at Murder," he needed to save her from a group of women who held her hostage, and in "Room Without a View" he rescued her from a prison cell. In "Small Game for Big Hunters," Emma was saved from two villains when Steed, emulating Tarzan, swung through the trees to rescue his imperiled partner. In "The Girl from Auntie," Peel was kidnapped, and Steed spent the entire show trying to find her. Because Mrs. Peel was rescued on a regular basis, she was reinscribed in stereotypical and traditional women's roles. She needed to be rescued; Steed did the rescuing. As tough as she was, she was not tough enough to be equal to him or other men. Thus, she did not threaten the masculinity of the male viewer, which is dependent, in part, on perceiving himself as distinct from and superior to the female and all that is associated with femininity.

Although Mrs. Peel's toughness was diminished in numerous ways, it would be a mistake to understand her character as suggesting *no* changes in how women should act and behave. She was still tough, unusually tough for a woman of the sixties. Her physical prowess was such that she could take on six men at once and defeat them all. Rigg once commented, "I never think of myself as sexy. . . . I identify with the new woman in our society who is evolving. Emma is totally equal to Steed. The fighting is the most obvious quality. I always win my fights, and, personally, I enjoy it—the idea of taking on six men when you know you're going to win" (qtd. in " 'Good-Chap' " 94). Rigg's words help to explain Emma's allure to women and demonstrate how she was a very different character from most other women on television in the 1960s. However, I have pointed out the ways that Mrs. Peel also helped to reinforce stereotypes about women. As we continue our exploration of some of the early precursors to the tough women of the 1980s and 1990s, we shall find that Mrs. Peel's paradoxical character is shared by many other women in the popular media, including Charlie's Angels.

Charlie's Angels: "Girls, Guns, and Great Clothes"

I confess—although my mother disapproved, I watched *Charlie's Angels* every chance I got. My mother frowned at the violence and sexuality that characterized much of the show, but, as a preteen growing up in the 1970s, I was fascinated by the Angels. Here were women who seemed remarkably free and independent to an eleven-year-old. Although men appeared on the show, John Bosley (played by David Doyle) was the only regular male character—unless you take into account the strange, disembodied voice of Charlie. The Angels were at the center of the action. I remained glued to the tube, seeing something very different in *Charlie's Angels* than in the other shows I watched; no woman on *The Brady Bunch, Bewitched, Gilligan's Island,* or *The Partridge Family* had a chance to attend the police academy, as did the Angels. Instead of viewing the Angels as mindless powder puffs, I perceived them as empowered women, acting out the dictates of the feminist movement—the influence of which I felt all around me. (I still remember proudly declaring that I was a feminist when I was in first grade.) My experience as a viewer of *Charlie's Angels* points out the paradoxical role this show played in the seventies. Even though they joined the police academy, pursued criminals, and excelled as super-sleuths, the way the Angels looked in bikinis was more important than their intelligence. This section explores some of the reasons for the appeal of the Angels and their show, arguing that *Charlie's Angels* depicted pseudo-tough women to imply that their toughness was less effectual than men's. In this fashion, the show addressed the very real societal uneasiness about Second Wave feminism.

The Charlie's Angels phenomenon began when the first show aired on ABC on 22 September 1976. The series ran until 24 June 1981, for a total of 115 episodes over five years. The program was created by Aaron Spelling, the producer responsible for *The Mod Squad, The Love Boat, Fantasy Island, Dynasty, Beverly Hills 90210,* and *Melrose Place.*[6] *Charlie's Angels* was an instant hit. By November 1976, 59 percent of American households were watching Farrah and her pals (Durkee 117). Fifty million households tuned into the program during a typical week, making it one of the most highly rated shows in 1976 (Sackett 222). The plot of the successful show was fairly basic, even sophomoric. The Angels worked for Charles Townsend, an anonymous ultra-wealthy bachelor who communicated only by speaker phone and was never seen by the Angels. The show always began with a voice-over from a man whom the audience later recognized as Charlie: "Once upon a time there were three little girls who went to the police academy . . ." Although his face was never shown, Charlie was often glimpsed cavorting with scantily clad women whom he variously described as his Swedish maid or new secretary. Charlie was a debonair ladies' man, but his impact on the Angels was limited because he was only a disembodied voice. The only man the Angels saw regularly was Bosley, their pudgy middle-aged liaison with Charlie. Every week the Angels were confronted with a new mystery or crime to solve, usually resulting in their going undercover, and every week they solved the crime, punished the evildoers, and rewarded the good guys. The show's popularity was always based more on the sexual appeal of the actresses who played the Angels than on the intricacy of its plots. The show featured actresses Farrah Fawcett, Shelley Hack, Kate Jackson, Cheryl Ladd, Tanya Roberts, and Jaclyn Smith as Angels. The original Angels were Fawcett, Jackson, and Smith, who played Jill, Sabrina, and Kelly, respectively (Figure 1). When Jill left the Angels, she was replaced by a string of other characters, including her younger sister, Kris (Ladd, 1977), Tiffany Welles (Hack, 1979), and Julie Rogers (Roberts, 1980).

For a time, it was difficult to avoid seeing the Angels everywhere, including on school-lunch boxes, mugs, posters, and magazines. They appeared on the cover of *People Magazine* over two dozen times (Durke 113). The Angels themselves were not able to escape their sudden fame and were pursued by endless requests for autographs, photographs, and letters. A *Time* cover story reported, "Fans mob the girls when they go into the streets for location work. The mail runs to 8,000 pieces a week" ("TV's Super Women" 71). The program itself was also at the center of

Figure 1. Publicity shot of the original Angels (Farrah Fawcett, Kate Jackson, and Jaclyn Smith) (*Charlie's Angels*).

attention. The fact that a national newsmagazine devoted its cover to *Charlie's Angels* confirmed its success as "the hottest new television show of the season" (67). "The show is not just a winner but a certifiable phenomenon," the article declared. "Seldom has a brand-new entry broken into Nielson's top ten in its first week and then stayed there, steadily improving its position with each subsequent airing" (67).

Today, *Charlie's Angels* remains popular in syndication, and reruns of it still play on my local television station not one afternoon a week but five. (The Angels were so popular that a sequel to their show appeared in the late 1980s on Fox Television. *Angels '88,* however, did not demonstrate the lasting power of the original show and quickly faded from sight.)[7] Fans remain obsessed by the show. One fan has an extensive web site devoted to the Angels. Another, Jack Condon, collects *Charlie's Angels* memorabilia on a massive scale; he owns coffee mugs, lunch boxes, bathmats, and radios plastered with the Angels' pictures. He has over fifty thousand magazine and newspaper clippings that feature the Angels, videotapes of every show from the series, and a room in his house is a shrine to the Angels ("Where's Charlie?" 68).

How are we to explain the appeal of *Charlie's Angels,* both when it first aired and today, more than twenty years later, when most of the television shows of the 1970s have mercifully faded into the dimmest of memories? Like *The Avengers,* one of the primary reasons for *Charlie's Angels'* success is sexuality, as a number of critics have pointed out: "Sex, pure and simple, seemed to be the principal ingredient in the considerable success of this detective show" (Brooks and Marsh 143). The Angels never lacked in sex appeal: "Scantily clad, [Farrah] and the other Angels were trapped on a cruise ship with a homicidal maniac. Scantily clad, they raced stock cars and skated in roller derbies. Scantily clad, they fled from evildoers on horseback and in rafts and in brakeless cars that were always headed downhill" ("Television's Top 25 Stars" 60). The sexual appeal of the women was stressed as frequently as possible, such as in the infamous "Angels in Chains" episode, where the three Angels go undercover as prison inmates in Louisiana. The jail is run by sadistic guards, and the prison is a front for a prostitution ring operated by the warden; the sadomasochistic and lesbian undertones are difficult to miss. This episode shows how the media make women, like the Angels or Mrs. Peel, sexually alluring to men by weakening their toughness, emphasizing their sexuality, and transforming them into sex objects for the male gaze. "Angels in Chains" and other similar episodes sent the ratings for *Charlie's Angels* soaring. Only the show's creator disagreed with his critics who saw *Charlie's Angels* as nothing but sex, sex, sex. He once commented, "in the whole five years of the show, none of the characters ever had an affair. *Charlie's Angels* was Puritan, absolutely Puritan" (Spelling 138). Notwithstanding Spelling's assessment, sex appeal was definitely one of the reasons the Angels were so successful.

And then, of course, there was Farrah: "Hers was the smile that blinded. Hers was the face that cut men down to sighs, the body that launched 8 million swimsuit posters, the hair that inspired countless doomed imitations, and, most of all, hers was the jiggle" ("Television's Top 25 Stars" 60). With her mane of tousled blonde hair and gleaming smile, Farrah was the best-known Angel and the one most commonly perceived as a sex object. She was a key reason for the success of *Charlie's Angels.* She offered an alluring, sexualized version of the girl next door, blonde and beautiful.

Sex appeal alone does not adequately explain the allure of the show. It was also popular with millions of viewers because it depicted a fashion utopia. In the magical world of the Angels, the women were always perfectly groomed. Their hair was perfectly coifed. Their fingernails were perfectly manicured. How they managed not to chip a nail while chasing down the bad guys was a miracle of modern science. The Angels always wore designer outfits. Far be it from Farrah to schlep around in a pair of old sweats and a torn t-shirt. The Angels presented a fantasy of ideal femininity; viewers never saw the makeup artists, hair stylists, clothing designers, or the many others who labored to create the Angels' look. Viewers saw only the fantasy that was the Angels—a fantasy that appealed to both men and women. Of course, the Angels' lives were also far more exciting than the mundane lives of most people, which gave viewers an opportunity to watch a fashion show and escape temporarily to a world much more interesting than their own.

Was the show more than a winning combination of "girls, guns, and great clothes," as one writer suggested ("Television's Top 25 Stars" 60)? Many feminist critics and others have understood the Angels phenomenon as nothing but sexism run amuck, with the show exploiting both its actors and women in general. As one commentator writes, "Kelly and Jill (and later Kris) were exposed, abused, and exploited in various combinations and various ways in episode after episode" (Meehan 80). There is more to the Angels, however, than just fluff. As I mentioned before, viewers of the 1970s could watch the program and carry away messages that were not hopelessly reactionary. Yet I am aware of the often overt sexism of the show. My ambivalence is shared by feminist critic Susan J. Douglas. In her book *Where the Girls Are: Growing Up Female with the Mass Media* (1994), she brings attention to her own mixed emotions:

> There is no doubt that the show was escapist rot of the first order, combining plots a three-year-old could follow with plenty of cheese-cake. But neither its sexual titillation nor its See-Spot-Run plotlines adequately explain why this show, at this time, became the media and cultural phenomenon that it did. Looking back on *Charlie's Angels* after nearly twenty years, we find some interesting and pleasant surprises mixed in with the string bikinis and those hideous bell-bottoms. (213)

Douglas argues that it was watching "women working together to solve a problem and capture, and sometimes kill, really awful, sadistic men, while having great hairdos and clothes" that made women watch the show (215). She also points out that the Angels' appeal lies in their ability to "do what men do . . . [while] they are still very much women" (213). Here, Douglas is beginning to describe the tough side of the Angels that interests me. The Angels did much of their own footwork to solve their cases, they were nearly always more intelligent than their male colleagues and opponents, and, despite the fact that the show was produced by a man and many of the writers were men, the Angels were not completely controlled by men. Though they had a subordinate relationship to their mysterious boss, Charlie (even the show's title established his proprietorship over them), the Angels were generally free to pursue their own plans because Charlie was only a disembodied voice. No matter how much they submitted to society's dictates about acceptable behavior for women, the Angels had a great deal of autonomy. It is too easy to look at the show with a 1990s mindset. We need to remember that in the 1970s the Angels represented a step forward for women. After all, they were graduates of a police academy and were far more independent than the majority of women on television at that time.

Let us now turn to the show itself, exploring how it represented pseudo-tough women—women who acted tough but also supported society's gender norms.

There can be no question that the Angels performed many tasks that were considered tough. In the episode "Angels on the Air," one Angel rides a Harley motorcycle. In "Haunted Angels," Sabrina wrestles briefly with an escaping criminal. In "Angels on Vacation," the Angels shoot down two kidnappers. Similarly, in "Angels Belong in Heaven," the Angels do not hesitate to use their guns while apprehending a villain. In "The Jade Trap," Sabrina rappels down the side of a high rise. In "Angel Come Home," Jill is a race-car driver in Europe. Despite the influence of the feminist movement, in the mid-1970s when the show aired, such acts by women were relatively uncommon (although there were exceptions to this rule), whether in real life or on television. Depicting toughness represented a step forward, albeit a small one. Showing the Angels engaged in such tough activities also helped to establish a precedent for the much tougher women who would appear in the popular media in later years.

Although the Angels were tougher than most of the female characters on television, the threat that their toughness posed to gender norms was deliberately lessened in many ways. As with *The Avengers*, one of the most significant ways that their toughness was undercut was by the show's emphasis on masquerade and "going undercover." Watching the show today, I am struck by the number of times that the Angels go undercover or disguise themselves in order to solve a crime. In the episode "Dancing in the Dark," for example, Sabrina disguises herself as a wealthy heiress, and Jill masquerades as a disco expert at a dance studio. In "The Jade Trap," Kelly pretends to be a wealthy Southern belle, while Kris masquerades as a grieving widow with a fortune in jade. In "Angel Come Home," Kelly pretends to be a tabloid reporter. In "Haunted Angels," Kris masquerades as a researcher to catch a phony psychic. Douglas has observed that the Angels seem more interested in disguise than a child just before Halloween:

> In the first season they went undercover as prison inmates, WACS in basic training, and roller derby queens. The girl they were helping was almost always from

> what was called 'a simple background,' meaning less sophisticated and of a lower socioeconomic class than they, although the angels' class was somewhat indeterminate. So they didn't just go undercover into an occupation not theirs, they also went undercover into another class. (214)

Douglas's words help to elucidate the role of masquerade in this show. Going undercover—masquerading as someone else—shows the constructed nature of identity. All is illusion. The constructed nature of the Angels' identities is highlighted; they are not what they seem to be. Their toughness is brought into question because masquerade forces its audience to question the nature of identity, as they questioned Diana Rigg's identity in *The Avengers*. Toughness, the show hints, is perhaps as artificial as the Angels' roles as hookers, nurses, or roller derby queens.

The Angels' tough image was also undercut by an emphasis on their femininity and sexuality. They portrayed women who were clearly interested in using their beauty to attract men. For example, in "Target: Angels" Jill (not for the first time) uses her sexual wiles to get what she wants when she flirts with a cabdriver so that another Angel can steal his car. Like Jill, the other Angels regularly use their sexual appeal to solve crimes; thus, the Angels are sexual objects in a world where being a sexual object is associated with subordination. The Angels appear less tough and capable than they might if they depended on their brawn or brains to solve crimes. They also appear less tough because their heterosexuality and heterosexual desirability are repeatedly stressed in a culture where heterosexual desirability in a woman often signifies submissiveness to a dominant man. For instance, in the episode "Target: Angels," both Sabrina and Kelly have boyfriends who are highly visible, reassuring the audience that the Angels are "normal" women, despite their guns and detective badges. In the episode "The Jade Trap," Kelly falls for a handsome cat burglar, and in "Angel on High" she is smitten by a stunt pilot. This constant focus on the Angels and their relationships with men lessens the Angels' tough image by emphasizing their emotional, feminine attributes in a society where emotionality and femininity are not associated with toughness. Interestingly, a tough man such as James Bond can have a sexual relationship with a woman and not harm his tough image. This gendered difference reflects a culture in which men are expected to be the sexual aggressors and women the passive recipients. Showing a tough man involved in a sexual relationship with a woman highlights his tough, aggressive character, but a sexual relationship between a woman and a man rarely enhances her tough image and more often detracts from it.

The Angels' toughness is also undermined because no matter how many crimes they solve or how many criminals they capture, they are still the prey for seemingly countless men with nefarious intent. Sometimes it seems as if the Angels cannot jog down to the local grocery store to pick up a six-pack of Tab without encountering some man trying to gun them down or run them over with a Mack truck. *Charlie's Angels* is a modernized version of *The Perils of Pauline,* where each episode brings new dangers and new villains. With a bad guy lurking behind every bush, one might assume that the Angels would become accustomed to their situation and perhaps a bit nonchalant about it. Such is not the case. In "Target: Angels," Jill screams when a gunman chases her and Sabrina does the same when a dead man falls out of a closet. (Would John Wayne have screamed?) In "Angels Belong in Heaven," a hitman pursues one of the Angels. In "Angels on the Air," Kelly, masquerading as a radio newscaster, is chased by a man who tries to run her down. In "An Angel's Trail," Jill stops to fill up her car's gas tank and ends up being taken hostage by an escaped killer and his two sons. Kris is threatened with rape by a former criminal; Sabrina is menaced by a man with a gun. (Why is it that most of the greater Los Angeles population seem to want the Angels dead? After I watched sixty or seventy episodes, I began to understand.) Although the Angels always manage to elude their captors and never suffer any lasting harm from their close brushes with danger, the fact that they are portrayed as prey week after week reduces the Angels' tough image.

However, the Angels do shoot guns, ride Harleys, and perform other acts that were and still are considered tough. And the Angels manage to solve their cases when faced with the most blatant male sexism. For example, in "An Angel's Trail," Kris (Cheryl Ladd) is looking for her missing sister, Jill. Kris must deal with a doubting policeman who questions whether a woman should be engaged in a potentially dangerous activity. Her reply: "Look, I'm a private detective. I can take care of myself." In another episode, "The Seance," an insurance man is openly scornful of "female detectives." Despite his disparaging comments, the Angels discover far more than the male police officers who have already combed the crime scene. In these episodes and others, the Angels prove that they can take care of themselves. I believe such images of capable women in the 1970s played a part in expanding the cultural perception of women's toughness and women's roles in society.

The Angels also demonstrate their toughness by frequently helping to protect or rescue communities of women. In "He Married an Angel," the Angels capture a conman who targets women. In "Angels on the Street," Kelly and Tiffany masquerade as street prostitutes to stop a pimp who beats up the women he employs. In "Dancing in the Dark," the Angels help out a middle-aged woman being blackmailed by her former boyfriend. These episodes and others depict the Angels protecting women who appear powerless in the face of a male threat. Although these episodes show the tough side of the Angels, they also emphasize the weakness of women. Only the Angels are tough enough to handle the problems they encounter; other women appear hopelessly weak and inept. In this fashion, the Angels' toughness is highlighted by suggesting the helplessness of most women, revealing that the Angels are the exception, not the rule.

The Bionic Woman features a woman who appears even tougher than the Angels, but, again, her toughness is diminished by the emphasis on her femininity. Masquerade and going undercover are stressed in this show, as they are in *The Avengers* and *Charlie's Angels,* suggesting that toughness is only a disguise for the Bionic Woman.

The Bionic Woman: A "Bionic Bimbo"?

> I think everyone has a fantasy about being bionic. Wouldn't it be kind of nice to be able to run 60 miles an hour or hear conversations a mile away?
>
> —Ken Johnson, creator and producer of *The Bionic Woman* (qtd. in Cohen 107)

She could rip apart a phone book with her bare hands. Vaulting the highest fence did not even cause her to break into a sweat. To me, the Bionic Woman appeared far tougher and more independent than the Angels, and I watched her show avidly, doing my part to make it one of the most popular shows of 1976. I remember a time when it was difficult to avoid the Bionic Woman and her male counterpart Steve Austin, the Six Million Dollar Man (Lee Majors). Like the Angels, Jaime Sommers (played by Lindsay Wagner) appeared on lunch boxes, posters, coffee mugs, and coloring books. You could even purchase books that featured the Bionic Woman's exploits, like Eileen Lottman's novel *The Bionic Woman: Extracurricular Activities* (1977). If this were not sufficient bionic booty, you could buy a host of other products, including a Bionic Woman figure with a bionic ear that went "ping" just like the TV Bionic Woman's.[8] For your Bionic Woman action figure, you could purchase a classroom, a sports car, a bionic beauty and repair station, and a whole host of fashion outfits. You could also join the Bionic Woman Bionic Action Club and read the comic book series about the Bionic Woman that was published for a short time.[9] There was no doubt about it: the Bionic Woman was hot. One reason for her popularity was that she, like the Angels, was far tougher than most women on television in the 1970s. However, she also perpetuated feminine stereotypes, as did the Angels and Mrs. Peel. Jaime was a combination of the taboo and the socially acceptable. She could outrun any man (except Steve) and punch a hole in a brick wall, yet she was a conventionally beautiful woman who did not strongly challenge traditional notions about women's desirable appearance. Although the Bionic Woman was not as feminine and sexually attractive as Farrah Fawcett's character in *Charlie's Angels,* she still conformed to social dictates about how an attractive woman should appear and act. The Bionic Woman seemed to subvert typical gender stereotypes —but only on the surface.

Jaime Sommers originally appears as the Bionic Woman in a few episodes of *The Six Million Dollar Man* (1974–1978). She is introduced as a tennis professional and a childhood friend of Steve's. The two fall in love just before Jaime is seriously injured in a sky-diving accident. Steve begs Oscar Goldman (Richard Anderson), head of the OSI (Office of Scientific Information), to make her whole again by replacing her injured arm, legs, and ear with bionic parts. Oscar consents, but Jaime enjoys her bionic parts for only a short time before her body rejects them. Presumably, she dies in the emergency room, leaving Steve grief-stricken. But Jaime does not die; she recovers, having lost all memories of her relationship with Steve. Like the widow Mrs. Peel, Jaime is now free to perform missions for Oscar and the OSI, partly out of gratitude for her bionic parts (which cost only slightly less than the Six Million Dollar Man's).

Jaime begins a new life working in Ojai, California. She is a "teacher during the week, secret agent on the weekend" (Cohen 98). This split between the Bionic Woman's weekday and weekend activities is reminiscent of when Mrs. Peel left *The Avengers* to pursue her married life. Both characters are divided between socially acceptable activities (being a wife or teacher) and less sanctioned activities (being a secret agent). Whether in the 1960s or 1970s, television did not present female characters who strayed too far from socially acceptable roles for women. A woman might be a secret agent on the weekend, but during the week she still pursued a stereotypical women's role of being a teacher. In this way television supported and perpetuated gender norms by presenting them as perfectly "natural."

Like *Charlie's Angels, The Bionic Woman* (1976–1978) was highly successful. In the first season, the show had a 45 percent share of the television audience (Sackett 223).[10] When it first appeared, it was one of the season's hits ("The "$500,000 Timex" 85). Lindsay Wagner's salary was truly bionic: $500,000 a season, $200,000 more than Lee Majors received (Sackett 223). At that time, Wagner was the highest paid actress in a dramatic series (Phillips and Garcia 45). Today, there is still sustained fan interest in both *The Bionic Woman* and *The Six Million Dollar Man*—so much so that there is a web site set up specifically for Jaime Sommers and Steve Austin, with volumes of information about the shows, including photographs, sound bites, and a detailed synopsis of the plot of each episode.

The Bionic Woman was a success partly because Jaime was a far more independent and central character than most women in 1970s shows. The Angels never appeared as self-sufficient as the Bionic Woman, who never had a Charlie to tell her what she had to do. Lynda Carter, starring in the 1970s television show *Wonder Woman,* never came close to matching Jaime for independence. Wonder Woman spent most of her time trying to help Major Steve Trevor; she did not have much time for her own pursuits. In *Laverne & Shirley,* the stars were two buffoons who were no match for a superhero like the Bionic Woman. Even Pepper Anderson (Angie Dickinson) of *Police Woman* was not as independent as the Bionic Woman. Pepper always had to report to her male cohorts, who constantly needed to rescue her from danger when she went undercover (typically as a prostitute or call girl). When we compare the Bionic Woman to other women featured in 1970s shows, we begin to recognize how unusual she was. As a star of an action-adventure show, she was breaking new ground by showing that women could be tough heroes like James Bond or Steve Austin. Of course, earlier there had been Mrs. Peel, but she had always been accompanied by Steed. The Bionic Woman was usually on her own.

Jaime, however, was a problematic version of a tough woman, as Susan Douglas explains: "In 1976 came television's most ingenious resolution to the tension between feminism and antifeminism. What we got was the bionic bimbo, the superhuman woman with lots of power, maybe even a gun, flouncy hair, a mellifluous voice, and erect nipples" (211). Douglas points out some of the contradictions in Jamie's character. She was able to run sixty miles an hour, yet she also was a beautiful woman who affirmed many stereotypical notions about femininity and the desirability of beauty in women.

Characters such as the Angels and the Bionic Woman were representative of a 1970s culture that was deeply troubled by toughness in women. Thus, toughness had to be made to seem less consequential and less controversial than it actually was. One way to lessen the potential threat of Jaime's tough image was through the use of masquerade and disguise. Like the Angels, Jaime frequently adopts different disguises. In the episode "The Bionic Beauty," she masquerades as a beauty contestant to discover who is trying to deliver top secret technology to enemy agents. In "The Ghost Hunter," she pretends to be a governess and goes to work in a mansion that might be haunted. In "Sister Jaime," she poses as a nun to trace missing diamonds that have presumably been stolen by a priest. As it does for the Angels and Mrs. Peel, masquerade shows the malleability of Jaime's subjectivity and suggests that her tough image might be just another façade, as indeed it is. Jaime's experiences with masquerade also weaken her tough character because she often masquerades in typical female roles (nurse, nun, singer, governess). Associating Jaime with stereotypical feminine roles assures the audience of her innate femininity.

The Bionic Woman's toughness is reduced by stressing her femininity in other contexts. For example, in one episode she sings "Feelings" and pretends to be a nightclub singer (Phillips and Garcia 45). This episode is a clear attempt to diminish Jaime's tough superhero status. Her image is further softened because she rarely has to use her brawn to capture villains. Instead, she trips or tricks the evildoers who challenge her ("The $500,000 Timex" 85). Her continued friendship with Steve Austin, which always verges on becoming the romantic relationship it once was, also serves to soften Jaime's image. These elements were part of the show's plan to reduce Jaime's toughness in order to broaden her appeal. Philip De Guere, a writer who worked on the program, commented, "We finally decided that the non-superhero approach was the way to go. That's how the series eventually worked. She was ladylike and operated her bionics discreetly. The conventional wisdom at the time was that an audience wouldn't buy a real strong, aggressive female character" (qtd. in Phillips and Garcia 45). Making Jaime "ladylike" was one way that *The Bionic Woman* helped to perpetuate the mythology that women should be feminine and demure, even when the show on the surface seemed to challenge the same ideas.

Like *The Avengers* and *Charlie's Angels, The Bionic Woman* helped to diffuse the threat that women were becoming too tough, a threat made more evident, as I have mentioned previously, by the demands of Second Wave feminists. Turning to comic books, women's magazines, films, and novels, we shall find that the same strategies are used repeatedly to reduce or control a woman's toughness and to suggest that it is no match for that of a man. In such a fashion, popular culture reduces the threat the tough woman poses to societal norms. Popular culture, however, frequently makes use of tough or pseudo-tough women, whether Xena, Martha Washington, Ripley, Sarah Connor, Elektra, or the Bionic Woman, as a sensational way to promote products, including films, books, and other media. She is a sellable commodity because society is fascinated by the tough woman, despite being dismayed by her. The popular media have the ability to convey perfectly the ambiguity people feel about tough women in real life.

Television and Social Change

The television programs analyzed in this chapter show how important it is to recognize the popular media's power to present images of women that have the potential to change social reality. The media are so influential because the ideology they convey is naturalized, made to seem "real."

The versions of reality offered by the popular media often present a society that appears transparent, easy to understand and interpret. For example, *Leave It to Beaver* seemed to show the "reality" of American family life in the 1950s. *The Brady Bunch* supported the ideological notion that the desirable family was composed of husband, wife, and children. *Bewitched* promoted the idea that a woman, even a powerful witch, should stay at home and take care of the house while her man was out earning a living. Of course, none of these shows presents "reality," but television offers us a view of the world that many people mistake for reality. For this reason, shows such as *The Avengers, Charlie's Angels,* and *The Bionic Woman* do have the potential to influence social reality. Though these shows might appear highly fantastic at times, they are still likely to be read as suggesting suitable or not-so-suitable roles for women. Such popular shows—no matter how "fluffy" they might appear—deserve critical attention because they are helping to constitute how viewers understand both acceptable and unacceptable roles for both women and men.

This chapter has pointed out the often paradoxical nature of tough women in the popular media. Mrs. Peel, the Angels, and the Bionic Woman were all tough women who had the potential to serve as new role models for how women should act. These characters suggested that being tough was acceptable for a woman. At the same time, they helped to reaffirm stereotypes about the sexuality and femininity of women, attributes that worked to diminish the impact of the women's toughness. This paradoxical message seems confusing at first until we acknowledge that the popular media are never feeding their audience a single message about women's roles; instead, the media convey countless different messages, with some contradicting others. "Television exists first and foremost as availability, as saying everything to everyone," writes Stephen Heath (270). As our exploration of toughness continues we find that ambiguity remains an essential element of tough women in the popular media. We are always confronted with a messy and contradictory message about women's toughness that seems to take one step forward and two steps back.

My examination of the contradictory image of women's toughness continues in the next chapter, which focuses on popular women's fashion magazines and how they have portrayed women's toughness in the 1980s and 1990s. Studying these magazines makes clear that the tough girl is ubiquitous. Whether on television, in magazines, or in dozens of other sources, the tough woman is performing similar cultural functions, helping both to change how people perceive women's gender roles and to support mainstream notions about how women should act and look.

Chapter 3
Pretty Tough
The Cult of Femininity in Women's Magazines

While thinking about the representation of toughness in American culture, I recently visited my local Barnes & Noble bookstore to peruse its extensive collection of women's magazines. Gazing at bank after bank of magazines with covers portraying nearly identical female models was an eerie experience. *American Woman, Glamour, Cosmopolitan, Self, Vogue, Vanity Fair, Mademoiselle, She, Seventeen, Allure, Redbook, Belle, Woman's Own, New Woman, American Cheerleader, Marie Claire, Elle, Black Beauty, Pride, Ladies' Home Journal*—some of these I recognized, others I did not, but all of the cover models looked remarkably alike, despite having a variety of hair styles and clothes, and sometimes different racial backgrounds. One attribute these models had in common was their lack of toughness. They were glamorous, beautiful, feminine, and graceful—but not tough. Studying the faces that stared back at me from the display racks led me to think about the role of toughness in today's women's magazines. Is toughness as completely excluded from the pages of these magazines as their covers would lead me to believe?

Flipping through the magazines, I discovered that despite the lack of tough girls on their covers, tough women do appear in the articles, advertisements, and photographs in these magazines—especially in high-fashion magazines such as *Vogue* and *Vanity Fair.* In one copy of *Vogue,* a heavily tattooed woman glares at readers from a Calvin Klein advertisement (To Be 220). In another issue of *Vogue,* a woman garbed in boxing gear confronts the reader, as if challenging her to a match (Evolution 343). In an article from *Elle,* androgynous models wear clothing that combines "[m]asculine tailoring and feminine touches" ("Masculine" 352). As I studied women's magazines from past years, I discovered numerous other images of tough women from the 1980s and 1990s. Obviously, tough women were not as rare as I had first assumed.

Examining these "tough" women more closely, however, I identified a variety of ways in which their toughness was undermined. Although these magazines have recently begun to show more tough-looking women, this does not mean that they are questioning the innate biological differences between men and women and their "natural" relationship to masculinity and femininity, respectively. The magazines present a fantasy of toughness. They create a Never Never land where models can present a performance of toughness—but it is only a performance. In this imaginary universe, which is clearly demarcated as a fantasy, women can appear dressed up with all the accouterments of toughness, but the models' location in fashion magazines undermines their toughness, reminding readers that everything they see is a fantasy of style. In addition, the magazines perpetuate the notion that toughness in women is sexy, which assures the audience that women are not abandoning their traditional roles as sex objects for men just because they are tough. This equation between women's sexuality and toughness works in a similar fashion in *The Avengers, Charlie's Angels,* and *The Bionic Woman.* The relationship between toughness and sexuality diminishes the threat that tough women pose to the dominant social order by suggesting that a woman's sexual availability and physical attractiveness will be in no way diminished by her tough actions and appearance.

Women's magazines are an especially intriguing medium to study when reflecting on the essence of toughness because they play an important role in helping to formulate gender in our culture. Yet they are still typically viewed as unworthy of scholarly attention because they are popular reading material aimed at women. In her well-known study of women's popular literature, *Loving with a Vengeance: Mass-Produced Fantasies for Women* (1982), Tania Modleski discusses the typical critical response to popular women's texts: "Women's criticism of popular feminine narratives has generally adopted one of three attitudes: dismissiveness; hostility—tending unfortunately to be aimed at the consumers of the narratives; or, most frequently, a flippant kind of mockery" (14). She wrote these words in 1982, but they remain germane today. This perspective is gradually changing as a greater number of feminist scholars have begun to recognize the importance of what Marjorie Ferguson calls "one of the most significant yet least studied social institutions of our time" (1).[1]

Women's magazines are an important source of information for anyone interested in our society's changing gender roles. As Naomi Wolf writes, "women's magazines are the only products of popular culture that (unlike romances) change with women's reality, are mostly written by women for women about women's issues, and take women's concerns seriously" (71). Because of this, women's magazines show how millions of women construct their identities according to the feminine norms touted by the magazines. It is difficult for *any* woman in American society to avoid these magazines: even women who argue that they never read them are still influenced by their omnipresent images. Because of their prevalence and popularity (many of the most popular ones have readerships in the millions), women's magazines hold a powerful position when it comes to negotiating the relationship between women and toughness because they prescribe how tough their readers and other women should look and act.

The advertisements that compose the bulk of most women's magazines are just as important as the stories and their accompanying photographs in determining the construction of gendered identities. Advertising in women's magazines plays an influential role in formulating, maintaining, and altering how readers understand the construction of socially acceptable gender norms. Advertisements function in a way similar to their surrounding text, but they also have different rules:

> Advertisements use the material of everyday life, but they draw upon this material in a highly selective fashion. That which is chosen for inclusion is reintegrated into the signifying system of advertising, where this material then provides the basis for the creation of new meanings. . . . Advertisements do not, therefore, simply reflect the social world but re-create it, reconstitute it, and communicate this manipulated version to the audience.[2] (Budgeon 56)

Advertisements develop a unique universe that might contain different messages about gender than the articles and photo spreads that accompany them. We must study advertisements and their surrounding texts together, analyzing the concurrent and convergent messages they convey about the constitution of toughness.

Advertisements in women's magazines often seem most adventuresome about portraying challenging and controversial images of tough women because advertising is always happy to use controversy to sell underwear, perfume, cosmetics, women's suits, or other commodities. Advertising's "very staying power derives from its ability to mimic the social. As society changes, advertising becomes the happy chameleon, always delighted to don spring's new colors" (Barthel 13). Advertising might act like a chameleon that follows social change, but we need to be alert to the ways that advertising can also lead to social change.

Not only advertisements, but women's magazines in general do more than alter how gender is constituted in American society. They can also change how gender is perceived. As Wolf observes, women's magazines have long been "one of the most powerful agents for changing women's roles" (64). She suggests that the magazines can change what is considered acceptable or unacceptable behavior for women. As women's magazines are widely read, they have ample opportunity to convince millions that the views expressed by the magazines are just, fair, and truthful. The magazines depict a monolithic perspective on the world, presenting their contents as "the truth," leading readers to believe that these texts present a mimetic view of the world; the magazines do not suggest that there is a world full of people with different perspectives. In *Subculture: The Meaning of Style* (1979), Dick Hebdige describes the importance of the media in changing how their audience members perceive the world: "The media play a crucial role in defining our experience for us. They provide us with the most available categories for classifying out the social world. It is primarily through the press, television, film, etc. that experience is organized" (84–85). Women's magazines are very much a part of this process.

Women's magazines can deliver messages that encourage social change—either progressive or conservative (and often both). Because of the complexity of women's magazines and their various target markets, a magazine might convey many messages within a single issue. Thus, it should come as no surprise that a magazine might feature a picture of a short-haired woman astride a Harley and a decidedly feminine woman with long, flowing locks in the same issue. One critic writes, "Women's magazines posit a collective and yet multivalent female subjectivity, which they simultaneously address and construct" (Ballaster et al. 172). We shall discover that many messages are contained in women's high-fashion magazines concerning women and their relationship to toughness, not all of them consistent. Although they play with tough images of women, women's magazines often use those images to affirm the desirability of femininity for women and to help maintain traditional gender divisions between men and women.

The Cult of Femininity

"Women must 'perform' femininity, and fashion is part of that performance," write Caroline Evans and Minna Thornton (13). To understand the role that women's magazines play in perpetuating femininity as the ideal for women, it is helpful to turn to Marjorie Ferguson's book *Forever Feminine: Women's Magazines and the Cult of Femininity* (1983), in which she discusses the association between femininity and women's magazines. According to Ferguson, "Women's magazines collectively comprise a social institution which fosters and maintains a cult of femininity. This cult is manifested both as a social group to which all those born female can belong, and as a set of practices and beliefs: rites and rituals, sacrifices and ceremonies, whose periodic performance reaffirms a common femininity and shared group membership" (184). If we concur with Ferguson, women's magazines (and also men's, such as *GQ*) are deeply invested in perpetuating the idea that femininity is aligned with women and masculinity is aligned with men. Women's magazines base their appeal on being the vehicles that provide the entryway into the mysterious world of femininity, providing "the syllabus and step-by-step instructions which help to socialise their readers into the various ages and stages of the demanding—but rewarding—state of womanhood" (Ferguson 185). Ferguson describes the rituals women undergo to perpetuate the ideology of femininity: "Individual members are socialised into their personal and collective identities through shared rites, rituals, parables, maxims, catechisms, badges and totems, in the same way that they are habituated into making the monthly or weekly dues they contribute towards the maintenance of the edifice itself" (186). The cult is kept alive by its millions of adherents and the social apparatus, such as women's magazines, that these women support.

As long as the primary purpose of women's magazines is to sell the many commodities that are essential elements in the creation of femininity, they will be hostile to women who too openly flaunt the fact that femininity is not the "natural" and right state of women but is, instead, only one of many choices that a woman can make in creating her subjectivity and self-presentation is a dangerous notion to a magazine empire built on selling the products needed for a woman's endless pursuit of femininity.

Women's magazines offer a fantasy that fosters in their readers a desire for a state of being that can never be achieved. In their pursuit of the spectre of perfect femininity, women are encouraged to buy both the products that the magazines promote and the magazines themselves. Since toughness is strongly associated with a lack of femininity, tough girls are a threat to this capitalist edifice; thus, female toughness must be carefully controlled so that it poses little danger to the cult of femininity that women's magazines help to build and reinforce.

Women's magazines are also successful in strengthening the connection between femininity and women because they make femininity alluring to many readers. In her book *Decoding Women's Magazines From Mademoiselle to Ms.* (1993), Ellen McCracken provides an accurate description of how women's magazines persuade their audience that the magazines' vision of femininity is highly desirable and deserves to be emulated:

> Readers are not force-fed a constellation of negative images that naturalize male dominance; rather, women's magazines exert a cultural leadership to shape consensus in which highly pleasurable codes work to naturalize social relations of power. This ostensibly common agreement about what constitutes the feminine is only achieved through a discursive struggle in which words, photos, and some-

times olfactory signs wage a semiotic battle against the everyday world which, by its mere presence, often fights back as an existential corrective to the magazine's ideal images. (3)

In other words, entire magazines are designed to offer readers a highly enjoyable reading experience that functions to perpetuate femininity as the norm; even the cagiest reader finds it difficult to resist the fantasy world of femininity in these magazines. In a similar fashion, a men's magazine like *GQ* functions to heighten the appeal of conventional masculinity.

One may ask *why* tough women appear at all in women's magazines, if the magazines are intent on maintaining the notion that femininity is the norm for women. One would think that images and narratives about tough women would undermine the emphasis on femininity. We shall find that the opposite is actually true. Tough girls do appear, but typically women's magazines use toughness to reaffirm the connection between women and femininity. In addition, toughness is often associated with women's sexuality, which makes toughness less threatening to the dominant social order than it might first appear to be—a strategy already described in the previous chapter.

Another reason tough girls appear in women's magazines is because the magazines promote more than one version of womanhood. Today, perhaps even more so than in the past, no single representation of womanhood expresses what it means to be female, and women's magazines prosper from the growing complexity of what womanhood entails: "The journal and fashion industries thriv[e] on the instability of the very idea of what a woman [is]: the 'new' woman, the working woman, the sports woman, the family woman, the sexually liberated and educated woman [are] all as much created and exploited by the journals as by the advertising apparatus" (Griggers 96). The world of women's magazines has always been open to different depictions of womanhood—a strategy that helps to sell the magazines and the commodities that they advertise to the broadest audience possible. In creating a complex, multifaceted image of what it means to be a woman today, women's magazines have made room for many new images of womanhood, including those that apparently emphasize toughness. No matter how varied these images might seem, however, they must function within narrow boundaries. Thus, a "tough" woman might appear, but she must be model-beautiful and slender.

These superficially tough images of women do not seriously endanger the dominant cult of femininity because tough women are only a minute percentage of the women who appear in the magazines. Studying hundreds of different magazines, I found that tough women were a tiny minority, despite their growing prevalence in recent years. The magazines I perused had dozens of pictures, advertisements, and articles that featured feminine women who did not appear remotely tough; women with teased manes of hair, long lacquered nails, and slinky dresses were impossible to miss. I had to search for tough girls; I went through many magazines that did not picture a single one. The more traditional magazines such as *Family Circle, Good Housekeeping, Ladies' Home Journal,* and *Woman's Day* rarely contained images of tough women. Even lifestyle and fashion magazines (*Cosmopolitan, Essence, Glamour, Mademoiselle,* and *Redbook*) portrayed few tough women. Not surprisingly, images of toughness were more apparent in *Elle, Vanity Fair,* and *Vogue*—magazines that feature daring, risk-taking high fashion—but this does not mean that these magazines necessarily have a more progressive attitude about women's roles. We need to recognize that high-fashion magazines are careful to distance the toughness they display from the reality of everyday. To gain a comprehensive image of the tough girl in women's magazines, this chapter studies a variety of women's magazines, concentrating on the high-fashion magazines because tough women appear more commonly in them.

The paucity of tough women in *all* of these magazines is disturbing because it suggests that little support exists in the popular media for women who dress and act in ways that are regarded as tough. Although some of their traits are portrayed as desirable, tough women are depicted as outsiders to the cult of femininity and are shunted to the edges of the fictional universe of the woman's magazine. This marginalization of the tough girl presents her as an anomaly. Tough women rarely appear in television advertisements, for instance, in contrast to the common appearance of tough men. Even the television commercials that could logically portray a tough woman generally do not. For instance, the endless advertisements for home gyms usually feature a man whose pumped-up pecs bulge impressively; his leotard-clad partner is far less muscular, and she often sports lipstick and carefully coiffed hair. The dearth of tough women is one of the most visible (or invisible) signs that tough women are not socially acceptable. This chapter primarily focuses on women who *appear* tough, and despite their increasing appearances in women's magazines, they still are marginalized and have in no way gained the same societal acceptance as more feminine, softer-looking women.

Women's magazines marginalize tough women by rarely depicting them. More commonly, the magazines depict women who adopt a few attributes associated with toughness. This lack of "real" tough women is one sign of a magazine universe that is uncomfortable with the masculine-coding of toughness. These magazines only represent tough attributes that can be toned down in one way or another, assuring readers that displays of toughness pose no serious challenge to the cult of femininity that the magazines uphold. The magazines present a feminized version of toughness, which is not genuinely tough. Instead, women's toughness is depicted as a masquerade. In some ways, the magazines present an inverse to the image of toughness presented in *Charlie's Angels* and *The Bionic Woman,* in which the central women acted (somewhat) tough, but did not look tough. In women's magazines, the women look (somewhat) tough, but it is clear that their image is only skin-deep. By exploring how women's magazines describe and portray leather fashions and mannish or masculine clothing for women, this chapter will offer readers a better understanding of how the popular media manipulates the signifiers of toughness.

Leather and Lace: Undercutting Tough Styles

To understand the depiction of women's toughness in fashion magazines, it is important to consider how they describe women's leather fashions.[3] Fashion magazines often portray women wearing leather attire and must in some way negotiate the aura of toughness associated with leather. In American culture, leather is strongly associated with masculinity and tough men. Mention the word "leather" and images of motorcycle-straddling Hell's Angels are apt to spring to mind. Leather is tough and masculine. How, then, do women's magazines present leather fashions for women?[4] Does the bad boy image of leather make it too tough, too rough for the glamorous models who fill women's magazines?

The representation of leather is interesting because, like all clothing, leather does far more than keep a person warm. Leather signifies a great deal about its wearer. In "Fragments of a Fashionable Discourse" Kaja Silverman discusses the multiple purposes of clothing; "Clothing and other kinds of ornamentation make the human body culturally visible" (145). She observes, "Dress is one of the most important cultural implements for articulating and territorializing human corporeality—for mapping its erotogenic zones and for affixing sexual identity" (146). No form of attire makes a body more visible than leather, which suggests both toughness and sexuality. Valerie Steele writes about the appeal of leather, "Many people find black leather sexy for both men and women. . . . Not only does leather have a certain tactile appeal as a 'second skin,' but it may also carry a variety of erotic connotations. From Marlon Brando's black leather jacket to Saint Laurent's black leather miniskirt, the message combines seduction and danger" (62). Steele adds that leather has acquired "tough, even sado-masochistic connotations" (62). Leather signifies many characteristics, but it is always linked to toughness, particularly in men. Leather must be presented with care in women's magazines because it potentially threatens the magazines' dominant feminine imagery with its tough connotations.

Many articles and photo spreads explicitly tone down the association between leather and toughness. One article in *Glamour* entitled "Leather or Not" states, "Bikers, hit your brakes. The new leathers are coming through and they're miles from tough. This year's keepers are refined, tailored" (254). An article in *Seventeen* titled "The Leather Report" assures its readers that leather is not as tough as they might assume, commenting "Bye-bye, biker chick: Leather's new look is more tender than tough" (137). Calling into question the common linkage between bikers' culture and leather is one way that women's magazines try to reshape leather's image, making it kinder and gentler.

When leather does appear, magazines soften its tough image by posing leather-clad women with men, especially in what appears to be a romantic entanglement. An article in *Mademoiselle,* "Zip! The Motorcycle Jacket—Truly Cool Again" (188), depicts four women in motorcycle jackets. Three are portrayed in sexually suggestive poses with men, and one woman is photographed alone. In this article and others, the man acts as a signifier of heterosexuality and limits the toughness of the women models by disavowing the implicit linkage between toughness and lesbianism.

Another common technique for diminishing leather's connection to toughness is to emphasize the femininity of the woman wearing the leather clothing. For example, in an advertisement for Calvin Klein from *Vanity Fair,* a female model wears leather gloves and has a black leather biker's jacket flung over her shoulders (Calvin Klein 16–17). She wears a low-cut black dress, has long hair, and is classically beautiful and feminine. In this interplay between masculinity and femininity, femininity is the dominant signifier. There is no suggestion that this statuesque beauty is threatening traditional gender roles, despite her masculine leather jacket. The masculinity of the jacket only heightens and accentuates her predominantly feminine appearance. In an advertisement for Calvin Klein jeans, a model wears a tough black leather jacket and rides a motorcycle, but her long hair and flawless face suggest that she is still all woman ("Best & the Worst" 122). Similarly, in a story from *Vogue* that describes fashion trends, a model straddles a motorcycle and wears a black leather jacket that would make the Fonz envious, but the large gold earrings she wears and her makeup reveal that the model has not abandoned her femininity, despite her biker's garb ("Best & the Worst" 122). In another fashion spread from *Cosmopolitan,* a boyish model wears a biker-style leather jacket ("Runway" 223). She has a short boyish haircut, but her eye makeup is quite evident, as is her lipstick. In our society, makeup and lipstick are two important markers of hetero-femininity, undermining the model's potentially lesbian-masculine presentation. In another article from *Cosmopolitan,* a model wears leather pants, which come across as far more sexy than tough because she has a sultry, come-hither look ("Runway" 219). By stressing the femininity and heterosexuality of models who wear leather fashions, women's magazines convey to readers that leather attire, despite its tough tradition rooted in images of James Dean and other bad-boy heroes, only enhances a woman's femininity.

Another way women's magazines mitigate the toughness of leather attire is by frequently including pictures, fashion spreads, and articles that stress the importance of combining a leather item with a more feminine piece of clothing. In one picture, a frilly top accompanies a black leather mini-skirt with the reassuring caption: "Bad-girl black leather looks sweet when it meets a tiny top or ruffled shirt" ("The Leather Report" 139). A fashion spread from *Vogue* suggests that even "the traditional leather jacket softens up for spring" when made from white leather instead of black ("Pale" 316). In a fashion spread from *Vanity Fair,* a tough-looking leather bustier is combined with a silk skirt ("Funny" 91). Not only is the toughness attributed to the leather undermined when presented in the form of a bustier, a piece of clothing very much attached to femininity and sexuality, it is also undermined by associating it with the softness and femininity of silk. Combining styles associated with masculinity and femininity sends out a complex signal to viewers because the "values of 'masculine' and 'feminine' in style are ultimately bound up with the values placed on actual male and female roles in social and sexual life" (Williamson, *Consuming* 53). Masculine styles are connected with authority, prestige, and power—attributes associated with men. Feminine styles are connected with softness, delicacy, and powerlessness, which is why women in business often wear outfits that have masculine characteristics. Feminine and frilly outfits would typically be interpreted as wielding less power. Thus, combining the masculinity of leather with the femininity of other clothing is one way to diminish the masculine strength and authority that are often conveyed by leather.

Women's magazines frequently combine masculine and feminine styles, and not only with leather fashions.[5] For example, *Mademoiselle* contains a fashion spread that displays "tough but pretty party clothes that wear as well as *West Side Story*" ("Stay Cool" 159). Another spread from *Mademoiselle,* "White-Collar Cool," portrays one model in a denim jacket combined with a frilly lace collar and another model in a leather jacket paired with big earrings and a flouncy blouse. The spread has semi-tough headings such as "Want to make something of it? Punch up a pastel shirt with a tight, streetwise skirt" ("Stay Cool" 161). In a photo spread entitled "Pretty Tough" from *Seventeen* magazine, jean jackets are combined with bikinis to give a look that is attractive but cool. One model is dressed in a "beat black" jacket that "cruises over a pretty polka-dot maillot" (169). Another wears a "bleached-out denim jacket (skimming the midriff) [that] toughens up a sweet peach bikini" (170). In a fashion spread from *Cosmopolitan* entitled "Feminine Denim" (1993), a classic men's-style denim shirt is paired with high heels and bikini underwear (158). These examples show how customary it is for women's magazines to combine tough clothing with feminine, frilly attire—a sign of a culture that is ill at ease with women adopting too many characteristics associated with men and masculinity because of their association with lesbianism. The fashion styles that fill women's magazines suggest a great deal about how men and women have been segregated into separate spheres by gender. Even when tough fashions are not shown, their absence speaks as loudly as their presence, a sign that being tough is still not perceived as acceptable for women.

Being a Boy: Girls in Drag

Wearing men's clothing or severely masculine clothing is another signifier of toughness that women have adopted. For centuries women have worn men's clothing for many reasons: to travel more safely, to find employment, to express themselves, and for physical comfort and ease of movement. "Women have opted periodically—and during certain periods with great fervor—to incorporate into their personas insignia of male status and masculinity" (F. Davis 33). Wearing men's clothing or very masculine clothing is also a fashion trend that has appeared and reappeared in women's fashion throughout much of the twentieth century becoming more popular than ever in the 1980s and 1990s.

When I initially began thinking about this subject, I assumed that magazines would be hostile to women wearing men's clothing or very masculine-style attire. After all, American culture has long been uneasy about cross-dressing for both men and women, and for centuries cross-dressing has been tightly controlled and policed.[6] Even today, a woman who dresses in extremely masculine attire is likely to meet with public ridicule. But women dressed in men's clothing or mannish clothing do make appearances in women's magazines, particularly those devoted to high fashion. Clearly, women's magazines allow for gender play and even gender bending. As the authors of *Women's Worlds: Ideology, Femininity and the Woman's Magazine* (1991) suggest, "the women's magazine must be understood as a cultural form in which, since its inception, definitions and understandings of gender difference have been negotiated and contested rather than taken for granted or imposed" (Ballaster et al. 176). Despite the space that women's magazines devote to different images of womanhood, the same magazines make sure that cross-dressing and wearing mannish clothing are carefully contained. Women who garb themselves in masculine-style clothing are a distinct minority in women's magazines, and cross-dressing will probably never be more than an oddity.

In addition to challenging gender roles, one of the reasons mannish attire is potentially dangerous is because American culture assumes a strong correlation between lesbianism and masculine clothing for women. I am not arguing that women's magazines *always* wish to squelch the possibility of lesbianism. In "Commodity Lesbianism" (1991), Danae Clark points out the relatively frequent appearance of women in the fashion industry who look like lesbians: "In fashion magazines such as *Elle* and *Mirabella,* and in mail-order catalogs such as *Tweeds, J. Crew* and *Victoria's Secret,* advertisers (whether knowingly or not) are capitalizing upon a dual market strategy that packages gender ambiguity and speaks, at least indirectly, to the lesbian consumer market" (186). Clark discusses the ways that magazines use a strategy she refers to as "gay window advertising" in order to appeal to a larger audience: "Generally, gay window ads avoid explicit references to heterosexuality by depicting only one individual or same-sexed individuals within the representational frame. In addition, these models bear the signifiers of sexual ambiguity or androgynous style" (183). Clark builds a persuasive argument about gay window dressing and how magazines seek to appeal to the largest possible audience of consumers, whatever their sexual orientation might be. It is equally important to recognize that magazines that might sometimes, whether knowingly or not, use an image that could be interpreted as lesbian are also deeply invested in maintaining the heterosexuality of their focus. A few images that could be interpreted as lesbian do not interfere with the countless images that are strongly coded as heterosexual. In a similar way, mannish or masculine clothing can appear in women's magazines, but it is still overwhelmed by the more feminine attire that is far more prevalent.

Women's magazines must carefully negotiate how to present women in attire that appears mannish. In *New Woman,* one fashion spread featuring masculine-style clothing assures readers, "Though inspired by classic menswear fabrics and tailoring, this fall's fashions are anything but mannish" ("Men's Department" 106). Being mannish must be avoided at all costs, which is why an article from *Essence* entitled "My Style" (1996) suggests that a woman might soften up a man's suit by combining it with "a lacy camisole and pretty jewelry" (142). Another article from *Harper's Bazaar* about menswear for women proclaims, "Menswear influences are being seen again, now with distinctly feminine interpretations" (Lebowitz 208). This article also emphasizes the femininity of women by focusing on the makeup that a woman should have on while wearing men's clothing or clothing influenced by men's styles. Magazines walk a tightrope. They wish to feature clothing and styles commonly associated with men because this is one mildly scandalous way to sell a new look, but they do not want to suggest that women are usurping men's roles. Because women's magazines are built on maintaining femininity as the cultural norm, portraying women who appear too mannish, too masculine, or too tough is antithetical to the magazines' entire aim.

Dressing in men's clothing is such a delicate issue to negotiate that numerous fashion spreads in *Mademoiselle, Cosmopolitan,* and other women's magazines address the subject of how girls should wear boys' clothing. In the *Mademoiselle* article "Full Pants Ahead," a photo spread is developed around women wearing masculine-style clothing, showing that such clothing need not interfere with a woman's femininity. The most peculiar story I have read on women wearing men's attire appeared in *Essence.* In this photo spread, the actor Mario Van Peebles, dressed as a private eye, tracks down a group of women who have been stealing suits from men's wardrobes. The last page of the piece features a photograph of Van Peebles wearing only his boxer shorts as he flees from the women he has been pursuing. They flaunt his clothing, which they have stolen. The caption reads: "Seems the 'game' had to teach Sonny a lesson. There's nothing wrong with women wearing menswear" ("The Great Suit" 91). Notice that the women, not the man, end up with the pants, which represent power and authority. This article suggests a great deal about society's fears concerning what happens in a topsy-turvy world where the girls wear the pants. Fifty years ago such a portrayal would have been unthinkable. Today, when a woman's magazine makes such a statement, it encourages readers to think about the significance of clothing and to rethink their relationship to it, perhaps even to wonder whether men's clothing is also acceptable for women.

When women in men's clothing do make an appearance in women's magazines, a variety of strategies are used to defuse the danger they pose to the divisions between men and women ordained by society:

> Notwithstanding fashion's frequent encouragement to women to borrow items and modes of men's dress, the norms of Western society demand that gender identity be grounded finally in some irreducible claim that is clearly either male or female, not both or some indeterminate middling state. . . . It is characteristic, therefore, for cross-gender clothing signals, even the more common and variegated women's borrowings from men, to be accompanied by some symbolic qualification, contradiction, jibe, irony, . . . that in effect advises the viewer not to take the cross-gender representation at face value. (F. Davis 42)

One way to assure readers of the femaleness of a subject is to include a touch of femininity to limit the toughness of men's clothing or mannish clothing worn by women. As long as the femaleness and the femininity of the models is evident, then the cross-dress attire becomes nothing more than a costume. For example, the women who model the male-style clothing in "Full Pants Ahead" are all notably feminine. Though they are wearing such traditionally male clothing as ties, trousers, and pin-striped men's shirts, there is no possibility that a reader could mistake these women for men. A few of the models even flaunt clear signs of femininity, such as a purse. Similarly, a fashion article in *Essence* that describes "suits with soldier chic" (114) makes sure to inform its readers that girls will still be girls, even while wearing highly masculine attire: "Whether military-inspired with epaulets, multiple pockets, gold buttons and an army green-and-khaki palette, or borrowed from the boys with tweeds and pinstripes in grays and camel, these new uniforms speak of power and a strong work ethic. A formfitting turtleneck sweater or a low-buttoning shirt becomes the perfect complement" ("What's New" 114). Women's magazines are masters at presenting an image or a description that both suggests and undermines masculinity and toughness.

Another way to reduce the threat posed by women dressing like men is to suggest that such behavior is sexy and fits neatly into a heterosexual context. A number of high-fashion magazines feature photographs and articles about cross-dressing women that acknowledge the sexual allure of such behavior. In one example, a fashion spread from *Cosmopolitan,* pantsuits for women that highlight the sexual desirability of the women are featured. The designer Ralph Lauren includes a picture of a woman model wearing a severely masculine blazer, complete with tie and handkerchief ("Runway" 224). There can be little doubt that Lauren and the other designers who create clothing for women are trying to attract an audience that finds such male designs appealing. Yet another example of an article that emphasizes the sexual allure of men's attire, from *Vanity Fair,* describes the Parisian fascination for "girls with a penchant for dressing up in boyish attire. Their hair Eton-cropped, their legs trouser-clad, they stride along the boulevards with all the loose-limbed assurance of the young Kate Hepburn. This, too, is the tomboy spirit which informs the best of fall's fad for masculine-style women's clothes" ("Tailor" 68). Even a magazine like *Vanity Fair,* recognized for pushing the boundaries of what it can represent, is quick to reassure its readers: "No matter how tailored, tweedy, or manly they are, one is always aware of the female beneath" ("Tailor" 68). Here, again, being perceived as too masculine or too mannish is the ultimate taboo. Even the most androgynous of cross-dressed women must be careful to reveal that they are biologically female.

Along with emphasizing the heterosexual desirability of cross-dressed women, women's fashion magazines diffuse the toughness and gender-bending threat of cross-dressing by the very nature of their form. Because fashion magazines in our culture are closely linked with maintaining the myth of femininity, it is almost impossible to *avoid* reading the cross-dressing segments as brief theatrical interludes between what the magazines represent as the "reality" of femininity. The whole structure of the magazines prepares readers to recognize that anything other than femininity for women is only a theatrical display.

We also need to recognize that fashion magazines are able to take something potentially threatening (wearing men's clothing) and turn it into nothing more than the latest fashion of the week:

> Because style is a cultural construction, it is easily appropriated, reconstructed and divested of its original political or subcultural signification. Style as resistance becomes commodifiable as chic when it leaves the political realm and enters the fashion world. This simultaneously diffuses the political edge of style. Resistant trends (such as wearing men's oversized jackets or oxford shoes—which, as a form of masquerade, is done in part for fun, but also in protest against the fashion world's insistence upon dressing women in tightly-fitted garments and dangerously unstable footwear) become restyled as high-priced fashions. (Clark 193)

Mainstream women's magazines appropriate the tough girl and turn her into an unthreatening commodity that can be bought and sold. Like the 1970s television shows examined in the previous chapter, women's magazines limit the threat posed by toughness in women by suggesting that toughness should not and does not interfere with a woman's adherence to femininity. Neither Charlie's Angels nor the leather-clad models that fill women's magazines like *Mademoiselle* and *Vogue* are going to overthrow the cult of femininity, because both the show and the magazines are deeply interested in perpetuating the mythology of femininity.

"Tough and Tender"

We have discovered how women's magazines use the imagery of toughness to create new fashions and to sell commodities ranging from leather jackets to silk shirts. However, these magazines are not suggesting that it is acceptable for women to be tough—rather, they repeatedly undermine the idea that women can be tough by linking toughness to femininity. An article in *Mademoiselle* describes the combination of toughness and softness that women should strive to achieve: "Femininity used to be thought of as soft, frilly, and—all too often—ineffective. But nowadays there's nothing weak about it. In fact, some of the most admired women around are the ones who manage to combine qualities both tough and tender" ("Pretty" 168). *Mademoiselle* and other magazines do not want femininity to be reconceptualized too dramatically. These magazines demonstrate how the popular media create new images for women, yet simultaneously perpetuate traditional roles.

It is a mistake to perceive the images of tough women in magazines as *only* perpetuating stereotypical views of women. I argued in the previous chapter that Emma Peel, Charlie's Angels, and the Bionic Woman, despite the way that their toughness was undermined, could still be perceived as possible strong role models for women, particularly when they first appeared. Even the general societal reaction of the 1970s that the Angels were nothing more than bimbos did not prevent viewers past and present from understanding the Angels as positive models for women. Similarly, although I have argued that the majority of high-fashion women's magazines work to undermine the toughness of women, there is no reason that readers cannot carry away very different messages from these texts. It is entirely possible to read the magazines' portraits of nontraditional tough women as empowering to women. My interpretation of the magazines, I hope, reveals the complexity of the depiction of tough women in women's magazines and other popular sources.

Despite creating images of tough women that some readers might find empowering, women's magazines also maintain the gender status quo by insisting on obeisance to the cult of femininity. Women's magazines undermine toughness because it threatens the foundation upon which they are built, and they are not the sole media form that suggests toughness in women is merely skin-deep. I have discussed how popular television has created images of pseudo-tough women. Next, to understand how the media portray pseudo-tough women only to undermine their toughness by showing that women are no match for men, we turn to films about women who kill—films that frequently star women who are not afraid to murder and maim. Rather than show that toughness is acceptable for women, these films affirm exactly the opposite. Hollywood's killer women demonstrate that women who adopt the masculine attributes of toughness are literally insane. As we shall find, killer-women films are all about punishing women who aspire to toughness.

Chapter 4
Lady Killers

Tough Enough?

In China in the early 1990s, "Dagger Ladies" became all the rage with the affluent, who could afford to shell out the 1000 yuan ($172) monthly salary to support one. Dagger Ladies—female body guards who fetch the mail, answer the phone, and perform other such office tasks, but who can also throw a mean right hook when necessary—are trained by a number of specialized schools. One school bragged that it instructed its seventy trainees not only in "shooting, parachute jumping, judo and boxing but also in law, psychology, etiquette and foreign languages." Dagger Ladies caught on to such an extent that three thousand women applied for the 130 openings in a Dagger Lady training course. The Dagger-Lady-wannabes did not seem put off that the class cost 3,500 yuan ($620), which represented three-and-a-half months of the earnings they could expect as Dagger Ladies. The *Chicago Tribune* article about this phenomenon was quick to reassure readers that a Dagger Lady would not lose her femininity: "She's a devil with a dagger and a whiz in martial arts. She often wears high-heel shoes and mini-skirts." As the title of the article informed readers, a Dagger Lady was "tough as steel, but still a lady" (Schmetzer 6).

Though not training to be Dagger Ladies, American women, too, have shown a new interest in learning how to fight, flocking to classes with names like Cardio Combat, Aerobox, and Executive Boxing—exercise classes that teach fighting skills along with providing a workout. Cardio Combat features "chops, punches and kicks" (Eller 124), while Aerobox and Executive Boxing introduce boxing, a sport generally considered off-limits to women. If women choose to concentrate on self-protection, a variety of classes are offered that teach them to fight back. Krav Magna is a "technique used by the Israeli Army" that instructs assault victims to lash out at the attacker's groin, kneecap, or eyes (Eller 125). Other classes offered include Model Mugging, in which women learn to fight back by attacking and attempting to disable a male instructor posing as a mugger (Eller 125).

Today, tough, aggressive fighting women are all the rage in Hollywood.[1] One writer observes, "In recent years, the rampaging female has become a new cliché of Hollywood cinema, stabbing and shooting her way to notoriety" (Birch 1). Another comments, "Hollywood has long been fascinated by women who kill. In the last ten years, however, deadly dolls have filled the screen. Willingly, even gleefully, they pick up the rocket launcher, the gun, the knife, the fork" (Holmlund 127).[2] Yet another writer, Julie Baumgold, discusses the growing numbers of what she refers to as "killer women" in such films as *Thelma & Louise* and *La Femme Nikita*. She writes, "They have borrowed the competence of the Fonda-Streep women and turned it to killing. They are no longer molls and helpers, no longer love puppies who commit crimes of passion; they are combat-trained outlaws" (26). What explains the increasing prevalence of the tough killer woman in films from the 1980s and 1990s?[3] Does her appearance signify new freedoms for women? What does she reveal about how tough women are perceived by Americans today? This chapter seeks to answer these questions by exploring the depiction of the killer woman in popular films, showing how her presence perpetuates the notion that women who adopt the tough attributes typically associated with men will literally go insane.[4]

Like the previous two chapters, this one is concerned with tracing the myriad ways that society seeks to limit the threat of toughness in women by showing that women are only pseudo-tough, lacking the "true" toughness of men. In the last two chapters, we discovered how toughness in women was repeatedly toned down by emphasizing the connection between women, sexuality, and femininity. This chapter demonstrates another way that toughness in women is controlled: killer-women films often depict women who are clearly insane or over the edge because they have become too aggressive, too masculine, or too tough. These women, the films show, must be punished for their aggressive gender-bending behavior. Punishment, however, is not the only tactic for dealing with such socially transgressive females. Killer women can be depicted as sex kittens under their tough demeanors, as were the Angels. They also can be presented as less tough than the boys. We shall find that films about killer women rely on these three tactics to assure viewers of the stability of the patriarchal order.

Despite the increasing number of killer women in recent films, this character type is by no means a new invention but one with deep roots in Hollywood. Notable predecessors include the scheming, manipulative women of *film noir,* such as Phyllis Dietrichson (Barbara Stanwyck) in

Double Indemnity (1944) and Gilda (Rita Hayworth) in *Gilda* (1946). In the 1960s, the killer woman took different forms. As Ma Barker, Lurene Tuttle was a killer in the film *Ma Barker's Killer Brood* (1960). Bonnie Parker (Faye Dunaway) was also a killer in *Bonnie and Clyde* (1967). The killer woman has been a staple of James Bond films for decades. A beautiful femme fatale lurks around every corner in Agent 007's world. In *For Your Eyes Only* (1981), Melina (Carole Bouquet) is an expert with a crossbow and does not hesitate to kill the man who murdered her parents. Fatima Blush in *Never Say Never Again* (1983) is a sadistic murderer who would do anything to kill Agent 007. Grace Jones plays the sinister May Day in *A View to a Kill* (1985). In *GoldenEye* (1995), Xenia Onatroop (Famke Janssen) delights in murdering the men with whom she makes love, often squeezing them to death between her muscular thighs.

Obviously, killer women are a recurring motif in Hollywood. However, contemporary killer women are growing in number and have become far more aggressive—changes indicative of altering cultural values. In her book *Spectacular Bodies: Gender, Genre and the Action Cinema* (1993), Yvonne Tasker writes about women in action-adventure films, "There is a whole range of determinants informing the production of the woman as action heroine in recent cinema. Her appearance can be seen to signal, amongst other factors, a response to feminism and the exhaustion of previous formulae" (152). Tasker's words are applicable to killer-women films in which the killer enacts society's worst fears about feminism: strong women prove to be not only career women, but also murderous harpies. In this way, these films offer viewers an extreme scenario about what happens when women usurp roles that have been long considered the province of men.

We can better understand how killer-women films offer an opportunity to enact cultural fantasies about the excesses of feminism in light of Alice Jardine's theory of male paranoia. In " 'She Was Bad News': Male Paranoia and the Contemporary New Woman" (1981), Amelia Jones describes how male paranoia operates:

> The new woman's films are structured by what Alice Jardine has called "male paranoia"—the fearful response of patriarchy to the loss of boundaries endemic to the condition of subjectivity in contemporary, so-called postmodern, American life. . . . Male paranoia is a defense aimed at rebuilding the subject/object dichotomy that threatens to dissolve as more and more women (and men, for that matter) take on both masculine and feminine roles. (297)

Jones argues that the films "represent patriarchy's last-ditch efforts to rebuild or shore up the tottering ramparts by which the masculine is assured a dominant socio-economic position in social relations" (298). She suggests that the new woman's films "repeatedly attempt to pose resolutions to the problem of gender identity by reinscribing women in traditional roles or eliminating deviant women to remove their threat to the family structure" (315). Jones's thoughts are germane to killer-women films that reassure viewers that women who display too many tough, masculine characteristics will get their just rewards, usually ending up in prison or being killed. In this fashion, the films serve to shore up the gender status quo and to warn women that adopting tough attributes is still unacceptable.

But there are other reasons for the current success of the killer-woman film. It offers a new thrill at a time when Hollywood is searching for the sensation-of-the-year in order to sell more films to jaded viewers. As Baumgold notes, "In part, the male-mogul motive is commercial. To appeal to women repulsed or bored by male action movies, they have created these warrior women. . . . There are contradictions in this new woman. She may wear her heavy jacket with something flimsy. She is hard but breakable" (29). Producers might wish to attract a broader audience to action-adventure films, but, at the same time, they do not wish to stray too far from the gender stereotypes that have served them well in the past. What they create are women killers who might wield a knife or shoot a gun but still remember the importance of appearing feminine and physically desirable to men. Because the sexual allure of killer women is frequently stressed in Hollywood films, these films present images of women and femininity that are less subversive than might initially appear to be the case.

The Killer Woman as Sex Kitten

The threat posed by the killer woman is mitigated in part because she is commonly portrayed as very sexually appealing to men. Christine Holmlund observes, "the murderesses in [killer women] films are, to a woman, white, lithe and lovely, because Hollywood sees female violence as erotic and defines 'erotic' within narrow parameters" (128). Holmlund points out that Hollywood takes the dangerous toughness of many killer women and limits its potential threat to the social order by suggesting that women might be killers, but they are still attractive to men. Often the association between women and violence only heightens their sexual appeal. As we have already discovered, the same connection between women and danger is used in *Charlie's Angels* to heighten the sexual appeal of the show's stars.

By making the women sexually desirable and stressing that they are attracted to men, the films assure viewers that women are sexual objects. Laura Mulvey discusses the objectification of women in the cinema in her essay "Visual Pleasure and Narrative Cinema" (1975): "Traditionally, the woman displayed has functioned on two levels: as erotic object for the characters within the screen story, and as erotic object for the spectator within the auditorium" (11–12). Mulvey's words provide an apt description of the killer woman. She might be a killer, but this does not interfere with how the film portrays her as an erotically appealing object for the pleasure of men. Moreover, killer-women films show not only sexually appealing women, but also women who display a keen interest in sexual relations with men, demonstrating that their tough attitudes and actions fail to interfere with their primary role as sex objects for men.

Throughout the past two decades, the sexually voracious killer woman has become a common character. *Prizzi's Honor* (1985, director John Huston) tells the story of Charley Partanna (Jack Nicholson) and Irene Walker (Kathleen Turner) who fall madly and impetuously in love, knowing nothing about each other's past lives. Irene turns out to be a hired assassin, and her new husband works for the Mafia as a hitman. As a married couple, Irene and Charley continue their careers as assassins. The film emphasizes Irene's sexuality and heterosexual desirability. She is a stunning blonde, and she and her husband have torrid sex every chance they get. The couple is often filmed kissing or hugging or with their arms around each other. The message is clear: Irene might be an assassin, but this does not prevent her from being the perfect wife and sexual partner, stereotypically feminine roles that detract from her tough self-presentation.

In other films, the sex-kitten nature of women is emphasized. The image of the woman who kills without a qualm, yet, in reality, is little more than a *Playboy* pinup come to life appears everywhere in the media, especially in the movie theater. Few films make the connection between sexual exploitation and the woman killer more apparent than *No Contest* (1994, director Paul Lynch), a low-budget movie in which the star, Shannon Tweed, was advertised as Playmate of the Year. She is a sex goddess, whose primary purpose is to be drop-dead gorgeous in the various skimpy outfits she wears. Although she takes on a veritable army of men who have captured the participants of a beauty pageant, and, of course, wins the pageant, it is difficult to watch this film and think of Tweed as anything other than a well-endowed woman for teenage boys to ogle. Her character development is obviously less significant than her status as Playmate of the Year.

The notion that killer women are sex kittens first and killers second is stressed in many films, even in 1990s movies that seem to offer tougher images of womanhood than *No Contest*. For example, in the film *Mortal Kombat* (1995, director Paul Anderson), the heroine appears to be as tough as her male compatriots, until we discover that she is really more sex object than warrior. This movie, based on the best-selling video game by the same name, features three martial arts experts who must defeat a host of evil creatures from an alternative universe who are trying to take over the world. One of the three heroes, Sonya Blade (Bridgette Wilson), is a woman.[5] She starts off tough, independent, and self-assured, but during the film her image undergoes a transformation. She is repeatedly viewed in a sexual light by the male fighters. For instance, the lead bad guy, a sorcerer, reveals that he has plans for the "beautiful Sonya." His lascivious intentions are clear. Tough men do not face the kind of sexual threat that tough women face constantly (think of Ripley in the *Aliens* series). The repeated sexualizing of tough women affirms the woman's role as sexual object; no matter how tough she might appear on the surface, she still can be subjected to the ultimate indignity of rape.

Sonya's tough image is also weakened in other ways. Despite her toughness, she lacks any unusual musculature, which is particularly evident when her body is compared with the well-muscled physiques of the men whom she encounters. In *Spectacular Bodies,* Tasker observes that well-developed muscles serve as a visible sign of an action heroine's vulnerability, demonstrating her need to protect herself from some threat (152). But muscles also serve as an important signifier of strength and power in our culture. Showing a tough woman with no bulging biceps is one way to make her appear less masculine, less threatening, and less tough, even if she is a crack shot or a champion kick boxer. Yet another way that Sonya is made to seem less of a threat than her two male comrades is that she appears in only one fighting match with the villains, while the two men engage in many; the men are still very much center stage.

Sonya is finally "put in her place" when she is kidnapped by the evil sorcerer, and her two friends must save her. At this point, Sonya's credibility as a tough hero is entirely destroyed, and her role as a sex kitten is made overt. Even though she had been depicted earlier as independent and in control, when she is kidnapped she does not put up a fight. When she is rescued, she is, for some unknown reason, dressed in a skirt (rather than the no-nonsense uniform she had on earlier) and wearing makeup. Her hair, rather than being pulled back into a sleek ponytail, is a teased mane (I do not know how she managed to work in a trip to the beauty parlor). And suddenly we find that she has fallen in love with one of her two male friends. Sonya's toughness has been entirely deconstructed; at the end, she does not appear to be much of a threat to anyone; she looks more like a model who might appear in *Cosmopolitan* or *Vogue.* The final message of the film is not that women *can* be tough, but that they *cannot* be tough; ultimately, they fail and need to be rescued by men. A woman's primary purpose is to be a sexual creature for the men who are doing the "real" fighting. Thus, we see how deceptive the depiction of tough women can be in the popular media; a woman might start out tough, but she does not end up that way—her "true nature" eventually emerges.

The Killer Woman as Insane Harpy

Another insidious way to portray tough women is to suggest that such women are insane and deserve punishment.[6] In this fashion, a film might allow a woman an unusually tough role, but often only so that she meets with the punishment that, the film suggests, she deserves for transgressing society's dictates about acceptable behavior for women.

Interestingly enough, the women who are portrayed as being so wild and out of control that they appear insane are almost always femme fatales, meaning that they are highly sexually appealing to men and often seem to be perfect mates—until they reveal a seriously flawed personality. In her book *Femmes Fatales: Feminism, Film Theory, Psychoanalysis* (1991), Mary Ann Doane provides a description of the femme fatale's role: "The femme fatale is the figure of a certain discursive unease, a potential epistemological trauma. For her most striking characteristic, perhaps, is the fact that she never really is what she seems to be. She harbors a threat which is not entirely legible, predictable, or manageable" (1). Doane points out some of the reasons that the femme fatale is such a threatening character. At the same time, however, there is something reassuring about the femme fatale because she adheres to various feminine stereotypes; for instance, she is always glamorous and extremely feminine. Thus, the femme fatale simultaneously subverts stereotypical notions of womanhood and upholds them. The femme fatale's danger is a fleeting one because, as Doane observes, she is punished:

> The femme fatale is situated as evil and is frequently punished or killed. Her textual eradication involves a desperate reassertion of control on the part of the threatened male subject. Hence, it would be a mistake to see her as some kind of heroine of modernity. She is not the subject of feminism but a symptom of male fears about feminism. Nevertheless, the representation—like any representation—is not totally under the control of its producers and, once disseminated, comes to take on a life of its own. (2–3)

As we shall find, Doane's words are an appropriate description of what happens to the femme fatales who are featured in killer-women films. The threat they pose to the social order is rarely allowed to last beyond the film's conclusion. Also, the femme fatale is typically shown to be insane, suggesting that her tough attributes are not "normal" for women but signs of a pathological condition.

Many films show that the toughness displayed by femme fatales is just one sign of their insanity. These movies became particularly popular in the late 1980s and 1990s. *Black Widow* (1987, director Bob Rafelson) was enormously popular when it first appeared, leading to a spate of copycat films. In the movie Debra Winger plays Alexandra, a dowdy, drab federal agent who is so wrapped up in her work that she does not take time off from her work even to go on a Friday night date. Everything changes when she starts to track down Catharine (Theresa Russell), a mysterious, beautiful, wealthy woman who marries rich husbands and then murders them. Catharine changes her look and image to attract each man she marries. She is a chameleon, able to change her style to appeal to any man. She fulfills the fantasy of each man she marries and then murders him, coldly and ruthlessly. Although she is a sexy blonde temptress, she is marked as tough and masculine because of her active sexual desire (particularly her desire for Alexandra), which is frequently emphasized in the film. As Lynda Hart observes, "Masculinity is as much verified by active desire as it is by aggression" (x). Thus, *Black Widow* and other femme fatale films typically depict feminine women, but what is often assumed to be their innate masculine toughness is betrayed, revealing that these are by no means "normal" women.

The Black Widow is doubly marked as evil because she is obsessed not only with money but with killing men. Undertones suggest that Catharine is lesbian or bisexual, such as when she gives Alexandra a kiss on the lips at her own wedding. The Black Widow has much closer relationships with women—even with Alexandra, whom Catharine knows is trying to capture her—than with men. The show implies that an erotic obsession exists between the two women that has gotten out of control. Catharine says that their sexually charged relationship is one that she will always remember, even when Catharine's schemes cause Alexandra to be imprisoned for a murder she did not commit.

The connection between lesbianism and women's aggression is explored in Lynda Hart's book *Fatal Women: Lesbian Sexuality and the Mark of Aggression* (1994), in which she discusses the history of the presumed connection between the lesbian and the female criminal. According to Hart, "one ghost in the machine of heterosexual patriarchy is the lesbian who shadows the entrance into representation of women's aggression" (iv). She comments that the lesbian is "the silent escort of the violent woman" (x). This is true in *Black Widow* and in many other killer-women films, one of the most notorious being *Basic Instinct* (1992, director Paul Verhoeven), in which Catherine Tramell (Sharon Stone) is a cold-hearted bisexual murderer whose weapon of choice is an ice pick. These films and others often imply that the femme fatale's violence stems from her lesbianism, which rarely goes unpunished. As a murderess and a potential lesbian or bisexual, Catherine is not allowed to escape punishment: at the film's conclusion, her plans are exposed and she is held by the police—presumably to be tried for her crimes. Thus *Basic Instinct* reveals that any woman, like Catherine, who transgresses gender boundaries by becoming a killer, must be punished.

The pattern in *Black Widow* and *Basic Instinct* recurs in other movies. *Double Impact* (1991, director Sheldon Lettrich) also depicts an insane femme fatale. Kara (Cory Everson), a bodyguard for a corrupt businessman, is a crazed murderer and sadist who delights in killing. Another film with an insane, vicious woman killer is *Romeo Is Bleeding* (1993, director Peter Medak).[7] This film features the steamy sexual relationship that develops between a policeman, Jack Grimaldi (Gary Oldman), and a hired killer, Mona Demarkov (Lena Olin). Mona is a classic femme fatale—with long nails, plunging neckline, bright red lipstick, and spiked heels. A husky-voiced siren who uses sex to control and manipulate men, she is also a sadistic killer who cares for no one and laughs hysterically when trying to strangle Jack. She is so vicious and so uncaring, that when Jack murders her at the end of the film one feels a sense of relief that this vicious woman has died. She was out of control—insane, wild, and vengeful.

All of these femme fatale films demonstrate that women who are too tough will be punished. The films also show that such women are literally insane. Femme fatale films depict tough women, but only to show what the films suggest are the women's pathological conditions. Moreover, as Amelia Jones points out, the films confirm male paranoia: tough women are basically psychotic and must be punished in order to uphold society's conventions about how women should act.

Tough, But Not as Tough as the Boys

In another version of the lady killer film, the woman is revealed to be less tough than her male companions. In *The Professional* (1994, director Luc Besson), Matilda (Natalie Portman) is an adolescent girl whose family has been killed by corrupt police. The family is so dysfunctional that Matilda hardly sheds a tear (except for her baby brother), so she is free to get down to business: she befriends Leon (Jean Reno), a professional hit man *par excellence,* to learn how to become a professional killer (Figure 2). She learns how to shoot a rifle, how to load a gun, and other tricks of the assassin's trade, but Matilda is still completely overshadowed by Leon, the true professional, who must rescue Matilda repeatedly.[8] The film emphasizes Matilda's soft side. For instance, she is shown carrying around a stuffed animal and watching Saturday morning cartoons. In other words, she is just a normal everyday girl underneath her tough veneer and poses little

Figure 2. Matilda (Natalie Portman) learns her trade (*The Professional,* Columbia Pictures).

threat to Leon's male power. In *The Professional* and other films, it is apparent that tough women maintain rather than challenge the status quo.

The belief that women are not as tough as men is also apparent in *La Femme Nikita* (1990, director Luc Besson), a French film that was popular in the United States. Nikita (Anne Parillaud) is a ruthless, vicious female junkie. She is wildly out of control and faces life imprisonment after killing a policeman, but she is given a second chance by a French secret police agency that coerces her into working for it. She is taught how to shoot guns and how to be an assassin, but she is also taught how to be a seductive femme fatale (Figure 3). She is literally rebuilt, reminding us of the way Henry Higgins rebuilds the cockney flower girl Eliza Doolittle in *My Fair Lady.* In both cases—*My Fair Lady* and *La Femme Nikita*—the intervention of a man is necessary to socialize a young working-class woman. Nikita is redesigned through her constant interactions with a man known only as "Bob" and an unnamed older woman. Both train Nikita for three years; she is never allowed to leave the police compound

Figure 3. Nikita (Anne Parillaud) plays a femme fatale (*La Femme Nikita,* Vidmark Entertainment).

during that time. Nikita, like Eliza, is taught how to pass in upper-class society. Nikita moves from sporting a studded black leather jacket and heavy boots to wearing slinky dresses and high heels. Not surprisingly, one of the skills she learns is how to apply makeup. She goes from looking like a street punk to looking like an elegant and sophisticated young lady. But she is also a killer. She embodies the ultimate male threat—a seductive, attractive woman who lures men to their deaths with her feminine wiles.

After Nikita is released from the training facility, she leads a happy "normal" life with her newfound boyfriend. During the day, she is an assassin for the mysterious agency for which she works. Ultimately, her lover reveals he knows about her clandestine career and explains that it makes no difference to him. At this point, Nikita is obviously distraught by the viciousness of her profession and wants out. At the film's conclusion we assume she has fled in order to escape the agency and its employees. Nikita's actions at the end reveal the artificiality of her tough pose; the film demonstrates that Nikita only thought she was tough.

When the "right" man came along, she was suddenly transformed into a "normal" woman, far more interested in concocting a tasty meal for her lover than plotting her next assassination. Patricia Mellencamp describes the message of *La Femme Nikita* as "tough but tamed by femininity" (*Fine* 116).

Mellencamp's words are also an appropriate description of the dynamics of *The Quick and the Dead* (1995, director Sam Raimi), one of several Westerns that appeared in the mid-1990s starring women in what were traditionally roles for tough guy actors like John Wayne and Clint Eastwood. Rather then being a transgressive redepiction of the Western, *The Quick and the Dead* confirms that women are not capable of holding onto the tough guy roles long played by men.

The film begins with a scene showing a man firing at a woman on horseback, a woman we later discover is Ellen (Sharon Stone). The man thinks he has killed her, but she gets up, slugs him, manacles him to his wagon, and then mounts her horse, leaving him to swear and curse as she rides off. Already, the woman is being set up in the image of the lone gunslinger. We have to remember, however, that the woman playing the role of the gunslinger is Sharon Stone—one of the top sex symbols of Hollywood (Figure 4). It is impossible for Stone to escape her reputation, which Stacey Lassally, TriStar Pictures' president of production, admits the studio promotes when she comments that Stone's character "has very wide appeal . . . [because she] has sex appeal and she also kicks ass" (quoted in Jordan D5). The film further bolsters Stone's status as a sex symbol by having her appear in a very chic Western outfit, never looking dirty or sweaty, whether she has been riding for hours in the hot sun or has just killed a desperado. Stone always looks like a model first and a gunslinger second.

Ellen rides into a small Western town where she and other gunslingers are competing in a shooting contest for a $123,000 prize, which goes to the contestant still alive at the end of the contest. The prize money is offered by the despicable John Herod (Gene Hackman), a cruel gunman who owns the town and runs it with the aid of his henchmen. It is clear that Ellen has a personal vendetta against Herod, which she tries to resolve by entering the contest in which he will also participate. When Ellen states that she wants to sign up for the contest, Herod sneers, "There's no rule against ladies, except women can't shoot for shit." The lines are drawn. Ellen's fight is going to prove not only her skills as a gunfighter, but also that women are just as tough as men. Before this point she has shown her toughness repeatedly in the film by coolly avoiding the sexual advances of several men and doing some fancy shooting that prevents a man from being hung. Yet, just the fact that Ellen has to handle a number of sexual advances from men functions to establish her as a very different charac-

Figure 4. A gunslinger (Sharon Stone) looking for revenge (*The Quick and the Dead,* TriStar Pictures).

ter from the traditional tough hero of the Western, who rarely fears sexual attention.

But Ellen's tough character is strongly modified as the film continues; the film's director is obviously not intent upon making Stone into an Eastwood or a Wayne. Instead, her femininity is stressed again and again.

For instance, at one point she wakes up in the morning in the company of a handsome young gunslinger known as the Kid; although the film does not show whether the two had sex, the implication is clear. Stone is also constantly depicted as less sure of herself than the men. She shows a great deal more emotion on her face, reminding viewers that, despite her gunslinging talent and ability to slug out a man, she is still a woman and therefore emotional.

Ellen's femininity becomes even more obvious as the film continues. After Herod kills a bragging gunfighter, Ellen looks terrified. Shortly afterward, she has a dream flashback in which she is a little girl, complete with doll and long dress, remembering her father being killed. We later learn that Herod murdered her father. Thus, she becomes a gunslinger only because of her obsessive desire to kill her father's killer. Her toughness is depicted as something that is forced upon her — something, we are led to assume, she would not have adopted if she had been able to avoid the trauma in her childhood.

Ellen's femininity is again emphasized when Herod invites her to dinner. She is shown taking an ornate silk bustier from her dresser. When she goes out for dinner, she wears a long dress with a low neckline and looks every inch a "lady." Here, viewers are reminded that Stone is a sex symbol and a woman. When Ellen is eating dinner, we see the gun that hangs by her side, with which she presumably plans to shoot Herod. The toughness associated with having a gun, however, is diminished by the generous glimpse of her garter-belted leg. She fails in her attempt to kill Herod and flees. At this point, she appears to be no more than another scared woman who cannot stand up to a man's toughness.

Eventually, Ellen returns to town and kills Herod, but we see less of her fight than the gunfight between Herod and Court (Russell Crowe), one of Herod's ex-gunfighters who has turned preacher. The two minutes the film devotes to Ellen's battle with Herod are less significant than the many minutes the film devotes to emphasizing that she has been pushed to extreme measures because of her father's death. The film implies that toughness is not a "natural" part of her identity, or the identity of any other woman.

The Quick and the Dead and many other films that feature killer women are intent on demonstrating that women, no matter how tough they might appear, are only superficially tough. In this fashion, the cultural myth is kept alive that women are no match for their male counterparts — a myth that helps to ensure that women are kept out of positions of power in government and industry because they are not sufficiently tough. Killer-women films are only one of myriad popular culture forms that help to support a social class system in which women are still very much second-class citizens.

Tougher Girls?

I do not suggest that *all* recent killer-women films are solely helping to perpetuate gender norms. Films are complex and carry many meanings, and the films studied in this chapter could be interpreted in different ways. Furthermore, a number of killer-women films have been produced that seem intent on creating tougher, stronger women characters. A classic example is *Thelma & Louise* (1991, director Ridley Scott), which suggests that women can be just as tough as men (Figure 5). One critic describes the appeal of Thelma Dickinson (Geena Davis) and Louise Sawyer (Susan Sarandon): they "grow stronger, tougher and funnier with every mile they drive" (Shapiro 63). However, no matter how tough these women might appear, they die (presumably) at the end of the film. Even though they make the decision to drive off a cliff rather than risk imprisonment, the decision reveals how impossible it is for tough women to survive and thrive in Hollywood.

Other recent films have developed central women characters who appear even tougher than Thelma and Louise. In *Galaxis* (1995, director William Mesa), Brigitte Nielsen plays a superhuman space alien who is searching for a mysterious crystal that means life or death for her people. Following in the footsteps of Superman and other superheroes, she is invincible. This blonde-haired woman, who stands over six feet tall, dwarfs most of the men in the film; however, her superhuman powers are acceptable because she is an alien. No real woman, the movie suggests, would be able to perform Nielson's deeds. Another approach to toughness in women is adopted in *The Demolitionist* (1996, director Robert Kurtzman). In this film, Alyssa Lloyd (Nicole Eggert) is a tough female undercover police agent who is killed by some particularly repugnant punks. After she dies, she is brought back to life as a superhuman crime fighter who takes out whole gangs of bad guys. Wielding two guns and wearing a suit of body armor, she is almost as tough as the Terminator, except for her emotions, which threaten to overwhelm her. The only reason she is allowed to become a killer crime fighter is that she is dead. She is also deeply concerned about romantic issues; she was going to be married before criminals killed her lover—the event that turned her into a vengeful killer. Now, she bemoans the lack of romance in her new life. At one point, she looks at a bridal display and then shoots it up, obviously feeling that phase of her life is over.

Despite the ways they break some gender barriers, *Thelma & Louise, Galaxis,* and *The Demolitionist* show a society in which toughness in women makes people uneasy. The depiction of tough women in films is a visible sign of a culture in which gender roles are no longer as stable and fixed as

Figure 5. Tough girls (Geena Davis and Susan Sarandon) doomed to die (*Thelma & Louise,* Metro-Goldwyn-Mayer).

in previous decades, a culture in which women seem increasingly intent on taking over men's roles. One way to control the threat posed by tough women is to demonstrate that they are not as tough as they seem. Killer-women films repeatedly show that the tough and masculine killer is really all woman beneath the façade. This emphasis implies that *all* tough women are not as tough as they appear and therefore pose no significant threat to male hegemony as far as toughness is concerned. Thus, we discover that even films that present apparently tough women often only depict such characters in order to systematically tear down the tough image and reveal the "real" woman underneath.

If women insist on being too tough and aggressive, killer-women films tell us, the transgressors will be punished. This emphasis on punishment is one way that killer-women films help perpetuate gender norms even when the films seem to be undermining such norms by depicting tough, aggressive women. The films also show that such women are too tough and masculine and hint that these are attributes that women in general should avoid. The movies warn female viewers not to become too tough or too strong, or they will be punished, like the women in the films.

When killer-women films are not intent on showing the punishment meted out to killer women, they often demonstrate that such women, despite their apparent aggression, are still primarily sexual objects for men. Paradoxically, tough attributes are used by the mainstream media in a variety of ways to heighten the sexual allure of women. This emphasis on the sexual desirability of tough women, whether in women's magazines or killer-women films, is yet another way that the media diffuse the danger inherent in tough, independent women—women who can take care of themselves and do not seem to need any man, not even Rambo. By stressing the sexual desirability of women and showing that they are still at the beck and call of a man to whom they are sexually attracted, the popular media inform their audience that although tough women are aloof and unavailable on the surface, their toughness undergoes a meltdown when, inevitably, they fall for a man.

This chapter, with Chapters 1 and 2, have explored the various ways that pseudo-tough women are used in the popular media. Initially such women appear to be tough, but upon closer scrutiny, their toughness is usually superficial and does little to disrupt the gendered social order. To find tougher versions of womanhood, I shall look at the characters played by Jodie Foster and Gillian Anderson, two actors who, as FBI agents Clarice Starling and Dana Scully, present much tougher images than is the norm for women and are far tougher than the fashion-obsessed Angels. However, even Starling and Scully, we will find, are portrayed as less tough than their male counterparts.

Part II
When the Going Gets Tough

Chapter 5
A Tough Girl as One of the Boys
Jodie Foster, Gillian Anderson, and the Threat of Masculinity

They could be sisters: both shoot guns, both are agents in the FBI surviving in a world made up primarily of men and both handle cases that deal with the freakish and abnormal. They even look alike. Clarice Starling from the film *The Silence of the Lambs* and Dana Scully from the television series *The X-Files* and the actresses who portray these characters, Jodie Foster and Gillian Anderson, respectively, share a long list of similarities, including having their own web sites set up by their adoring fans.[1] How can we explain these similarities and what they suggest about Foster and Anderson's roles as tough women? Moreover, what do these similarities suggest about how women's toughness is constituted in the media? In this chapter I argue that Jodie Foster, and to a lesser extent Gillian Anderson, have become icons of tough women in American society, and how their characters are portrayed has a broad impact on the ways that society thinks about tough women. This chapter also points out how these actors have been "softened up" to make them more appealing to a mass audience, as have many other tough women, including Cagney from the television show *Cagney and Lacey* and Jo from *The Facts of Life*.

One of the reasons I take Anderson and Foster as examples is that they play types typically associated with men, and in these roles they display many attributes assumed to be masculine or tough. Anderson's character in *The X-Files,* Dana Scully, has been called "the incarnation of Cartesian rationality" (Hitt 94) and "one of the most cool-headed heroines ever on a TV series" (Gliatto, "X-Ellence" 75). Not only is she cool, she also adopts many masculine attitudes and gestures. Anderson's tough characterization of Scully has not prevented the character from becoming very popular.

Foster has also been associated with a masculine self-presentation in both her own life and her films, particularly in her portrayal of Clarice Starling in *The Silence of the Lambs* (1991). A critic commented about Starling, "you get the sense that she wouldn't be distracted by a man if Nick Nolte himself crossed her path" (Klawans 246). Despite Foster's masculine persona, which I shall discuss in greater depth later, she has not alienated viewers and has become one of the most successful women in Hollywood. As film critic B. Ruby Rich writes, "The iconographic significance of Jodie Foster as 'persona Americana' cannot be overstated" (6).

How does American culture deal with the masculinity as displayed by two of its most famous stars of the 1990s? How do the media depict Anderson, Foster, and other tough women so that they do not challenge gender norms too greatly, potentially turning away the mainstream audience? Studying actors Foster and Anderson, I believe, can tell us a great deal about the continuing media uneasiness with the tough woman in the 1990s and demonstrate ways the media attempt to contain her. Although Starling and Scully appear far tougher than Charlie's Angels or the Bionic Woman, these two more recent characters must grapple with some of the same issues of toughness that their predecessors did. Starling and Scully mirror a society in which toughness is still chiefly considered a male attribute and where tough women are considered abnormal.

Jodie Foster: "The Man in the Family"

When thinking about women's toughness, one might think of Jodie Foster because of her overwhelming presence in American culture. During the decades of her acting and directing career, she has been highly visible and phenomenally successful, becoming one of the most influential women in Hollywood, which is still a bastion of male dominance.[2] Praise has been heaped on her by the popular media for her many successes. An article in *Harper's Bazaar* (1991) describes Foster as "an industry power-player and an unapologetically smart, independent woman" (Berger 168). One writer called her one of the ten most powerful women in show business (Thompson 114).

What is most interesting about Foster is not that she has had success as both an artist and a businesswoman, but that she has long presented a masculine, tough persona, in opposition to more mainstream visions of femininity. Despite this tough image, Foster has emerged as an icon of American culture, with her picture plastered on magazine pages, newspapers, and books. Images of her in the media are difficult to avoid and have helped to perpetuate her tough image, although she is not always depicted as tough looking. "Foster's images are constructed not only through her acting roles, nor only through her directorial choices, but also via her iconography that circulates through print media and fashion photography" (Lane 153). What explains this tremendous success?

In real life and in her films, Foster was associated with toughness and masculinity long before her appearance in *The Silence of the Lambs.* She has often been called tough; writer Rachel Abramowitz, for instance, describes her as "seemingly naked but tough" (60). Foster has repeatedly played roles that emphasize her toughness. *Taxi Driver* (1976) featured Foster as a street-wise prostitute. Later, in *The Accused* (1988) and *Little Man Tate* (1991), she played tough working-class women. A number of film critics have commented on the no-nonsense characters that Foster has portrayed. Christina Lane observes that the characters Foster played as a child were "tough and precocious" (150). B. Ruby Rich writes that Jodie plays "characters who are abused, manipulated, pimped, set up, raped or nearly raped, even killed. However often she may be victimised, though, she never plays the victim. . . . However vulnerable at the level of the body, every Foster character is smart and tough" (8). Rich writes further, "Foster presents us with characters who are strong-willed, not weak; active, not passive; direct, not coy; openly sexual, not repressed or puritanical. . . The [charge] of sexuality makes these tough characters vulnerable, while giving them the strength to sustain that vulnerability" (9). These quotations clarify the consensus that exists about Foster's toughness. Many people judge it to be one of her defining characteristics, which makes her success more intriguing in a society where tough women are often regarded by the mainstream with uneasiness or even hostility.

Foster's tough attitude and carriage are even more controversial because they are combined with a sometimes masculine persona. She has admitted that she has never been a traditional feminine woman: "I never had the gift of looking cute. I hate dresses and jewelry, and the only doll I played with was a G.I. Joe. And I've got this deep voice. That's why they call me Froggy at school" (qtd. in Corliss, "A Screen" 68). The masculinity of Foster's characters has been commented on by a range of writers. Kathleen Carrol, in a review of *Alice Doesn't Live Here Anymore* (1974), wrote that Foster, "looks like a boy and talks like a man" (qtd. in T. Brown 232). Another critic describes Foster's boyish image: "Foster's performances as a child actor are marked by a tomboyish excess" (T. Brown 232). Some people go so far as to compare Foster to a man. Liam Neeson, for instance, who costarred with Foster in the film *Nell,* which she directed, comments that "there's a turbulence in Jodie that comes from being the bread-earner, being the man in the family" (qtd. in Trebay 128). This repeated emphasis on Foster being masculine or man-like underlines the fact that she transgresses gender boundaries. Combined with her tough character, Foster's masculinity becomes a loaded sign of her Otherness because we live in a culture where women are supposed to be neither tough nor masculine. Toughness and masculinity in women continue to be taboo and are commonly regarded as signs of lesbianism in a society where lesbians are stereotyped as being mannish; thus, it is not surprising that Foster's sexuality has been an issue of discussion for many years (Lane 149).

She is tough and masculine—perhaps a lesbian. Foster breaks the rules of "proper" ladylike decorum every time; she is far tougher and more masculine than the actresses who typically find fame and fortune in Hollywood. Why has she become a megastar in an industry not famous for its support of strong women? Foster's success lies partly in her unusual ability to evade categories, a quality she shares with Anderson. Christina Lane argues that "a certain strategic sexual liminality informs much of Foster's career. . . Her persona encompasses such oppositions as masculine/feminine, public/private, gay/straight, in/out rather than submitting to their binary structure" (149). A screenwriter comments about Foster's combination of masculine and feminine attributes, "She seems small and sad; you want to protect her. Then you find she's a pretty and intelligent woman who knows kick boxing" (qtd. in Corliss, "A Screen" 72). Foster is able to present an image that combines both masculinity and femininity, and this contributes to her success. However, she is not too masculine or too tough. And her feminine image is often carefully cultivated by writers, photographers, publicity agents, studio directors, and a host of other people. Some of her roles have been notably feminine; as one critic remarks: "Perhaps it is a symptom of the media's tendency to feminize almost any female star, or perhaps it reflects Foster's own range and flexibility, but she often has . . . projected a persona that is quite feminine" (Lane 150). In addition she has posed for photographs, such as those for a 1994 issue of *Vanity Fair,* that portray her as "a beautiful, attractive, feminine woman" (Mellencamp, *Fine* 142).

The portrait of Foster that emerges is deeply ambiguous. She is tough and masculine at times, but she was also included in *US* magazine's 1991 list of the ten most beautiful women—a list not recognized for a particularly progressive ideology of what constitutes feminine beauty.[3] Viewers do not seem to know where to position her: Is she a tough tomboy or a beautiful feminine star? This ambiguity about Foster's persona is a central issue in *The Silence of the Lambs,* a film that can be read as a metaphor for what happens to a woman who dares to present a tough, masculine image, challenging the societal belief that only men should pose such characteristics.

The best-known tough image of Foster appears in *The Silence of the Lambs* (1991, director Jonathan Demme) in which she plays FBI agent-in-

Figure 6. FBI agent Clarice Starling (Jodie Foster) (*The Silence of the Lambs,* Orion Pictures).

training Clarice Starling (Figure 6).[4] This film has garnered a great deal of attention from scholars, primarily because of Foster's commanding performance, but the film also deserves scrutiny for what it suggests about how tough women should be contained.[5] Like many popular movies, the film depicts a tough woman only to limit the threat she poses to gender norms by stressing her sexuality and femininity. The same strategy is used with the depiction of Ripley in the *Aliens* films, which I discuss later.

Silence begins to build a portrait of Starling's tough persona from the opening scene, in which she is shown running on what is obviously a very difficult fitness trail, at what we later learn is the FBI academy. She colonizes the traditional territory of men by demonstrating her superior physical fitness on a trail that many men would find impossible to finish, and by invading the FBI, a long-time bastion of tough guys, not girls. She also challenges our culture's assumption that women should strive to be attractive to men at all times, since she wears a baggy sweatsuit and does not change clothes when she is called in from the track to meet with her supervisor Jack Crawford (Scott Glenn).

Almost from the film's beginning, steps are taken to dilute Starling's initial tough image. As she hurries through the academy to her meeting, she steps into an elevator that is packed with men, other FBI agents-in-training, who tower over Starling. The lingering shot of her in this situation leaves an impression of her as small and perhaps less physically capable than her much taller and larger comrades. She is also made to seem less tough after Crawford, the head of Behavioral Science, gives her the daunting task of interviewing Hannibal (the Cannibal) Lecter (Anthony Hopkins)—a notorious sociopathic serial killer who is now imprisoned. As she discusses her plans, it is clear that Starling plays the role of protégé to Crawford; she looks up to him and admits to wanting to become part of his department after graduation, which softens her tough persona by positioning her as a novice with respect to the experienced Crawford.

As the film continues, Starling's toughness is further encroached on by the emphasis placed on her femininity and sexuality. Some critics have suggested that Starling is not a sexual character: "Foster plays desexualized roles that safely contain [her] tomboy excess, roles such as that of the FBI agent Clarice Starling in *Silence of the Lambs,* a movie in which she runs, climbs, wields a gun, and deflects the romantic interests of men" (T. Brown 233). Although Starling pays little attention to the romantic allure of men, she is far from lacking sexual attractiveness. For example, when she first goes to the asylum for the criminally insane, where Lecter is being held, the warden mentions how attractive Starling is. When Lecter meets her, he clearly finds her appealing not only because she is intelligent but also because she is a heterosexually desirable woman; his desire works to foreground her femininity for the audience. In all these ways, the film works to lessen her toughness and reposition her as "woman."

Limiting Starling's tough image continues to be a concern of the film as it depicts her in such tough pursuits as target shooting, arresting a classmate in a mock exercise, and engaging in the most masculine of sports, boxing. These rough experiences are softened by the film's repeated emphasis on her femininity. When she is shown running with another woman, a team of male runners pass by and crane their necks to ogle the women. Similarly, when she is arresting her classmate in a class exercise, Starling "dies" because she has not seen the other "gunman" lurking outside her field of vision. When Starling is in boxing class, she is placed as the well-cushioned target of her male partner who is doing the actual boxing. The film remains ambivalent about her toughness and constantly reminds viewers that she is a beautiful woman who is less tough than her male classmates.

Her femininity is repeatedly an issue as she begins researching the gruesome serial crimes of Buffalo Bill, who is suspected of killing young women. In one scene, she is the sole female in a roomful of male police officers at the funeral of one of Buffalo Bill's victims. As the lone woman, she appears vulnerable and isolated, even when she takes charge of the men. This vulnerability is again evident during an autopsy, when Starling appears nervous and upset, clearly taking the death very personally. Crawford's voice is distant and professional, compared with Starling's shaky one. The male gaze is represented by the camera, which continually clicks as Starling records her professional observations; the camera's steadiness contrasts sharply with Starling's trembling. Her nervous behavior positions her as woman by linking her to the female victim and by showing her emotional vulnerability and empathy.

Starling's femininity remains at the forefront when Lecter offers to help her with the case of a missing young woman who is thought to have been captured by Buffalo Bill. Lecter insists on trading information with Starling. She must give him as much information about her past life as he gives her about the case. Here, she becomes an emotional woman who is forced to recall her secrets and reveal them to Lecter. Starling's emotional discussion of her life reduces her toughness greatly because one of the elements of toughness is assumed to be a lack of emotion, or at least tightly controlled emotions. Before Hannibal escapes, Starling discusses much of her past life. She reveals that she chose to join the FBI partly because of her desire to try to fill the shoes of her beloved father, a policeman who died in the line of duty when she was a small girl. This is reminiscent of Ellen in *The Quick and the Dead.* Each woman is forced to pursue a gun-toting career due to her obsession with justice; the inference is clear that women do not "naturally" become tough, as men do. Instead, the childhood memory of an extreme act of violence drives these women to become tough.

Starling is ultimately able to help solve the case not because of her toughness but because of her woman's intuition, which she uses when she visits the home of Buffalo Bill's first victim. Searching for clues in a bedroom that numerous other agents had combed many times, Starling is drawn almost immediately to the girl's music box; opening it, she finds photographs hidden in the lining. Critic Carol Watts writes that what drives Starling is curiosity (69), but I believe that more than curiosity is at issue. This scene of discovery reminds the audience that Starling is a woman and therefore possesses an understanding of other women, giving her the intuition that the music box might contain a secret compartment holding vital clues. Also, she has a connection to the victim that the male FBI agents can not experience, because, after all, the men have the comfort of knowing that they are not going to be Buffalo Bill's next victim.

The film continues to contain Starling's toughness at its conclusion, when she is forced to pursue Buffalo Bill by herself. Trapped alone in a house with him, she is portrayed as the victim. Wearing goggles that allow him to see in pitch darkness, he calmly and methodically stalks her, as she stumbles through his basement. Even after she kills Buffalo Bill her triumph is downplayed; Starling is made to appear young and less than tough when Crawford gives her a fatherly hug. However, the concluding scenes do not entirely detract from Starling's image; she has killed the murderer, which proves that she is tough and heroic. Foster comments about her role in the film, "There is a certain feeling about being the hero again and blowing somebody away. Not being the one who is left in the pit" (qtd. in Schruers 57). But Starling's toughness is undermined throughout the film by its repeated emphasis of her femininity, vulnerability, and smaller physical size.

In many ways, *Silence* can be interpreted as a metaphor for how Foster, Anderson, and other tough women in the media are controlled by the repeated emphasis on their femininity and sexuality. In Foster's case, no matter how tough and masculine she might appear to be at times, the media make sure to highlight her femininity and beauty, reducing her edge. The same tactic is used with Anderson, another woman who portrays an unusually tough character. Both of these women show that the popular media are uncomfortable with tough women and work to undercut their toughness.

Gillian Anderson: "Serious Suits and Frumpy Pumps"

Browsing through the stalls at an *X-Files* convention, one finds *X-Files* calendars, computer screen savers, postcards, comic books, key chains, lapel pins, trading cards, desk diaries, clocks, sweat shirts, t-shirts, books, and disappearing logo mugs (Kaplan 34).[6] If a mug or t-shirt is not sufficiently macabre, there is always a model of an alien head (Kaplan 34). If avid X-philes have not received an *X-Files* overdose at the convention, they can turn to the Internet for the *X-Files* information that they crave. The show has a significant presence on the Internet, where it is possible to look up dozens of *X-Files* sites, including the *X-Files* Singapore Homepage, *X-Files* Down Under, the Rutgers *X-Files* Homepage, Jon's *X-Files* Homepage, and the Superdeformed *X-Files* page. As is evident from some of the homepages, the success of this quirky television show is far from limited to the United States; it is a hit around the globe.[7] In England and Australia, *The X-Files* is one of the most-watched shows of the mid-1990s. In Spain and Japan, the show has also attracted a large following. In Japan, *The X-Files* was the first show from the United States to run in a prime-time spot in the past eight years (Updike 104). By 1994, broadcasting rights had been granted in fifty-six countries (Kantrowitz and Rogers 66). Not since *Star Trek* has a television show developed such a cult following. Avid X-philers do far more than just buy the occasional coffee cup adorned with Mulder's or Scully's picture; they buy *X-File* novels and comic books and spend hours online discussing their favorite shows in chat groups established on America Online and Delphi; if the fans want more, there is an *X-Files* music CD and an *X-Files* movie was released in June 1998. For many viewers, watching the *X-Files* goes far beyond the normal television viewing experience. It is an addiction. What explains the uncanny success of *The X-Files,* a show in which "everything operates according to the logic of paranoia" (Van de Walle 18)? How has the show's central female character, Dana Scully, contributed to the show's success and how has her image been moderated in order to limit her toughness?

Before turning to Scully, I will look briefly at the reasons for the success of what a critic calls a "moody, mysterious 'Twilight Zone' for the 90's" (Dowd 37). Influenced by shows such as *The Twilight Zone, The F.B.I., The Night Stalker,* and *Twin Peaks, The X-Files* first aired on 10 September 1993. The show was what one writer described as a "gripping and moody creep-fest on paranormal occurrence, mutants, extraterrestrials and other weirdos that go bump in the night; and a telling indictment of authority in general, and the government in particular" (A. Johnson, "Real" 3). Director Chris Carter's creation was an instant success. When *The X-Files* first aired, it received very positive critical attention. One reviewer wrote of the new show that it kicked off "with drive and imagination, both innovative in recent TV" (T. Scott 36). Another reviewer called the show a "wry, intelligent, and creepy drama . . ." (E. Davis 49). Since its introduction, *The X-Files,* which won the Golden Globe Award for best television drama in 1995, has become one of the most discussed television shows of the 1990s, with scores of people writing about the program's unusual appeal.[8]

The reasons for the show's success are many. During a time when people are ever more distrustful of government, *The X-Files* feeds on that uneasiness by creating "an Orwellian, Kafka-esque alien nation that's populated with suspicious folks who have too much time on their hands and a deep sense that something is horribly, horribly wrong" (Wild 79). The show's director has discovered that his audience enjoys being told

Figure 7. Publicity shot of partners Fox Mulder (David Duchovny) and Dana Scully (Gillian Anderson) (*The X-Files*).

that all their worst fears about government and society are true. *The X-Files* confirms our worries that far darker ghouls and beasties lurk in our society than we ever imagined. In a society that has long been fascinated by UFO's, Big Foot, vampires, and other similar unexplained phenomena, *The X-Files* promises to tell the truth. As C. Eugene Emery, Jr. writes, an "ominous mix of the paranormal and the paranoid . . . gives 'The X-Files' its edge and has fueled its popularity" (18). In a world that only grows more confusing and difficult to understand, *The X-Files* hints that all our worst suspicions are true. For the hour it runs each week, viewers can revel in the notion that the government is every bit as corrupt as they imagine.

Our desire to confirm our suspicions about the worst excesses of the United States government explains only part of the show's appeal. The central characters and the relationship between them are also important. The show features Dana Scully (Gillian Anderson) and Fox Mulder (David Duchovny), FBI agents who are tracking down the mysterious, unsolved cases known as the X-files (Figure 7). Scully is a medical doctor; Mulder is a psychologist. He is a believer in the paranormal; she is the doubting Thomas. These two characters and their interpersonal dynamics are essential to the show. I am, however, particularly interested in the depiction of Scully because she frequently is overshadowed by Mulder. Moreover, the actor Duchovny—as one *Cosmopolitan* article describes him, "a brainy hunk [who] is a scholar-turned-sex-symbol"—is far more the focal point of the show than Anderson (Grant 144). Yet, in many ways, she is the more intriguing of the duo because her representation is more controversial. He is doing what men are expected to do; she is not doing what women are expected to do.

Mulder's preeminence is hard to question. He is the dominant character in the show and has received the bulk of popular attention.[9] His number one position is made clear in numerous ways. When the two characters are walking, he takes the lead, with Scully following a few steps behind. He is typically the one who begins the questioning of suspects and informants. He is the first to come up with theories and explanations for the bizarre phenomena they encounter, and he is usually right while she is generally wrong. Finally, with his moody image, he is very much the suffering Byronic hero, a direct descendent of Heathcliff. Compared to such a dramatic figure, Scully appears less significant and less *Angst*-ridden; her concerns are more mundane. He always questions the status quo; she is more likely to accept it. She believes in Cartesian rationality; he believes in the irrational and the unknown. This is a difference that makes Scully appear to be the less interesting of the two, but such a perspective shortchanges her importance. "Without both Mulder and Scully, 'The X-Files' would be lost in space," as one journalist writes (A. Johnson, "Real" 3). Although Mulder dominates the show, there are many ways in which Scully is a more intriguing character because of her tough and often masculine persona.

Gillian Anderson's tough image, like Jodie Foster's, has been contained to assure the audience of her femininity. Like Foster, Anderson has had difficulties because she presents a no-nonsense image. She was not the first choice of the executives at the Fox network, who "initially wanted someone with less radiance and more vavoom as Scully" (Gliatto, "X-Ellence" 78) or, as Anderson phrased it, someone "taller, leggier, and bustier" (qtd. in Gliatto, "Occult" 98). Some Fox officials wanted "someone who could hold her own in a fashion show with the cast of *Melrose Place*" (Lowry 15). The show's producer, Chris Carter, managed to convince Fox that Anderson was perfect for the intense, no-nonsense Scully. But the battle did not conclude after she was cast: "Doubts about Anderson didn't end with her casting. Even as footage started to come back from the pilot filming there was . . . 'tremendous negativity toward Gillian' from some quarters—questions as to whether the character was too cold or if she was likable enough" (Lowry 16). The debate over whether Anderson was right for the part demonstrates how uneasy American culture is with the tough woman and how society pressures her to conform to what are perceived as desirable feminine norms. This is one reason it is necessary to study women like Foster and Anderson. Whether knowingly or not, they are helping to influence how women's gender roles are perceived by the public.

Since Anderson's debut on *The X-Files,* the attempts to lessen her tough image have continued. For example, Stephanie Mansfield's article about Anderson in *TV Guide* featured a centerfold picture of the actress in a low-cut dress that revealed a great deal of cleavage. Anderson was not depicted as tough in either the picture or the accompanying article. As we shall find, the show has been involved in a sustained attempt to blunt her tough edge, making her into a more traditional female sidekick for Mulder. This image softening is one example of the mainstream media's tendency to perpetuate the ideology that only men are truly tough. It is too simple, however, to argue that television (or any other media form) only presents reactionary images of women. Instead, television is inherently paradoxical, presenting a wide variety of women's roles, some antithetical to others. In a single show, such as *The X-Files,* there are always contradictory messages about women's roles.

For instance, *The X-Files* often emphasizes Scully's tough image. One writer comments, "special agent Dana Scully may be the most humorless woman on television. In her serious suits and frumpy pumps, she exudes a certain self-righteous discipline" (Mansfield 12). While at times Scully's attire supports her tough image, at other times she is shown fashionably and tastefully dressed, often in a way that makes it extremely difficult for her to chase suspects and other evildoers. Scully's clothing both emphasizes her toughness and suggests that her femininity and identity as a woman have not been altered just because she is in the FBI, the government agency most strongly associated with toughness. At the FBI, Scully, like Starling, works in a world of men; among Scully's male colleagues are Fox Mulder, Assistant Director Walter S. Skinner, the Cigarette-Smoking

Man, Agent Alex Krycek, Deep Throat, and the Lone Gunmen. Depicting Scully and Starling in all-male environments tends to highlight their toughness; they can compete with the boys. At the same time, however, they are seen as exceptional women; thus, their toughness is understood not to be a common trait of women.

In a world where women's sexuality is commonly associated with their subordination, the relative lack of sexuality shown by Scully and Starling strengthens their tough images. Scully does have a single date, with Rob in the episode "Jersey Devil." Starling has none. Scully and Starling do, however, have what appear to be hero-worship relationships with Mulder and Crawford, respectively. These relationships always seem on the brink of becoming romantic, suggesting that Scully and Starling's sexuality is present, if suppressed. Scully's attire, her all-male environment, and the lack of emphasis on her sexuality are just three of the ways that she is made to appear tough, but her tough image is blunted around the edges.

Softening Scully's tough image has been and continues to be an issue for the show, particularly in its 1996 season. Earlier in the series, Scully was more likely to be portrayed as tough, even unusually so. For example, in the episode "Beyond the Sea" (7 Jan. 1994), Scully is calm and collected even when her father dies. Before his funeral she shows up at work, looking emotionless and under control. Mulder is visibly surprised to see her and asks her if she should not be at home. Scully maintains her cool demeanor and insists that she should stay at work. Throughout this episode and others in the series' early days, Scully has a flat demeanor, curiously lacking in expression. She rarely smiles. Her image is particularly startling because, although we are acquainted with tough guys who show little emotion (John Wayne springs to mind), we are not accustomed to seeing unemotional women. We expect Scully to burst into tears after her father's death or at least to appear distraught; we do not expect her steely expression.

In this early episode Scully adopts many characteristics that we associate with the tough man. She acts in a completely independent fashion, venturing off by herself for example, to discover kidnapping victims held in an abandoned building; she does not call Mulder to assist her as she is more likely to do in later episodes. When the kidnapper is captured, it is again Scully who plays a leadership role, leading and directing a group of FBI agents. In the entire episode, Scully is central and Mulder plays the secondary role, a relationship that is usually reversed in later episodes. Scully also has a prominent role in the early episode "The Erlenmeyer Flask" (13 May 1994). She rescues Mulder when he is being held prisoner by a government agent, and her medical detective work at the Georgetown Microbiology Laboratory is vital to solving the case of a mysterious disappearing man who might be an alien-human hybrid. Scully also plays a central, tough role in "Lazarus" (4 Feb. 1994) when she is the FBI agent who shoots the bank robber. In these early episodes, she is unusually tough, far tougher than the female characters in similar action-adventure television series.

Her image has gradually grown less tough as the show has continued its run. By 1996 she was being portrayed in more stereotypically feminine ways. For example, her emotional and sexual feelings for Mulder suddenly become an issue in "War of the Coprophages" (5 Jan. 1996). In this episode, Mulder and Scully's relationship is marked by increasing sexual tension. He asks her at one point over the phone, "What are you wearing?" The sexual tension is accentuated as Scully repeatedly asks Mulder about the woman scientist he has met, commenting sarcastically, "Her name is Bambi?" When Scully encounters Bambi outside the research facility where Mulder is waiting, Bambi asks if she should go in. Scully remarks coolly, "No, this is no place for an entomologist." The main issue here is that Scully feels jealous of Bambi. She has become far more given to emotions traditionally associated with femininity (such as jealousy) than she ever was in the first season, when she was more impersonal in her relationships.

In 1996, Scully became more emotional not only about Mulder but about many other subjects, too. In the episode "Apocrypha" (16 Feb. 1996), she is depicted as emotional when she suspects that she is chasing the gunman who killed her sister. Assistant Director Skinner, who has been shot by the same man, notices Scully's obvious anger and cautions her, "If you can't keep your head, it's okay to step away." Here Scully is shown as an emotional female who cannot be trusted to make difficult decisions. She again becomes overly emotional in "Wetwired" (10 May 1996) when she develops paranoia because she has been brainwashed by an electronic signal sent through the television. She grows irrational and violent, even shooting at Mulder. He must convince her that she is seeing a warped vision of the world. Finally, she dissolves into tears as Mulder remains cool and unemotional. In another episode, "Home" (11 Oct. 1996), Scully is obviously shaken up because she and Mulder are investigating the murder of a baby, and she thinks about what it would be like to lose a child. This reaction positions Scully as a socially acceptable woman, more interested in the human aspect of losing a child than in solving a crime. Mulder strengthens this image of Scully as the emotional mother figure when he quips, "I never thought of you as a mother before." Later, he refers to her as "mom." These displays of emotion by Scully are one way that the studio has toned down her toughness and helped to reassure the audience that Scully is a "normal" woman. She needs to be "normalized" because the mainstream media are uneasy with presenting a woman, like Scully or Starling, who seems to blur the division between men and women by projecting a tough, even masculine image. Still, such women do appear because they provide titillation for an audience that is both fascinated by and uncomfortable with tough women.

Scully's toughness is also reduced because she plays a less important role in the action than Mulder. She is less likely to be out in the field; she is more likely to be sitting back in her lab. In "Talitha Cumi" (17 May 1996), Mulder ventures off to Rhode Island while his partner stays at headquarters. She is shown sitting at her computer terminal; Mulder is shown outside, making a risky deal that ends in a long drawn-out fist fight. In "War of the Coprophages," Scully talks to Mulder by phone for the first half of the show, only joining him and his more dangerous pursuits halfway through the episode. In "Wetwired," she is left recuperating in bed as he goes searching for the people responsible for Scully's paranoid actions. She appears again only momentarily at the end of the episode. In "Piper Maru" (9 Feb. 1996, part I), Mulder performs more adventuresome feats than Scully. He travels to Hong Kong; she stays in California.

These examples demonstrate the ways that *The X-Files,* which is supposedly about the exploits of two equal partners, works to centralize Mulder while marginalizing Scully. Positioning her as secondary to him is far from an inconsequential act. It perpetuates the notion that men are the ones to lead, while women follow. This is an idea that is so deeply imbued in our culture that it is almost impossible to imagine the reverse situation. It is hard to think of Scully as the active partner, while Mulder stays at home with the computers, because American culture is inundated with images of men as the "natural" leaders, an image that *The X-Files* helps to promote.

Scully is further marginalized because Mulder, not Scully, is the one involved in the majority of the action scenes. For example, in "Herrenvolk" (4 Oct. 1996), an alien killer easily knocks Scully to the ground and chases Mulder. Mulder and the alien have a fast-paced pursuit and battle; Scully is left to fetch the car. Later, Mulder leaves for Canada to solve a mystery there; Scully stays in the FBI office where she again works on her computer. In "Unruhe" (27 Oct. 1996), Scully adopts a much more passive role than Mulder. A killer whose thoughts are mysteriously recorded on photographic film is on the loose. Scully is captured by the killer and needs to be rescued by Mulder; rarely is this scenario reversed, with Mulder requiring his partner to rescue him. Again, these episodes are far from innocent, because they reinforce traditional ideology that men are the ones who are the heroes, not women.

Although *The X-Files* tones down Scully's tough image to make her more palatable to a mainstream audience, she still retains some of her toughness. She is not only intelligent and knowledgeable but also able to

Figure 8. Scully (Gillian Anderson) in the field (*The X-Files*).

take of herself, whether in the field or in her office. Most women on television come across as highly incapable, unsuited to be heroes because they are helpless in emergencies (Figure 8). Not Scully. In "Piper Maru," she identifies the make of a downed military plane when Mulder cannot and knows a great deal about the radiation poisoning from which a group of French sailors are suffering. She continues to be depicted on the show as tough and cool. In "Quagmire" (3 May 1996), for instance, Scully and Mulder go after a Loch Ness-style monster nicknamed "Big Blue." Scully plays the cynic in this episode, confessing to Mulder that she once believed in the Loch Ness monster: "I did as a kid, but then I grew up and became a scientist." Scully is cool, detached, and sarcastic, far more so than the vast majority of women on television.

Another way that her tough image is maintained is that she, like Starling, looks directly at men. Women are not supposed to stare at men; they are supposed to defer. "Feminine faces, as well as bodies, are trained to the expression of deference. Under male scrutiny, women will avert their eyes or cast them downward; the female gaze is trained to abandon its claim to the sovereign status of seer" (Bartky 68). Scully's direct gaze presents a clear challenge to male authority and rule. She is also depicted as tough because she is an FBI agent, a career choice that automatically positions her as tough in our culture. Thus, there are many ways that *The X-Files* is reluctant to give up Scully's tough image, but that image is never one that the show is completely at ease with; *The X-Files* constantly seeks to reassure the audience that Scully is a feminine, "normal" woman.

Though the toughness of Starling and Scully is downplayed, I wish to caution against understanding these two characters as *entirely* lacking in toughness. Despite the ways in which their images are softened and made more feminine, these women still possess considerable toughness. Even though their femininity is stressed, they are far tougher than the women who usually appear in the popular media. I wish to acknowledge the strengths of such characters and how such characters help to demonstrate that women are competent, in control, and tough. However, the same shows that depict positive messages about the ability of women to be tough and capable also suggest that women cannot be as tough as men.

Now it is time to move beyond the twisted universe of *The X-Files* and travel to the final frontier: space. The next two chapters explore the depiction of tough women in science fiction in an effort to discover whether the alternative genre of science fiction is more conducive to representing truly tough women than other media forms. Science fiction, after all, is a genre that prides itself on its ability to reimagine the future and to think about realities that have never actually existed. In this kind of speculative universe, surely tough women could also be reimagined.

Chapter 6
Tough Women in Outer Space
The Final Frontier

Remember *Barbarella* (1968), the cult science-fiction classic in which Jane Fonda—long before her aerobic studio days—reigned as the Queen of the Galaxy? This job, as far as we could see, required Fonda to prance around in not much of anything and flaunt her body. *Barbarella* is typical of early science-fiction films and novels, which frequently portrayed women as little more than curvaceous sex kittens, just waiting to seduce (or be rescued by) the next man who landed on their planet. Perhaps because of its predominately male audience, at least in early decades, science fiction has not often been regarded as progressive in its depiction of women. But the scenario for women has changed a great deal in the last few decades; we have moved beyond *Barbarella,* and many new roles are open to women in science fiction. Whether as hotshot pilots, commanders, or space mercenaries, tough women fill outer space.

Although they are not as numerous as tough men, a significant number of women in science fiction adopt non-traditional roles and can be categorized as "tough." In Iain M. Banks's novel *Against a Dark Background* (1993), Sharrow is the leader of a fighter squadron and is more than capable of taking care of herself with the FrintArms HandCannon that she packs. In John Varley's novel *Titan* (1979), Captain Cirocco Jones graduates at the top of her class in the astronaut corps; her childhood training includes "handguns and karate" (47). Elizabeth Stone, "with a command presence measured in stellar magnitudes" (19), is captain of her own ship in R. M. Meluch's story "Traitor" (1995) and is "supremely comfortable in her authority" (19). In C. J. Cherryh's novel *Downbelow Station* (1981), Mallory is the tough captain of a military spaceship. In P. M. Griffin's story "Lizard" (1995), Ranger-Sergeant Liza Morrigan—Lizard—scales an almost vertical cliff after abandoning her burning transport craft, and then goes after the pirates who have destroyed her home colony. Sharrow, Jones, Stone, Mallory, and Lizard are some of the many tough women who have infiltrated science fiction, whether in books or films.[1]

Tough women have become a common feature in a genre that historically has featured tough men in leadership roles as bold captains of starships and brave space pilots. What are the reasons behind the increasing prevalence of the tough woman in science fiction? Does her more frequent appearance suggest that our society is beginning to accept women who adopt roles that have been more commonly associated with men? Or does she serve a more conservative purpose? By exploring the image of the tough woman in the trilogy of *Aliens* films and the television show *Star Trek: Voyager,* this chapter analyzes the ways in which tough women are represented in science fiction. In particular, I argue that science-fiction's depiction of tough women offers a new way to conceptualize gender roles and what it means to be a woman. Yet, at the same time, science fiction films and television shows often reinforce the notion that tough girls are essentially softies, notwithstanding their tough demeanor, and can seldom compete against the "true" toughness of men.

This chapter focuses on *Aliens* and *Voyager* for a number of reasons. Both the film series and the television show feature controversial tough women. *Aliens* stars Sigourney Weaver as Ellen Ripley, whose tough persona in the movies is widely regarded by critics as having changed how women are depicted in films. Her portrayal has been widely praised; in a typical remark one critic calls Ripley "an exemplary figure for women in her rugged independence, cool courage under fire, and resourcefulness" (Bundtzen 12). Some writers, however, are less enthusiastic about Ripley's characterization, calling her little more than a "flex-and-fire warrior" (Edelstein 41). *Voyager* also stars a controversial tough woman, Kathryn Janeway (Kate Mulgrew), the first female captain on *Star Trek.* For many years, the producers of the *Star Trek* shows refused to cast a woman for the captain's position out of fear that their largely male audience would not be able to relate to a woman ("Mulgrew" 4). When Janeway was finally introduced as a captain, a heated battle raged about how her gender would influence her ability to be a leader. Both Ripley and Janeway deserve study to examine why they have aroused such diverse and heated opinions.

Aliens and *Voyager* are interesting to compare because they feature different aspects of toughness. Ripley is a leader who is also physically tough. Janeway is a leader, but she lacks the same kind of obvious toughness that Ripley displays. Unlike Ripley, Janeway, despite being physically fit, almost never lugs around big guns or flexes her pecs in a t-shirt. Yet, Janeway is still very much a leader, and a tough one. Janeway and Ripley are useful to study to demonstrate the different ways that women's toughness is constituted in science fiction. They are also worth juxtaposing because each *appears* to take huge strides forward in the depiction of autonomous, brave women who adopt leadership roles. But are these depictions as progressive as they might first appear?

Before turning to Ripley and Janeway, I will examine why science fiction is a particularly important genre to study when focusing on toughness. In her book on the development of the science-fiction film, *Screening Space: The American Science Fiction Film* (1987), Vivian Sobchack observes: "The SF film is a film genre which emphasizes actual, extrapolative, or speculative science and the empirical method, interacting in a social context with the lesser emphasized, but still present, transcendentalism of magic and religion, in an attempt to reconcile man with the unknown" (63). Sobchack's words apply to all forms of science fiction. Science fiction tries not only to uncover the unknown, but also to interpret what is known. By this I mean that science fiction is concerned with sorting out the problems and concerns of the present world, interpreting gender concerns, race relationships, class conflicts, and other issues of our daily lives. Yet it is able to transcend the limitations of our everyday world. This is one of the primary reasons science fiction is crucial to study when analyzing women's changing roles; these new roles are often first visible in science fiction and other similar alternative media forms, such as comic books or underground 'zines.

As a barometer of social change, science fiction serves a unique purpose, as Sharona Ben-Tov argues in *The Artificial Paradise: Science Fiction and American Reality* (1995). Discussing science fiction's "position at a unique intersection of science and technology, mass media, popular culture, literature, and secular ritual" (6), she writes:

> In what source other than science fiction's rich, synthetic language of metaphor and myth can we trace the hidden, vital connections between such diverse elements as major scientific projects (spaceflight, nuclear weaponry, robotics, gene mapping), the philosophical roots of Western science and technology, American cultural ideals, and magical practices as ancient as shamanism and alchemy? (6)

As Ben-Tov affirms, science fiction suggests a great deal about social change, including the changing roles of women in both real life and the media.

Not only does science fiction reflect women's roles, but it has the potential to re-envision and even alter gender roles.[2] As critic Nadya Aisenberg comments, science fiction "affords [a broad] opportunity to upset gender stereotypes and, beyond that, present visions of societies different from the one we inhabit" (159). Because the gender roles presented in science fiction can lead to social change, they are a potential danger to the status quo. This is a primary reason that science fiction is a rich source for examining the ways in which women's toughness is being rescripted and exploring the resistance that such change still encounters.

Rambo She's Not

One of the most fascinating portraits of a tough woman in space appears in *Alien* (1979, director Ridley Scott) and the two sequels in the trilogy, *Aliens* and *Alien 3*. Sigourney Weaver plays one of the toughest women ever to hit the big screen in these films, and theorist Constance Penley calls *Alien* "stunningly egalitarian" ("Time Travel" 73).[3] Even *Glamour,* a magazine not widely recognized for its strong feminist sentiments, praises the *Aliens* saga, arguing that the three films "are just sci-fi popcorn movies, but their effect on female moviegoers has been profound. Ripley, in her no-nonsense cotton tank-top bodysuit, is the first woman we've seen left standing when all the guys are dead" (Krupp 163).[4] Ripley is an unusual heroine, but is she more than just a "smart Rambo" as one reviewer labeled her (Kael 79)? Is Ripley, as Weaver once claimed, "lucid and powerful and unemotional" (qtd. in Weber 15), a woman who deserves our respect and admiration? How does her tough image help to explain the ways science fiction has used tough women in general?

Alien begins with an introduction to Ellen Ripley and her fellow shipmates after the ship's computer awakens the crew from hypersleep, alerting them to a mysterious signal being broadcast from a nearby planet. Ripley blends in with the rest of her crew mates. She appears calm and composed, her no-nonsense image emphasized by her lack of makeup. She has yet to achieve the heroic stature that she will have in the rest of the film.

The first time Ripley's true toughness is revealed is when the captain and several crew members return to the ship after a visit to a crashed alien vessel, the source of the mysterious signal. One of the crew members has an alien organism attached to his face, and the captain wants to ignore quarantine procedures to get the injured man into the infirmary. Ripley, as acting commander while the captain is off the ship, refuses to let them in. In this nightmarish situation, Ripley's calm refusal to disobey rules and break quarantine contrasts sharply with the reaction of the only other woman on board, who snarls, half-hysterically, "Would you open the god-damn hatch? We need to get him inside." Even when Ripley is ordered by the ship's captain to open the hatch, she refuses. Like Sarah Connor of the Terminator films (discussed in the next chapter), Ripley is tough because she is willing to sacrifice her personal wish to save her fellow crew member for the greater good of the ship and its crew. Her tough-mindedness and adherence to the rules, however, prove to be futile when a male member of the crew, Ash, the chief science officer, opens the hatch anyway. Here, we notice one common characteristic of the tough woman in space. Ripley adheres to a higher code of morality than her fellows, and she is also able to make the difficult decisions that no one else will. For her, toughness is not just a physical attribute but a moral one. She speaks the truth, even when no one wishes to hear it.

The alien organism turns out to be a true horror, with acid for blood and a zeal for murdering the ship's crew members. After the captain is killed, it is up to Ripley to keep the remaining members of the crew alive. They are divided on how to treat the beast. One wants to use maximum brute force and kill it as soon as possible. Another, Lambert, the other woman, is shrill and hysterical. Her distorted, tear-stained face contrasts sharply with Ripley's steely calm, a contrast that only deepens when the camera moves from a close inspection of Lambert's face to Ripley's. They are opposites, and as critic Judith Newton writes in her essay "Feminism and Anxiety in *Alien*" (1990), Lambert "functions for the most part to define what Ripley is not—emotional, feminine, unheroic" (86).[5]

When the few surviving crew members recognize that they have been set up by the company they work for to bring back the alien, they decide to blow up the ship, taking their chances in the ship's shuttle. Again, Ripley remains calm while the rest of the crew falls apart. Whether Ripley or John Wayne, a tough hero remains cool and collected even when confronted by tremendous odds. Ultimately, Ripley's lack of emotion will save her. Only by moving away from the displays of emotion that are usually considered "normal" for women will she be able to become a tough hero, because our culture considers toughness and displays of emotion to be antithetical.

With all of her comrades dead, Ripley struggles to survive, managing to blow up the ship and escape in the shuttle. It is not so much her physical or mental toughness that allows her to survive but her moral and emotional toughness. As I have mentioned she was the only one who considered what was best for the entire crew when she refused to allow the contaminated crew member on board, an act that might have saved them all. If one accepts the common myth that women lack the moral toughness leaders require, a woman—like Lambert—is too emotional to make difficult ethical decisions. Ripley must adopt traits associated with masculinity and "act like a man"—unemotional and in control—to be considered tough and to be respected. Her masculine traits are contrasted with feminine ones, making the negative connotations of femininity (as displayed by Lambert) more overt. Ripley is forced into femininity's opposite, masculinity, which makes her like a man. In our culture femininity and masculinity are in opposition and therefore exclude one another.

Thus toughness for Ripley is not some new feminist ideal, where she takes the best parts of femininity and masculinity and forges them into a type of toughness that has not yet been seen. Instead, Ripley can be perceived as a man in a woman's body, reason enough for critics to complain about her being just another Rambo figure.[6]

Alien does not draw attention to Ripley's body until the end of the film, when she undresses for her hibernation sleep. Wearing only bikini underwear and a tank top, she wanders around the ship, allowing for some lingering shots of her barely covered bottom. This scene also emphasizes Ripley's more feminine, nurturing side when she places the ship's cat, Jonesey, whom she has rescued, into a deep sleep. This scene is an important one, because it repositions Ripley as a member of girldom. As Harvey R. Greenberg points out, "When Ripley steps out of her fatigues, she becomes intensely desirable and achingly vulnerable. The sight of her nearly nude body is highly arousing, in the context of the film's previous sexual neutrality" ("Reimagining" 93). In other words, Ripley has become resexualized as a woman. The message is that it is fine for a woman to act tough and take control in outer space, but she had better be a lady when she returns to society. Clearly, the film has not come to grips with Ripley's tough image.

Viewers have a scant few moments to ogle Ripley's posterior before they discover that the alien has managed to conceal itself on board the shuttle. Even during this moment of terror, the camera insists on reminding viewers that, yes, Ripley is a girl, by focusing on her skimpily clad crotch and thighs as she slowly inches her way into a space suit. The shot detracts from her tough image and shows viewers that Ripley is and will always be a sexy, feminine woman, which, at least in our society, suggests that she is a potential victim for men. This image stays with the audience while Ripley manages to eject the alien into the vacuum of space. The final emphasis on Ripley's sexuality does a great deal to limit the threat to gender norms posed by her tough persona. Ultimately, the film seems uncomfortable leaving viewers with an image of Ripley that is *too* tough.

The need to contain Ripley's toughness becomes more apparent in the second film in the trilogy, *Aliens* (1986, director James Cameron), which has been praised as offering women empowerment and disparaged as offering women only an illusion of empowerment. Negative views of *Aliens* are best represented by Greenberg's essay "Fembo: *Aliens*' Intentions" (1988) in which he criticizes *Aliens* for being "hatched out of the day's conservative climate" (166). For Greenberg, the feminist potential of *Aliens* has been grossly overrated: "In view of *Aliens*' Neanderthal politics, . . . such interpretations represent far more serious misreadings than the earlier misprision of *Alien*" (170–71). His analysis points out some serious flaws in the second film, which presents Ripley as tough but is even more insistent than the first film on the need to contain that toughness by emphasizing her maternal, nurturing side.

Aliens starts with Ripley being discovered after a hypersleep of fifty-seven years. The members of the company she reports to are disbelieving of her story about an alien with acid for blood. When they lose contact with the colonists who now live on the planet where her crew originally discovered the aliens, the company begins to believe Ripley's story. The company begs her to return, because she is the only one who knows anything about the aliens. Reluctantly, she returns to the planet. This time, however, she is not alone. She is accompanied by a group of heavily armed, super-fit marines.

One of the most intriguing of the marines is Vasquez (Jenette Goldstein), a muscular Hispanic woman who appears every inch the prototypical butch lesbian and who has been described by a critic as a "stylized Chicana lesbian grunt" (Zwinger 84). Vasquez gives a performance that has been called "ball-busting" (Elley 35). She is first shown doing chin-ups. As they do for Sarah Connor in the Terminator saga, chin-ups mark Vasquez as tough; because they require upper-body strength which women are supposed to lack, many people regard them as a male exercise. Her toughness is emphasized when one of her male comrades asks her, "Vasquez, have you ever been mistaken for a man?" and she quips, "No, have you?" The chin-ups and Vasquez's cocky attitude set her apart from Ripley, who lacks Vasquez's brashness. In many ways, the two women are antithetical. Their difference is underlined when Vasquez points to Ripley and asks her comrades, "Who's Snow White?" Vasquez and the other marines resent Ripley's role as an elite consultant.

Vasquez is all tough, unreflective action. She just wants to know where the aliens are so that she can blow them away. Vasquez's toughness is the kind traditionally associated with the military; it is physical, action-oriented, and combative. Ripley's toughness is of a different caliber. She lacks the very apparent musculature of Vasquez, yet Ripley is equally tough. One of the important issues that *Aliens* addresses is what being tough actually entails. Almost every character in the film has a different way of going about it. Vasquez is all swagger. Ripley is a cooler, calmer character. Bishop, an android, raises the question of whether a machine can be tough and heroic. Rebecca Jordan (Carrie Henn), nicknamed "Newt," a little girl who has managed to survive for a number of weeks after the aliens have killed her family and all of the other colonists, presents yet another image of toughness. Through these characters and others, the film becomes a meditation on toughness and the nature of being heroic.

Vasquez's toughness is based on showy display, and is emphasized by her ability to lug around an enormous gun (so big that she needs to hold it with two hands and brace it against her hip) as the marines go in search of the aliens. Ripley, on the other hand, is shown with no gun at all. Vasquez sports a jaunty red bandanna around her head and a ripped shirt that shows off her bulging biceps. She is stereotyped as an impetuous, hot-blooded Latina and she stands out from the crowd. Although her sexual orientation is never mentioned openly, and the film hints that she might be having an affair with one of her male comrades, Vasquez is also stereotyped as a butch lesbian, more concerned with pull-ups than with intellectual pursuits. In contrast, Ripley lacks Vasquez's muscular build, but she does present herself as a leader. Each woman reveals herself as tough in a different fashion, again showing the multiplicity of ways to be tough. Their depictions reveal an opposition that is a force throughout the film.

Ultimately it is Ripley's less showy steeliness that will save the day. When Lieutenant Gorman's marines are being destroyed by the aliens, the military leader is frozen, incapable of action. Ripley takes over, rescuing the besieged marines, even though she has been ordered not to do so. Her toughness is evident when she is able to act under pressure. The marines recognize Ripley's authority, calling out for her, not Gorman, when they need to be rescued. When the marines are forced to stay on the planet's surface because their shuttle has crashed, Ripley remains calm and focused, her demeanor contrasting with that of a sobbing male marine who is nearly hysterical, just as Lambert is in *Aliens.*

Like Ripley, Newt is also tough, but in a different fashion. Only Ripley recognizes Newt's true toughness. After befriending her, Ripley becomes the girl's mother-figure, taking care of her, nurturing her, and rescuing her when necessary (Figure 9).[7] At one point, Ripley is seen carrying the sleeping child off to bed, just as a mother would. She becomes multidimensional because she is shown as being capable of love, and she becomes more plausible as a character. (In a similar fashion, the Terminator becomes a fuller character when the young John Connor befriends him.) Although Ripley's maternal nature toward Newt makes Ripley a more complex character, it is important to recognize how it marks her as a woman; Constance Penley has commented that "Ripley is . . . marked by a difference that is automatically taken to be a sign of femininity . . . *Aliens* reintroduces the issue of sexual difference, but not in order to offer a newer, more modern configuration of that difference" ("Time Travel" 73). Ripley's gender becomes even more of an issue in *Alien 3,* the final film of the trilogy.

It would be a mistake to consider the relationship between Ripley and Newt the film's central concern. Some critics stress the relationship so much that they are unable to recognize Ripley as an autonomous being who managed to survive long before Newt's introduction.[8] In "Blood Re-

Figure 9. Ripley (Sigourney Weaver) shows her maternal side (*Aliens,* Fox).

lations: Feminist Theory Meets the Uncanny Alien Bug Mother" (1992), Lynda Zwinger emphasizes that "it is only in order to preserve her position as new, nuclear, sentimentalized mom that Ripley appropriates military, masculine attributes" (84). Zwinger overlooks the many "military, masculine attributes" that Ripley possessed long before meeting Newt. Like Zwinger, Dennis Patrick Slattery emphasizes the centrality of the relationship between Ripley and Newt in his essay "Demeter-Persephone and the *Alien*(s) Cultural Body" (1992), in which he understands Newt as "the only image for which [Ripley] lives" (34). This argument does not take into account that Ripley, time after time, demonstrates that she lives for a variety of reasons, including her desire to save the world—and herself—from the aliens. Establishing the Newt-Ripley relationship as the central reason for Ripley's existence disregards her complicated personality; she is not solely a mother. Still, the mothering relationship does tone down her tough demeanor by emphasizing a role traditionally considered feminine and, therefore, not tough.

As *Aliens* continues, only Ripley, Newt, Bishop, and Corporal Hicks (Michael Biehn) escape being killed by the aliens. When Newt is captured, Ripley's toughness becomes even more apparent: although Bishop has arrived with the shuttle so that Ripley is free to leave, she returns for Newt. Her mission is not made any easier by the fusion reactor that is going to blow up in nineteen minutes and turn the entire station into a gigantic nuclear fireball. There is a lingering shot of her strapping numerous weapons to her body, preparing a grenade launcher, stripping down to a t-shirt, and generally getting ready for an all-out assault on the aliens. Ripley's toughness is at least partially conveyed here by her carrying large quantities of heavy armaments. Whether it is Sarah Connor preparing to battle the evil cyborg or Ripley arming herself to battle the aliens, bearing weapons signifies toughness for women, just as it does for men.

Despite all her firearms, Ripley is not represented in the same way as tough male heroes. For instance, while she is searching for Newt, her face lacks the expressionless, immobile quality that characterizes Rambo, the Terminator, and many other tough guys. Her face registers fear, anxiety, and horror. Because she is a woman, she is depicted as showing a great range of emotion, affirming her femininity.

Ripley's identity as a woman and a mother is further emphasized after she rescues Newt and the two accidentally step into the aliens' nursery, a vast room filled with leathery eggs and dominated by a huge female alien who hovers protectively over her clutch. There is a clear comparison between the alien and Ripley as mothers: they are both determined to protect their young at any cost. The two reach a tacit agreement—Ripley will not burn the eggs if the aliens let her pass safely through the chamber. But Ripley breaks the agreement and destroys as many eggs as she can. The mother alien, bent on vengeance, pursues Ripley and Newt and manages to hide on the shuttle that takes them back to the ship in orbit. Once on board, a battle takes place between the mothers as the alien tries to kill Newt and Ripley tries to protect her. With the aid of a powerful loader that entirely encases her body in steel, Ripley is able to duel with the powerful and virtually indestructible alien. After exchanging blows with the alien mother, Ripley opens the airlock to jettison her foe. Although the alien is clinging to Ripley's foot and the vacuum of space threatens to suck Ripley out of the ship, she survives. Here, she becomes a fantasy of toughness. The role of the fictional tough hero is to be stronger and able to bear more than any mere mortal. No matter what monsters she faces, Ripley will endure.

Ripley's ability to survive is also evident at the start of *Alien 3* (1992, director David Fincher), in which she is the lone survivor of her ship after her safety pod crashes on a penal colony planet. This film, however, differs in significant ways from the first two. While the others are based on showing Ripley's development as a tough hero, the last is structured around confining the threat posed by her toughness.

Throughout the film, Ripley's vulnerability is emphasized. For example, she is first shown as an unconscious, scantily clad body being handled by a number of anonymous males. The similarities to a rape scene are unmistakable. Ripley is now the only woman on a planet full of aggressive men, many of whom are sex offenders with long histories of raping or killing women. This setup alone emphasizes her identity as a woman and her potential vulnerability to the predatory male. Her gender is stressed when she stands up after being rescued and is completely naked, although all the camera reveals is her head. The sexual connotation of this scene is undeniable.

Her femininity continues to be stressed. The warden makes it clear that the colony's twenty-five prisoners are extremely dangerous, posing a particular threat to Ripley because she is a woman. She needs to think before promenading in front of them. When Ripley shaves her head to avoid lice, this act makes her more feminine rather than less, because she is shown standing naked in the shower afterward.[9] When she enters the prisoners' dining hall with her new haircut, her shorn head makes her appear vulnerable, not tough. Although a shaven head is a strong signifier of rugged masculinity, for Ripley it heightens her femininity, an effect that the Fox studio was clearly aiming for. When the idea of showing Ripley with a bald pate was first suggested, the studio conveyed to Weaver that she would be allowed to be bald only if she appeared attractive (Krupp 163). If she were unattractive, the bald look would have to go. The studio wanted Ripley to be tough, but not so tough that male viewers would not find her sexually desirable.

Ripley is further feminized through her interactions with the prison physician. Bluntly, she asks him if he is attracted to her. Then, the two have sex. This is one of many times in *Alien 3* when Ripley's sexuality is emphasized, a complete turn about from the earlier two films, where her sexual nature was generally downplayed. Now, she becomes more like a traditional female heroine; in *Alien 3,* Ripley loses some of her toughness and independence. She becomes sexualized to remind viewers that, yes, Ripley is still a girl.

Her identity as a woman is again highlighted when she is nearly gang raped by a group of prisoners and needs to be saved by another prisoner, who tells her to "run along" so that he can deal with the men. Although she slugs one of the would-be rapists before departing, she does leave. This is definitely *not* the Ripley from the two other films, who never would have let a man protect her. The message the scene conveys is that women—no matter how tough they might look and act—are always potential victims of male violence. Women are the prey; men are the predators. However, Ripley is not incapacitated by the attempted rape, which shows that her toughness has not been entirely reduced. The rape scene, however, does remind viewers that Ripley is "just a woman." Her gender is further emphasized after this scene when the burly prison superintendent confines her to the infirmary with the patronizing comment, "That's a good girl."

As the film draws to its finish, Ripley regains some of her toughness. She becomes a leader and must try to save the prisoners. It is up to her to make the men act in their own defense. She shows her toughness again when she runs a body scan on herself to discover whether she has an alien inside her, which she finds to be the case. She bursts into tears, but that does not stop her from going in search of the full-grown alien by herself. She also shows her toughness at the film's conclusion when she kills the adult monster and is offered a chance to live by the men from the company, who have just arrived. Because she knows they want the monster inside her chest for their bio-weapons division, she refuses their offer of life and takes a backward dive into a giant mold filled with hot lead, ending her own life and the life of the baby monster. Ripley's death is perhaps inevitable at this point. She has proven that she is too tough to survive even in outer space; she is doomed. Her death serves as a warning to women who, like Ripley, might rebel against gender constraints and adopt tough personas.

Despite her fiery finish, Ripley, because of her unusually tough depiction, paved the way for countless other women in science fiction who would follow in her footsteps. Her appearance did make a difference and helped to make science fiction (and other genres) more tolerant of women who were tough, independent, and in control. Now, let us turn to one such woman: Captain Kathryn Janeway from the television show *Star Trek: Voyager.* Studying Janeway, the first woman captain featured on a Star Trek show, can reveal a great deal about the increased acceptance of nontraditional tough women in the media and the persistent cultural fears about such women.

Captain Janeway Takes the Helm

Women played a number of roles in the original *Star Trek* series (1966–1969). For the late 1960s, the show was fairly progressive in using a black woman as the ship's communication officer, Lieutenant Uhura. The program featured many other women in less prominent roles, but it was always clear that women played second fiddle to the real stars who were Captain Kirk, Mr. Spock, McCoy, Scotty, Ensign Chekov, and Lieutenant Sulu. Uhura was a central character, but she never was as prominent as the men and spent most of her time stuck on the bridge of the USS *Enterprise* like an interstellar receptionist. One could never call her "tough." Although some of the women in the show had professional careers as nurses, diplomats, or scientists, they typically appeared more interested in swooning over Kirk than pursuing their work. As the Star Trek universe expanded, Kirk receded into the past and new men emerged to fill his role—first Captain Jean-Luc Picard (Patrick Stewart), and then Commander Benjamin Sisko (Avery Brooks). Although Picard and Sisko have significant differences, they both follow in Kirk's steps by being strong male leads. This orderly progression suddenly changed with the next addition to the Star Trek saga, *Star Trek: Voyager.* A woman, Captain Kathryn Janeway (Kate Mulgrew) was now at the helm of the USS *Voyager,* and the universe would never be the same.[10]

The *Star Trek* saga featured tough women before *Voyager.*[11] In the series *Star Trek: The Next Generation* (1987–1994), actress Denise Crosby played Lieutenant Tasha Yar, chief of security on board the ship. Critic Rhonda V. Wilcox argues that Yar represented a "clear-cut effort to put a woman in a position of physical strength" (55). She lasted less than a full season before being killed off and was not replaced by a similar tough woman. One of the reasons Yar was killed was because Crosby wished to leave the series; her role, she complained, was undeveloped (Wilcox 56). She did not want to spend the next five years repeating "The frequency's open, sir" (qtd. in Toepfer 57). Perhaps one of the reasons Crosby failed to become a more complex, fully developed character was because the producers did not know how to handle their creation of a tough woman who was more than a physical match for the men on board. Even while she was still on the show, Yar's tough image was often softened by showing her more feminine side. For example, in the episode "Code of Honor," she was kidnapped by a man who wanted her to be his wife, and she was represented as far less tough than he was. Although she was initially shown as tough when she won a fight with this man, she was later kidnapped and placed in the typical feminine role of victim. In another episode, "The Naked Now," she came down with an illness that made her appear drunk; the first thing she did was discard her trim uniform in favor of something slinkier. She also had a romantic affair with one of her fellow crew members, Data, lessening her tough edge and reassuring viewers of her femininity as well as her heterosexuality.

Yar was a less central character than the show's other primary characters. Lieutenant Worf, Data, Geordie La Forge, William T. Riker, Captain Picard, and Wesley Crusher were all men or, in Wesley's case, a boy. The ship's chief medical officer, Beverly Crusher, and the ship's counselor, Deanna Troi, were both played by women, but they were represented as feminine, nurturing women. A typical scene in the show would have Beverly and Deanna doing aerobics and talking about men, relationships, children, and similar feminine concerns. Other tough women occasionally made an appearance on *The Next Generation.* Ensign Ro was tough but appeared in only a few episodes. In the episode "Angel One" the crew encountered an entire planet that was peopled by dominant, aggressive women and physically small, weak men. The toughness of this planet of Amazons was limited by showing that one of the women from the planet was romantically involved with Riker and that another was the wife of a Federation man who had been stranded on the planet for many years. Despite their superficial toughness, both these women fell head over heels for any "real" man who beamed down to their planet.

From the beginning, it was clear that Janeway was going to be a far more central character from the earlier *Star Trek* women. Most important, she was actually going to be the leader, not just a follower. Although Janeway is prominent as the captain, *Voyager* is far from being overrun with women. The central crew members include Kathryn Janeway (Kate Mulgrew), B'Elanna Torres (Roxann Biggs-Dawson), Kes (Jennifer Lien, who left the show; Kes was replaced by Seven of Nine [Jeri Ryan] at the start of the fourth season), Tom Paris (Robert Duncan McNeil), Harry Kim (Garrett Wang), Chakotay (Robert Beltran), Tuvok (Tim Russ), Neelix (Ethan Phillips), and the holographic doctor (Robert Picardo). There are six men and only three women, yet Janeway's introduction led to an uproar that was heard far outside the *Star Trek* universe. Mulgrew's addition to the crew was further highlighted by the fact that she became the second woman to play the part: actress Genevieve Bujold, the first choice for the part, walked off the set after two days.

Popular magazines and television shows were fascinated by Mulgrew's introduction as captain but gave very different descriptions of her personality and character. One journalist, John Leonard, writing for *New York* magazine, offered only praise:

> Mulgrew, as Kathryn Janeway, is a splendid captain. We see her mind watch itself think in split seconds, as if hesitation were a form of sloth. She was born to command, with hair swept up like Edith Wharton's, eyes narrowed like a basi-

> lisk's, the best jaw on television this side of Karen Sillas; she's so crisp she crackles like a graviton, so svelte in her Federation woolens that she seems to chuck herself into action like a spear. (82)

Other journalists and magazines were less free with their praise. *People* magazine hastened to assure its readers that Mulgrew was "a natural space case" who freely admitted to not being able to operate a computer or fax machine; thus, the threat of power suggested by a woman as captain is modified by letting readers know that Mulgrew is really a technological klutz (Cunningham 116). *Working Mother* informed its readers that "Mulgrew infuses Janeway with an irresistible take-charge quality—sort of a young Katharine Hepburn in outer space" and also that both Hillary Clinton and her daughter, Chelsea, watch Mulgrew's show (Petrucelli 25). Associating Mulgrew with Katharine Hepburn and Hillary Clinton is an effort to place the starship captain in a category with other mainstream strong women, making her appear less of a challenge to male leaders. Even executive producer Rick Berman seemed intent on not making Mulgrew appear too tough, commenting, "Kate is the personification of grace under pressure. . . . We needed somebody who brought a sense of command and dignity to the role but also the nurturing qualities of a woman" (qtd. in Israel 46). Berman's words point out that Janeway shares some of Ripley's problems. For both, making them appear nurturing is a way to mitigate their very evident toughness.

A discussion of how Janeway is softened up would be incomplete without mentioning her haircut. Like the fight over Sigourney Weaver's bald pate in *Alien 3,* a debate emerged over Mulgrew's original hairstyle, her infamous "bun of steel." During the debate over her hairstyle, it sometimes appeared that how Mulgrew wore her hair was more important than the actress herself. One of the "hot items" of discussion during the second season of *Voyager* was about the replacement of Mulgrew's "bun of steel" with a softer, more feminine coiffure in some episodes. The debate over Janeway's haircut reflects the role hair plays in society as a signifier of femininity. As feminist theorist Frigga Haug argues in her book *Female Sexualization* (1983), hair is a cultural marker of considerable power: "Hair long ago lost its function of mere protection—in which its usefulness was defined in relation to heat and cold—and has become a symbol of femininity and masculinity—of potency, in its association with beauty" (111). In other words, a hairstyle signifies a great deal about a particular person's construction of his or her gender. A man flaunting flowing, long locks like Fabio's will be interpreted differently than the same man with a crewcut. A woman with long, blow-dried, bleached-blonde hair will be interpreted differently than the same woman with a shaved head. For Janeway, the "bun of steel" suggested her toughness and her adoption of a no-nonsense masculine image in the first season. The new "softer" look suggests that the show's producers were growing increasingly concerned about presenting Janeway as more feminine and less potentially intimidating.

Sometimes it appears that the show's producers are obsessed with emphasizing Janeway's femininity. For instance, when enjoying the holodeck, which can create any kind of scenario that a visitor imagines, she typically adopts romantic, feminine roles, a reminder to the audience that Janeway is still a woman, despite her tough demeanor. In the episode "Threshold," her femininity is again emphasized when she thinks longingly about having children. Another episode where her femininity is stressed is "Death Wish," in which she meets the notorious Q from *Next Generation.* Q is humanoid in appearance but is actually a member of a different species that has advanced far beyond humanity. He constantly wreaked havoc for Picard and now causes trouble for Janeway. Q's interactions with her are primarily based upon her womanhood. He is constantly commenting on her gender, questioning her ability to be a leader, and irritating her by calling her "Madame Captain" and "Kathy." His worst behavior, however, comes when he transports himself into her bed. She leaps up and pulls a robe over her skimpy satin nightgown. Her hair in this scene is not done up in her bun of steel but is long and flowing over her shoulders. The nightgown and hair strongly re-encode her as "woman." Janeway's femininity is made more evident when Q announces his infatuation with her and wants to start an affair, commenting "I never did anything like this for Jean-Luc. Maybe it's because you have such authority and yet manage to preserve your femininity so well." This episode highlights her sexuality and vulnerability by portraying her in bed. Even if Picard had awakened to find Q in bed with him, such a scene would be interpreted far differently than the scene with Janeway. Q is viewed as a male predator who might threaten Janeway sexually, but never Picard.

Another way that her toughness is limited is by contrasting her with B'Elanna Torres, the half-Klingon and half-human chief engineer. Torres is one of the Maquis, a rebel group that has been forced to join Janeway's crew in order to find its way home from a distant uncharted section of the galaxy. Torres serves as the foil to Janeway, just as Vasquez performs the same role for Ripley. Torres shows a much tougher image than Janeway ever does. As Lieutenant Paris comments in one episode ("Threshold"), "Torres doesn't cry." Torres has a hot-headed quality that Janeway lacks. In the episode "Prototype," Torres's tough, swaggering attitude is evident when Harry Kim says to her, "You may think that you're tougher than anyone else, B'Elanna Torres," but insists that he is just as capable as she is. She sneers, "Don't make me laugh, Starfleet." The division between Janeway and Torres is clear. In one episode, Torres is passionate about her desire to save a robot race from extinction. While Torres is heated and passionate, Janeway is dispassionate and cool—but she is still very much in control of the situation. She does not agree with Torres's desire to help the robots continue their race. Janeway and Ripley are far more rational than Torres or Vasquez. Janeway and Ripley appear far less tough when compared with their foils, who pose more of a threat to male hegemony.

Janeway's toughness, although mollified by repeated references to her femininity, does not vanish entirely. She remains a strong, effective leader. When she does not, disaster follows. For example, in the episode "Alliances" the captain tries to make an alliance with an enemy faction to ensure the safety of the *Voyager*'s crew. The plan ends disastrously. At the conclusion of the episode, she has learned her lesson. She upholds the "principles and ideals of the Federation" even when the crew is far from home; she adds, "As far as I am concerned, those are the best allies we could have." The captain represents law and order in a part of the galaxy in which law and order are rare (at least by Starfleet standards). Another aspect of Janeway's toughness is that she, like Ripley, is concerned with the greater good, something women stereotypically are not supposed to be interested in. For instance, in the episode "Dreadnought," Janeway plans to blow up her own ship to stop a missile from hitting and decimating a planet. After ordering everyone off the ship, she plans to stay on board and be destroyed with it.

Toughness for Janeway, as for Ripley, lies partially in the ability to be a leader, even in the most dire situations. Ripley must face the aliens; Janeway must confront other alien threats. In one episode, "The Thaw," the captain faces down a computer-generated embodiment called Fear in order to save a group of hostages. Janeway could have backed down from this encounter, just as Ripley could have avoided many of her encounters with the aliens, but Janeway does not even consider such a route. As Harry Kim remarks, "The captain would sacrifice herself to save the hostages." Janeway, like Ripley, is tough because she is willing to do what other people will not—including using force when necessary.

Despite her flaws, Janeway is tougher than similar women characters in leadership roles. The short-lived mid-1990s television show *Space: Above and Beyond,* for instance, had less plausible tough women. The show focused on a group of hot-shot space marines who comprised the 58th Squadron and their role in a war that raged between humanity and an alien species. Two of the marines were women: Shane Vansen (Kristen Cloke) and Vanessa Damphousse (Lanei Chapman). Although both were marines, they looked more like models. They were feminine in appearance and possessed none of Vasquez's masculinity or Ripley's androgyny. Damphousse appeared nervous, frightened, and less secure than her male comrades. She was portrayed as a rookie, which made her seem more tentative. (Vansen appeared more hard-nosed and was often the leader of the group in battle situations.) The two women carried guns, but they were only following in the footsteps laid out earlier by Fonda in *Barbarella,* looking more sexy than tough. Compared to such women, Captain Janeway is a definite improvement, even if *Voyager* is excessively concerned with emphasizing her femininity.

New Images of Women in Science Fiction

Because it thrives on alternative realities, science fiction at first appears to be a genre in which tough women might thrive. It is clear, however, that science fiction can also serve to reinscribe the gender roles that it questions. In many ways, Ripley and Janeway are tough, but their toughness is lessened by the emphasis placed on their maternal and nurturing sides. Each woman is made to seem less tough by the presence of a woman in a lesser role (Vasquez or Torres) who is far more blatantly tough, making Janeway and Ripley less of a threat to gender norms.

Although the *Aliens* trilogy and *Star Trek: Voyager* strive to assure viewers that women pose no significant threat to the "real" toughness of men, science fiction still has the potential to depict tough women who challenge gender stereotypes and, unlike Ripley and Janeway, are not re-feminized. One example of a science-fiction writer who creates tough women but is unconcerned with affirming their softer, more feminine side, is Nicola Griffith. In her novel *Ammonite* (1992), she recounts the story of Marghe Taishan, an anthropologist on a planet where all the men have been killed by a deadly virus. Marghe manages to survive in hostile weather conditions that would kill most people. She is one tough woman among many in *Ammonite.* Commander Danner is the tough leader of a human settlement on the planet. Aoife is the independent, strong-willed chief of her people. Vine is the sea-hardened captain of a sailing ship. One of the reasons Griffith is able to create such characters is because the men have all been conveniently killed off by the virus on the planet. No Stallone or Schwarzenegger can barge in to flex his pecs, strut about, and order the women around. Griffith's novel demonstrates that science fiction is a genre in which tough women can assume roles of power and influence.

The next chapter will analyze a series of post-apocalyptic science-fiction films that present tough women who, in many ways, appear even tougher than Ripley or Janeway. This chapter reflects on the increased prevalence of the tough woman in post-apocalyptic science fiction and examines how these films present tough women who challenge society's deep-rooted belief that only men can be truly tough. In this chapter I will continue to explore the power of science fiction to re-image women's roles and also to open up a broader spectrum of roles for women.

Chapter 7
Post-Apocalyptic Tough Girls:
Has the Road Warrior Met His Match?

The tough woman of the post-apocalyptic worlds of science-fiction films and books is hardly one of Charlie's Angels.[1] No designer fashions for her, and she probably has never seen the inside of a beauty parlor. She shoots an Uzi and is a match for any man bent on assault. She has better developed muscles than Martina Navratilova. In such texts, particularly those written in the 1980s and 1990s, the tough girl has become a common character. Although she is still outnumbered by tough men, her appearance marks a change from earlier years when women in science fiction were more likely to be victims than tough, independent heroines. In recent years, the tough woman has appeared in such films as *The Blood of Heroes* (1989), *Nemesis 2: Nebula* (1995), *Tank Girl* (1995), *APEX* (1993), *The Terminator* (1984), and *Terminator 2: Judgment Day* (1991). In each of these post-apocalyptic works, a tough girl plays a central role.

Tough women are also appearing in greater numbers in post-apocalyptic science-fiction novels. For example, Jane Unger in Bruce Sterling's *Heavy Weather* (1994) thinks nothing of rescuing her brother from a Mexican black-market medical clinic, using explosives and eventually carrying him out when he proves to be in no state to walk by himself. She lives in a twenty-first-century world where the greenhouse effect has devastated much of the environment, and her passion is chasing down tornadoes—the bigger the better. Another tough woman is Beverly O'Meara in David Alexander Smith's *In the Cube: A Novel of Future Boston* (1993). She earns her livelihood as a detective in the often brutal environment of a futuristic Boston. A cool, calm character, reminiscent of Raymond Chandler's Philip Marlowe, she is not afraid to use a gun and knows all the back streets, no matter how squalid.

What explains the increasing prominence of the tough woman in post-apocalyptic texts—works that feature a post-apocalyptic universe in which humanity faces unforeseen dangers and terrors? How does she offer new ways for women to act? Is this character as tough as she first appears? With these questions in mind, we turn to a study of the tough heroine in four post-apocalyptic films (the two *Terminator* movies, *The Blood of Heroes,* and *Nemesis 2: Nebula*). This chapter will show the ways that these films and other similar post-apocalyptic narratives depict tough women in order to contain the threat they pose to the dominant society and to stereotypical gender roles.[2]

Tough women in post-apocalyptic texts are particularly intriguing to study because typically they have been overshadowed by their male counterparts. Whether it is Deckard (Harrison Ford) negotiating the postmodern terrain of future Los Angeles in *Blade Runner* (1982), or Mad Max (Mel Gibson) traveling through the Australian outback of a devastated future world in the *Mad Max* trilogy of *Mad Max* (1979), *The Road Warrior* (1982), and *Mad Max: Beyond Thunderdome* (1985), the tough male surviving in a post-apocalyptic world has become a staple in films and books. Tough women are less common in such works, but, as I already have mentioned, they are beginning to appear with greater frequency. What do these women suggest about society's changing values?

Before turning to the texts themselves, it is worthwhile to reflect on why tough women (and men) are appearing in works that feature a grim vision of the future. One reason for the current peculiar fascination with a post-apocalypse future is our location in time, with the millennium's turn only a few years away. In such an environment, the apocalypse is "in." Lois Parkinson Zamora writes in *Writing the Apocalypse: Historical Vision in Contemporary U.S. and Latin American Fiction* (1989): "As the year 2000 approaches and we become accustomed to thinking of crisis in global terms, references to apocalypse seem to be increasing steadily, both in frequency and volume. . . . The end of this millennium has displaced 1984 as a focus of speculation, and apocalypse is in vogue" (1).[3] He points out the growing cultural fascination with the apocalypse and the growing speculation about the future beyond the year 2000. There is curiosity, fear, and dread about what lies ahead for the United States and the world, and reading post-apocalyptic texts is one way that people blow off a little steam about the changes they confront; there can even be a certain amount of pleasure in such an experience, as theorist Steven Goldsmith suggests: "Apocalyptic literature can be made a pleasurable refuge from violence, just as a good crossword puzzle offers welcome distraction from the anxieties of front-page news" (1). Perhaps one of the reasons for the boom in post-apocalyptic texts is that they offer a fleeting escape from a world that seems to grow only more complex and out of control.

Post-apocalyptic texts are also a sign that society already seems post-apocalyptic to some. Jean Baudrillard discusses this notion in his essay

"The Anorexic Ruins" (1989), in which he laments the fate of late-twentieth-century society: "We are no longer in a state of growth; we are in a state of excess. We are living in a society of excrescence, meaning that which incessantly develops without being measurable against its own objectives" (29). According to Baudrillard, society is madly producing far more than it can ever use, literally choking itself in a frenzy of production. He writes: "A lack is never dramatic; it is satiation that is disastrous, for it simultaneously leads to lockjaw and inertia" (30). He is horrified and amazed "by the obesity of all current systems" (30), which has resulted in an overabundance that threatens to overwhelm the world, and he perceives this satiation as inevitably pushing us toward our collective doom:

> The pole of reckoning dénouement, and apocalypse (in the good and bad sense of the word), which we had been able to postpone until the infiniteness of the Day of Judgment, this pole has come infinitely closer, and one could join Canetti in saying that we have already passed in unawares and now find ourselves in the situation of having overextended our own finalities, of having short-circuited our own perspectives, and of already being in the hereafter, that is, without horizon and without hope. (33–34)

Baudrillard is far from alone in expressing a general sense of uneasiness about the world's direction and a feeling that perhaps we have reached the point of no return. This attitude seems omnipresent in America, where people confront environmental pollution, high crime rates, cutbacks in industry, and other social ills. In such an environment, post-apocalyptic literature flourishes as people grapple with the often overwhelming feeling that they possess no future.

What Goldsmith and Baudrillard overlook in their reflections about the threat of apocalypse is the subject of gender. As this chapter suggests, gender plays an essential role in post-apocalyptic fiction, which becomes a terrain for both contesting present gender roles and helping to perpetuate them. In the often barbaric and excessive world of the post-apocalyptic narrative, women are freer to act tough and be independent because it is evident that the world has been turned topsy-turvy. In such a universe, girls are sometimes free to act like boys. Yet, at the same time, such a fictional world can be used to reaffirm traditional gender stereotypes. For instance, Mad Max and similar futuristic male heroes typically need to rescue women (and sometimes children) from harm. The reverse scenario is far less common.

Now, let us turn to the films themselves to discover how post-apocalyptic narratives explore gender differences yet still support the notion that even the toughest woman is no match for a tough man. I will examine the four films in order from the one that features the least tough woman to the film that depicts the toughest. Studying the films and the different ways they handle their tough heroines will lead to a better understanding of how gender is constituted in post-apocalyptic narratives and what such representations suggest about men and women and their roles today.

She Can Shoot, But Can She Knit?

The Terminator (1984, director James A. Cameron) charts the developing toughness of Sarah Connor (Linda Hamilton), a young woman who is being pursued by the Terminator (Arnold Schwarzenegger), a cyborg from the future that has been sent back in time to kill her. The Terminator pursues Sarah because she will one day give birth to the man who will lead the human resistance against machines after a nuclear holocaust in the distant future, when the machines have taken over the world. A resistance fighter, Kyle Reese (Michael Biehn), also has been sent back from the future to protect Sarah from the seemingly unstoppable Terminator, who is equipped with superhuman strength.[4] Sarah is introduced as she drives a motor scooter to the restaurant where she works as a waitress. Her Farrah-Fawcett hairdo makes her appear to be no match for the muscular Terminator, who exudes virility. Her femininity is emphasized; for example, she is depicted blow-drying her hair and primping in the bathroom. Because our society equates femininity with weakness, Sarah's actions make her appear less competent and self-assured than the Terminator.

Sarah's weakness is stressed early in the film when she is placed in the role of victim. The Terminator is stalking her late one night, and she is terrified. She calls her roommate and cries in a panic-stricken voice, "I'm really scared. I think there is someone after me." Shortly afterward she is attacked by the Terminator and is helpless, needing to be rescued by Kyle. Shouting, "Do exactly as I say," Kyle takes charge of Sarah. She continues to be passive in the early part of the film, but she starts to change when she cleans a wound of Kyle's. She says of the task, "This is going to make me puke," but she does not throw up and demonstrates that she is capable of taking charge of a situation. At this point, Sarah does not yet recognize the toughness within her. She denies to Kyle that she is tough even when he informs her that in the future she will teach her son to fight and organize others for combat. She says with disbelief, "Am I tough? Organized? I can't even balance my checkbook." Here, Sarah is the opposite of tough guy Rocky Balboa, who, we assume, was tough even in his cradle. Sarah must learn how to be tough, which suggests that toughness is not as "natural" for women as it often appears to be for men in movies and books.

Sarah becomes truly tough only after Kyle, who is now her lover, is injured. She takes charge as she recognizes his need for her help. She continues to act tough and to order Kyle around as the Terminator chases them into a factory. She is tough enough to survive Kyle's death and a horrific pursuit through the factory as the Terminator drags its half-destroyed body after her. Finally, she is tough enough to destroy the Terminator; she crushes him in a hydraulic press, snarling, "You're terminated, fucker." The woman who says these words is very different from the one who claimed that she could not balance her checkbook. Despite her newly found toughness, she has not been entirely removed from stereotypical gender roles. Her reasons for acting tough—to protect a loved one (Kyle) and her unborn child—are traditional women's concerns. She is tough, but the film assures viewers that she is tough *only* because her family is being threatened. This message is emphasized at the conclusion of the film when Sarah, noticeably pregnant, is driving a jeep through the deserts of what appears to be Mexico. As Margaret Goscilo writes in her essay "Deconstructing *The Terminator*" (1987), Sarah's "pregnancy encompasses her heroism, in reassurance that maternity differentiates and secures the feminine, however strong a woman may become" (49).[5] Sarah's toughness is controlled by her reinscription as a mother. Notably, *she* is not going to save the world; her son will.

A more interesting film, at least in terms of the development of a tough woman, is *Terminator 2: Judgment Day* (1991, director James A. Cameron). Sarah has toughened up considerably by spending years in Central America with various guerrilla groups, becoming what one writer called "a wild-cat, a tequila-swigging desperado, an Olympian avenger" (Morrison 70).[6] Sarah has made toughening herself a priority, recognizing that she must save her son, John—humanity's sole hope in its future war against the machines—and prepare him for his destiny. She has been transformed into an entirely new woman. "She can pick a lock, swing a broom handle and crush a skull, wire bombs [and] lug artillery" (Baumgold 26). These talents will be handy because she must protect John while another time-traveling cyborg, the T-1000, is equally intent on killing him.

The audience is introduced to Sarah in this movie with a frame that reads "Pescadero State Hospital." The camera then pans to a shot of the sweat-covered muscular arms of a woman doing pull-ups in what looks to be a prison cell. This shot in itself is unusual because it focuses the viewer's attention on the woman's arms and shoulders, rather than her breasts, emphasizing her muscularity and downplaying her femininity.[7] This effect is increased when the camera pans to a view of her taut back muscles, rather than her chest.

Not only is Sarah engaging in the prototypically tough activity of doing pull-ups (which is far tougher than, say, an aerobics workout with Jane Fonda), she also looks tough. She has muscles, wears no makeup, and has an angular, lithe form, which took actress Linda Hamilton grueling months to achieve. Some critics have viewed this presentation of Sarah's body in terms of her becoming "like a smaller version of the Terminator" (Telotte 31). J. P. Telotte understands Sarah as having "technologized herself, shaped herself into the best human cyborg possible in order to cope with the menace posed by the future's real cyborgs" (31). Sarah, however, has accomplished far more than fashioning herself into the best possible simulacrum of a machine. It is important to recognize her growing independence and autonomy. Although her pumped-up pecs might align her with the Terminator in some ways, they suggest her ability to stand up for herself; she is a different woman from the one encountered in the beginning of the first film.

As the unnamed woman continues to exercise, the audience views a male doctor strolling down the halls with his colleagues on his way to inspect her. When he opens the small window that looks into her cell and says a patronizing, "Good morning, Sarah," she turns to glare at him. With her hair unkempt, and an expression of hatred on her face, she appears insane. Her first words are, "Good morning, Dr. Silberman. How's the knee?" The doctor reveals that Sarah stabbed him in the knee with his own pen the week before. Here, Sarah is the wild woman, someone who will not submit to the male authority represented by the doctor, guards, and orderlies. Although on the surface the rest of the film is about the battle between the reprogrammed good Terminator (Arnold Schwarzenegger), who now fights to save Sarah and John, and the T-1000, the film is also about Sarah. Audience members learn that her tough image and attitude are too severe, too masculine, and too emotionless and, thus, must be softened in order for society to tolerate her.[8]

The next time the audience sees Sarah it becomes even more evident that there is a link between her non-traditional tough actions and society's assumption that she is insane (she is confined to a mental hospital for the criminally unbalanced). She is shown watching a video of herself becoming more and more enraged as Silberman forces her to recount her nightmares about how the world will end in a nuclear holocaust. Ironically, Sarah is the only sane person, because she knows that the future does hold such a disaster. She watches the video with no apparent emotion and, turning to the doctor, states calmly, "I'm much better now." When it becomes clear that he is going to renege on his promise to transfer her to the minimum security wing of the hospital where she could be visited by her son, she springs at Silberman, cursing and attacking him with her bare hands. Ultimately, she needs to be restrained by four orderlies. In this scene, Sarah is considered unbalanced because her views fail to coincide with what the majority holds to be the truth. She is also judged insane because she is tough and hard-boiled in a way that women are not supposed to be. The taboo nature of her character becomes more evident as the movie continues.

After extensively developing the growing relationship between young John Connor and the good Terminator, the film returns to Sarah. She appears catatonic while detectives question her about the deaths of John's foster parents, who have been murdered by the T-1000. In the next shot, she is heavily restrained in a bed where an odious guard licks her face; she continues to pretend to be catatonic. After being subjected to this grotesque act, she manages to escape. Breaking out of her cell, she knocks the obnoxious guard out cold and runs for freedom. After knocking out yet another guard, she prevents Dr. Silberman from calling for help by breaking his arm with a billy club. Then she cold-bloodedly siphons poison into a syringe, which she holds against Silberman's neck while she uses him as a shield to make her escape. The doctor is unable to understand Sarah's true toughness because it is contrary to his image of how he thinks women should behave. With the syringe at his neck as Sarah drags him down the hallway, he remarks, "It won't work, Sarah. You're no killer. I don't believe you would do it." He cannot accept that Sarah is no obedient little girl. Our collective society, represented by Silberman, finds it impossible to understand that women can be as tough as men. Recognizing such an idea threatens society's assumptions about the innate differences between men and women, differences upon which American culture is based.

During Sarah's orgy of violence, we see one of the reasons she appears tough. When she attacks men, she shows no emotion, even when the attacks are very violent. Because women are supposed to be emotional, Sarah's apparent lack of emotion works to establish her as something other than a woman.

After being forced to free the doctor, Sarah flees and encounters her son and the good Terminator. Together, the three escape from the shape-changing, liquid-metal T-1000. When they are under attack by the invincible T-1000, Sarah proves almost as tough as the Terminator. Both of them have guns and proceed to fire against the T-1000. Although Sarah is injured, she does not slow down; she runs to the hospital's underground garage where she orders a policeman out of his car "right now." Her toughness, however, is modified by her injury, which prevents her from performing at her peak level. Schwarzenegger's overwhelmingly tough bad-boy image in the film also mitigates Sarah's tough style; dressed in full leather, with dark sunglasses and a hyper-pumped-up physique, he is the epitome of male toughness, which minimizes but does not efface Sarah's tough image.

As the three make their getaway in a stolen car, Sarah berates her son for endangering himself by coming to her rescue, remarking, "I didn't need your help. I can take care of myself." At this point, we see how far she has traveled from traditional women's roles. She can take care of herself. Rather than portraying this strength as solely positive, however, the film depicts it as a flaw because it creates a breach between Sarah and her son. She has learned to take care of herself but only by losing her ability to show love and affection.

Sarah remains distant and aloof from her son as the three travel on. The Terminator, however, grows closer to John, becoming more human through its interaction with the boy. Sarah is presented as an "abnormal" mother. The movie conveys the message that her toughness carries a heavy price.

When the trio reach a desert hideaway where Sarah has stowed a secret cache of weapons, she smokes cigarettes, plays with a knife at one point, and spends a great deal of time assembling weapons. She is a conglomeration of signs that indicate toughness and masculinity. Her connection with weapons marks her as tough in American culture (Figures 10, 11).[9] Her competent handling of the guns marks her as "one of the boys" and reveals how much she has changed from the first film, where she was shown putting down in horror a pistol that Kyle had given her for protection and then picking it up out of curiosity, bewildered about how to handle it. At the end of *The Terminator,* a pistol is shown on Sarah's car seat as she drives off into the Mexican desert. She is not shown using it. In *Terminator 2,* Sarah handles even large guns with ease and owns an arsenal that would make the U.S. Army proud.

The development of Sarah's toughness, however, is at the cost of her building a close relationship with John, a lonely boy who wishes he could meet his real father and who views the Terminator as a father figure. Clearly, the film conveys mixed messages about the desirability of Sarah's tough character. It comes as little surprise that when she looks her toughest—at the end of the movie when she is dressed in fatigues and carrying an automatic weapon—she runs into trouble. Without a word to her son, she drives off on a mission to kill a scientist, Miles Dyson, whose discoveries will ultimately lead to the impending holocaust. Sarah abandons family and strikes out on her own, while in contrast, Miles is shown with his wife and child, cozy and secure at home. This scene of domestic tranquillity is rudely shattered by gunfire from Sarah. She has become too emotionless, which marks her as an outsider to family life. It is up to her son to bring her back to a "normal" female role. But Sarah already feels the schism between her adopted persona and her "natural" one. This is evident when she tries to kill Miles, ignoring his protesting wife and child. At the last moment, she is unable to do it and breaks into tears. John runs into the room, and the two embrace. Sarah has returned to her role as a mother and woman. Thus, although this film goes further than most

Figure 10. Sarah Connor (Linda Hamilton) gets armed (*Terminator 2,* TriStar Pictures).

action-adventure films in depicting a tough and capable woman who can take care of herself, ultimately, by emphasizing her femininity and Schwarzenegger's masculinity, the movie backs down from making her into another Rambo. She still possesses the emotion that sets her apart from male action heroes. (Schwarzenegger does not break into tears.)

Figure 11. Sarah Connor (Linda Hamilton) involved in a shoot-out (*Terminator 2*, TriStar Pictures).

Sarah's show of emotion and her acknowledgment of the importance of her relationship with her son are reminiscent of the woman hero of another post-apocalypse film, *APEX* (1993, director Phillip J. Roth), which features Natasha (Lisa Ann Russell) as a battle-hardened soldier who lives in an alternative world where the earth has been devastated by plague. Like Sarah, Natasha is more than capable of taking care of herself, yet her toughness is softened considerably by the fact that she was the hero's wife in the alternate universe from which he came.[10] A flashback of her making love with her husband is intercut with a scene of her in battle, reducing the threat of her being "less than a woman" because she carries a large gun and goes into battle with a group of men. Both *Terminator 2* and *APEX* emphasize the family ties of their tough leading women to show that they are not as tough as they might first appear.

Despite its attempts to defuse Sarah's toughness, *Terminator 2* does insist on her toughness in the denouement where she, John, and the

Terminator must fight the T-1000. Until the very end of the movie, she is depicted as tough while she fights to save her son's life. She wields a gun and shoots at the T-1000 for as long as she possibly can, but she is seriously wounded, leaving her relatively incapacitated and forcing the Terminator and John to protect her. She is tough, but she is not able to take care of herself as well as a tough guy like Schwarzenegger can look after himself. His ability points out her inability, reducing the threat that tough women like Sarah pose to society's codes of femininity.

She Can Kick Box, But Can She Cook?

A post-apocalyptic film that presents an even tougher heroine than Sarah Connor is *The Blood of Heroes* (1989, director David Peoples), which takes place in the barbaric remnants of the world after World War III. Most of the world is now desert, with a few scattered villages and underground cities. In this grim, barren universe, the sport of choice is a brutal, no-holds-barred game reminiscent of the gladiatorial games of ancient Rome. Although those who participate in the game are often maimed or killed, the heroine of *Blood* aspires to be a player, or a *jugger.*

Although *The Blood of Heroes* has been panned by critics, including one who called it a "megaviolent futuristic sports movie" (Novak, "Picks and Pans: *Blood*" 22), the film deserves attention because of the portrayal of its heroine.[11] The audience is first introduced to Kidda, an athletic young Asian woman (Joan Chen), at the beginning of the movie when she is shown preparing to play the game. She make a fierce, aggressive opponent as she plays, but eventually she is knocked down and must be helped off the field by her parents. At this point, her big dream is to travel to the city to play in the League, which is composed of only the best juggers. The members of the League teams are showered with luxuries that only the wealthiest of city people possess. Kidda is fascinated by some of the luxuries she hears about and asks, "Is there such a thing as silk?"

Kidda's presentation is different from Sarah Connor's in a number of ways. Kidda breaks the common Western stereotype of delicate and fragile Asian women, but she adheres to the stereotype of Asian women as dangerous, fierce predators. Her Asian identity makes her toughness more acceptable to a white audience; she is seen as Other because of her racial background. She also does not display the stereotypical heavy musculature of many tough characters, whether male or female; she is slight and not physically imposing. She is, however, very fast. As she says, "I got speed. I can run." Her speed is what makes her perfect for the role of the game's "quick," the person who must carry the "ball" (a dog's skull) down the field, eluding the opposing players. Kidda's small, wiry build and speed work to make her toughness more palatable to a mass audience; her lack of visible muscles causes less worry about her being overly masculine.

Kidda's toughness lies not as much in her brawn as in her tenacity. For several days she follows the team of juggers she has just played against until the team's leader, Sallow (Rutger Hauer), grudgingly allows her to join the team and become its quick. She is tenacious when subjected to brutal training as she learns how to be a better quick. Her toughness lies more in her determination than in her success. I do not suggest, however, that Kidda lacks physical prowess. What she lacks in bulk, she makes up for in aggression and stamina. In the first competitive game she plays with her new team, she beats up a man on the playing field and even bites off his ear, a perfectly acceptable act in this brutal sport.

One reason a woman like Kidda can get away with these actions is because the film repeatedly stresses that this is a world one step away from total anarchy, a world replete with physical deformity, suggesting the omnipresent decay. In this nightmarish universe, a woman can be tough, but only because the world has become incomprehensible, a horrid place where nothing functions as it should and laws of polite behavior for men and women have been ripped to shreds.

Even in this barbaric world, Kidda's toughness must be contained. Throughout the film it is evident that she is merely an apprentice to the older, more experienced Sallow. As often happens in the portrayal of a tough woman, such as Sarah Connor, Kidda's toughness is modified by the more extreme toughness of a male. Another way that Kidda's toughness is weakened is by showing her developing sexual relationship with Sallow—a relationship that allows Kidda to show her tender side. The film also contains her toughness by revealing that her character is the result of a corrupt social class system. This becomes evident in the city that the juggers visit in order to challenge the established League. The film emphasizes that Kidda and her teammates are at the bottom of the city's social hierarchy. Repeated shots show the pampered, lily-white members of the upper class watching the League fights and taking pleasure in the dirtied, bloodied fighters. There are also shots of the elites walking on an elevated, brightly-lit sidewalk, while the juggers are reduced to lurking in dark, dingy alleyways. The emphasis on class differences reassures the audience that Kidda, because she lives in a corrupt, decadent world where an aristocracy rules, has been pushed to extreme measures to survive; in a "normal" world, presumably, she would not be so tough.

When the big game finally takes place between the League players and Sallow's team, Kidda plays a major role; she is not shoved to the side and made to stay on the bench because she is a woman. The quick for the other team makes it clear that Kidda treads on dangerous ground when he leers, "Want to come kiss me, little girl?" She refuses to be intimidated and plays a hard, tough game—kicking, punching, rolling, biting, and breaking bones—doing whatever it takes to win. She does not hesitate to knee a man in the groin or slug another. She remains the dominant player throughout the competition and helps her team win the game, something that no other challenger has ever done. Her toughness, at this point, lies partly in her being an underdog who makes good, someone who wins against all the odds.

The conclusion of the film immediately after the winning game is ambivalent. Kidda has been noticed by the League, but does she wish to join their ranks? Does she want to become an object fawned-over by the aristocracy? Will she settle down with Sallow? Will she become a champion League player? These questions remain unanswered. The film's abrupt finish after the winning game leaves it to the audience to imagine what Kidda will do in the future. Her destiny remains vague, maybe because the director did not know what to do with such an unconventional woman.

She Can Throw a Punch, But Can She Darn a Sock?

A film that presents a tougher leading woman than the *Terminator* films or *Blood* is *Nemesis 2: Nebula* (1995, director Albert Pyun), which went directly to video release, perhaps because it portrays an extremely tough woman.

The film begins in the year 2077, when the world is ruled by cyborgs. A mother is taking her baby back in time to the year 1980. The mother has spirited her girl away because the child's DNA has been genetically engineered to make her into a super-woman, someone intelligent and strong enough to confront the cyborgs, who wish to kill her. Soon after their arrival in the past, the mother is murdered by desert marauders, leaving her daughter, Alex (Sue Price), to grow up with an East African tribe. Twenty years pass, and Alex is now a young woman, whose arms, stomach, back, and thighs bulge with muscles. Her sinewy build is an asset when she must sprint after a wild pig and stab it to death, or confront an enraged warrior. She is a crack shot with a gun and an ace at throwing a knife.

If she only had to worry about fighting combative warriors and running down any stray boars that came her way, she would have few worries. But Alex does have other concerns. Namely, she is being pursued by a cyborg from the future—because the cyborgs know that Alex is the one threat to their rule. The cyborg murders everything it encounters, mowing down Alex's entire village. She spends the rest of the film fleeing from the cyborg and trying to avoid the clutches of other more human villains.

If the viewer has any lingering doubts about Alex's ability to take care of herself, they are quickly dispelled when she proves that she is more than a match for man or cyborg. Early in the film, she displays her prowess by killing one man and knocking another out cold, accomplishing both feats while she is gagged, with her hands tied. Although such acts of derring-do by men are common in movies, it is unusual to see a woman performing them, particularly a woman who has no male assistance throughout the entire film. This is a way that the film presents a tough woman very different from Sarah or Kidda, both of whom are repeatedly helped by men.

After she rescues two women from the hands of mercenaries, much of Alex's time is spent in the company of these women, who are insipid and so poorly developed as characters that perhaps they are in the film to identify Alex clearly as Other. Alex is allowed to be so muscular only because she has been genetically enhanced; thus, she is not a "real" woman. The difference between Alex and the two women she rescues is highlighted when one of them, Emily, questions Alex about her muscularity. Emily is talkative, while Alex is usually silent—another characteristic of tough heroes:

> "You're pretty muscular, aren't you, for a girl?"
> "Am I?"
> "Looks like you've been out here a long time."

A knowing look then passes between Emily and her female companion, a look that acknowledges the difference between them and Alex. The comment about how long Alex has been "out here" (in the East African back country) positions her as culturally naive, someone who is not even aware of how unusual her physique is for a woman. Alex is Not Woman; she is something else entirely, limiting the threat she poses to traditional notions of femininity.

It is lucky for the other two women that Alex is around, because they could not survive without her. When the three of them venture into an old mining camp, Alex guns down an army of men, while at the same time eluding the cyborg, which blows up buildings and people indiscriminately. Alex thinks nothing of blazing away with two guns simultaneously and chucking a few grenades, too. In one memorable scene, she fires a gun while executing an acrobatic flip and hits her target square on. Although this is a feat that Sylvester Stallone, Chuck Norris, or Jean-Claude Van Damme would feel right at home executing, it is not one commonly performed by women. The significance of the scene changes because it is more difficult to interpret a woman being only another Rambo-like figure, blowing up buildings and lobbing grenades to protect the American way. Alex's gender changes all that. Just by *being*, she challenges notions of how women *should* act. Her appearance and gender are always throwing into question the limits of the traditional action-adventure film.

In the scene that best shows how Alex undermines societal expectations about women, she encounters two tough, muscle-bound men who are engaged in an arm-wrestling contest, the prototypical he-man sport. She pretends to offer sexual favors to the winner of the match in exchange for information about where the kidnapped Emily has been taken. As the winner struts after her, eager to earn his reward, he comments: "You know, we usually kill girls out here." To this, she responds "Do you?" before kicking him in the groin and bringing him to his knees. This man needs to learn a few lessons about how to treat a lady. Instead of offering the man sex, Alex punches him out. He is twice her size and even more muscle-bound than she is, yet she dispatches him with ease. Again and again, she proves more than able to take care of herself in a world filled with hostile and predatory men. Such a scene offers a moment of catharsis for women, in which they can imagine what it would be like to have the kind of physical power and confidence that Alex possesses. The scene provides female viewers with a feeling of empowerment, which is one reason the tough female hero appeals to women.

Ultimately, Alex's tough image proves too much for a film geared toward a mass audience. Her sexual desirability is stressed, which makes her a less threatening figure because it suggests her vulnerability and presumed availability. For example, she displays more than a generous amount of cleavage. There are also numerous "skin" shots of Alex, clad in the skimpiest attire, displaying a great deal of her tightly muscled flesh. In some ways, she can be interpreted as a stock character, following in the footsteps of many similar scantily clad women in other action-adventure films. This interpretation, however, does not take into consideration that she is genuinely autonomous and capable of taking care of herself. She is also extremely muscular, unlike most women who star in similar films. She is very much the center of the film, not merely a man's sidekick. For these reasons, this film suggests new ways that the tough woman is gaining power and validity in the 1990s. However, this dramatic image of a tough woman is available only on home-video; such an image is far less common in movies that hit the big screen, perhaps because a woman as tough as Alex is a character who makes many people uneasy. Alex transgresses the gender boundaries that our society holds to be "normal" and suggests that male and female identities may not be as closely aligned with masculinity and femininity, respectively, as has long been presumed to be true.

Post-Apocalyptic Women: Past, Present, and Future

Post-apocalyptic tough girls show science fiction's potential for reevaluating and questioning gender norms. Because the "normal" rules of desirable gender behavior do not always apply in a science-fiction world, film directors and fiction writers can create an imaginary universe in which they can explore how gender identities are created and what determines masculinity and femininity. Directors and writers are even freer to create alternative universes in a post-apocalyptic future where the rules of "correct" social behavior have been drastically warped—and in some cases, eliminated entirely.

Although alternative ways of being a woman or man can be explored in the post-apocalyptic future, science fiction also perpetuates the gendered norms of American culture. The *Terminator* films and *The Blood of Heroes* present tough heroines, but diminish their toughness by emphasizing their femininity and gender. In this fashion, the films paradoxically challenge typical gender roles, while also working to support them. *Nemesis 2* moves a step beyond the other films by depicting a tough woman whose personality is never softened by showing her maternal side or having her fall in love with a man. Alex is an independent loner, who is far more capable than the men or women who surround her. She demonstrates post-apocalyptic science fiction's potential to create women who call into question what it means to be a woman and who show that physical toughness is not limited to men.

I wish to conclude this chapter with a few words about another post-apocalyptic tough girl, because she embodies the battle between femininity and toughness that engages many tough girls. Tank Girl is the hero in the 1995 film of the same name, which takes place in the year 2033 in the Australian Outback, a bleak world where water has become the most valued commodity. When it first came out, *Tank Girl* was almost universally panned by reviewers.[12] Leslie Felperin's response was typical: "If Tank Girl were real she would have shot everyone rather than let this be released in her name" (55). Felperin was particularly critical of the actress who played Tank Girl: "Lori Petty, too squeaky-voiced and Nautilus-conditioned to pull it off as TG, comes off as a valley girl rebelling against middle-class parents by shopping in thrift stores" (55). Tank Girl, however, was not always so "squeaky-voiced and Nautilus-conditioned"; before her film debut, she was one of the toughest and raunchiest characters in an underground comic book series that was published under the name of "Tank Girl." Hollywood toned her down, creating a much milder character for moviegoers. Tank Girl's transformation reflects our society's continued uneasiness about tough women who challenge our widely held beliefs about how women (and men) should behave. Tank

Girl, Kidda, and Alex make our culture nervous because they suggest the malleable nature of our gendered identities and raise fears that women are capable of being far more autonomous and independent than they are usually portrayed. Even worse, they raise the specter that men are expendable. Thus, like Tank Girl, they are often reshaped to lessen the threat posed by their tough attitude.

In the next chapter we turn to a discussion of tough women in comic books, an even more marginalized genre than science fiction. Like science fiction, comic books provide an alternative venue where new ideas about gender can be explored. Comic books and other alternative media forms provide a space to expand the definitions of what it means to be a man or a woman and to explore how toughness is constituted for both. But even an alternative medium such as comic books can perpetuate traditional notions about desirable gendered behavior. As the next chapter demonstrates, comic books can be both the most progressive and most reactionary of art forms, especially with regard to their depiction of women.

Chapter 8
Tough Girls in Comic Books
Beyond Wonder Woman

"For boys, Wonder Woman is a frightening image," wrote Dr. Fredric Wertham in his attack against the comic-book industry, *Seduction of the Innocent* (1954). "For girls she is a morbid ideal. Where Batman is anti-feminine, the attractive Wonder Woman and her counterparts are definitely anti-masculine. Wonder Woman has her own female following. . . . Her followers are the 'Holliday girls,' i.e. the holiday girls, the gay party girls, the gay girls" (193). Wertham's words express an early uneasiness about the role of tough women in comic books. To Wertham and others, Wonder Woman seemed *too* tough and capable. If she did not slug a bad guy, she could depend on her magic golden lasso, which forced anyone to tell the truth. In the unlikely event that she had forgotten her lasso, she could always turn to her handy bullet-deflecting bracelets. Thus equipped, Wonder Woman, in her skintight costume and perfectly coiffured hair, could overcome any villain she encountered. No wonder she made Wertham uncomfortable.[1]

Wonder Woman is a precursor to the many women heroes and villains in comic books in recent years, including such characters as Marvel-Girl, Invisible Girl, Girlhero, Wonder Girl, Dagger, Darkstar, Catwoman, the Huntress, Bloody Mary, Shadow Cat, She-Hulk, Spider Woman, Rogue, Invisible Woman, and Wasp.[2] Many of these female characters are portrayed as surprisingly tough, adopting behaviors and characteristics that have been traditionally ascribed to men. Whether slugging a bad guy or giving an opponent a shattering kick in the head, these comic book women are aggressive and physically potent. In numbers undreamed of in previous decades, these tough women are making a mark in contemporary comic books. However, they still are not challenging the preeminence of tough male characters, including Batman, Captain Marvel, Captain America, Daredevil, Thor, Green Arrow, Aquaman, Hawkman, Superman, Doc Savage, Green Lantern, Plastic Man, and Spiderman.[3]

Despite being greatly outnumbered by her male counterparts, the tough female character plays an increasingly important role in comic books. What explains her notoriety? Does her presence in the alternative genre of the comic book offer more room for artists and writers to rescript notions of traditional femininity? This chapter seeks to answer these questions by exploring the changing representation of tough women in comic books and analyzing the depiction of three prominent women heroes or anti-heroes: Storm, Elektra, and Martha Washington. Storm appears in many of the X-Men adventures. Elektra is featured in a series of comics compiled in Frank Miller's *Elektra, the Complete Saga* (1989). Martha Washington's adventures are the focus of Frank Miller and Dave Gibbons's graphic novel *Give Me Liberty: An American Dream* (1992). Studying these characters, this chapter illustrates how comic books offer an opportunity to create new and subversive images of what it means to be a woman. However, we also find that many comic books use tough women only to perpetuate stereotypes, often portraying them as sexually uncontrollable blonde bombshells.

Why Study Comic Books?

Critic Frank McConnell argues that in recent years "some of the best and most human fiction in America, not to mention the rest of the world, is appearing not as 'novels' but as that more-than-faintly-contemptible form, the comic book" (21). Graphic novels and comic books such as *Watchmen* (1986) and *The Return of Superman* (1993) are far more sophisticated and far darker than Richie Rich and Donald Duck.[4] Many comic books and graphic novels have become as complex an art form as novels or paintings and are worthy of attention for both their artistry and the messages they convey about society.

Despite the growing intellectual sophistication of contemporary comic books and their rich historical heritage—including such canonical art as William Hogarth's etchings *The Rake's Progress* and *The Harlot's Progress*—they are still viewed with uneasiness and disdain by mainstream America (Gloeckner 246). They have gained greater acceptance in other countries, such as France, where college classes on comic books are a common part of the curriculum (Gloeckner 247). In America, many view comic books as "inferior products for the post-drool, pre-shaving set" (Nericcio 83). Although this attitude has been changing, particularly in recent decades, it still proves remarkably tenacious. "Comic books have been and continue to be one of the most marginalized of art forms. The assumption that the 'reading' of comics is a frivolous and inferior activity seems a given even among those who do not see them as a threat" (Schmitt 153). Even graphic novels widely acknowledged as masterpieces, such as Art Spiegelman's *Maus* (1971) or *Maus II* (1986), have far less social acceptance than most canonical novels.

In addition to being perceived by many as shoddy entertainment undeserving of critical attention, comic books are often considered perverse and lewd, a view that has persisted throughout much of this century. The idea that comic books could twist young minds reached its height in the 1950s when Wertham's *Seduction of the Innocent* was originally published. *Seduction* was at the center of a campaign by educators and parents to control the threat they assumed comic books posed.[5] Wertham's sensationalistic work claimed that reading comic books was a key factor in juvenile delinquency. The campaign for comic book reform instigated by his study even led to the formation of a Senate subcommittee to study the influence of comic books on youth. The subcommittee members were scandalized by the graphic content of some comic books, proclaiming, "this country cannot afford the calculated risk involved in feeding its children through comic books a concentrated diet of crime, horror, and violence" (Committee on the Judiciary 32). As a result of the hearings, the comic book industry came under greater scrutiny, as educators and parents tried to control what they perceived to be a threat to the "American standard of decency" (Committee on the Judiciary 25). Today, comic books are still viewed by many as morally suspect—dynamite waiting to blow up American morality.

Given the general suspicion that comic books are a form of subliterature that can corrupt youngsters, it comes as little surprise that critical attention to comic books is limited, but they deserve more scholarly attention.[6] As one critic writes, "Since the 1930s, the comics have been influenced by, and in turn, have influenced, mainstream culture in the United States. They reflect the popular themes, attitudes, and symbols of Western culture, which positions them within the prevailing current of the American media scene" (Boker 116). I argue that comics should *not* be ignored, as they have been and continue to be such an influential twentieth-century art form. Many people who have *never* read a full-length novel have read hundreds, if not thousands, of comic books. And who among us does not stop to read the Sunday morning comics occasionally (or even every week)? Comics are ubiquitous, and their changing content suggests a great deal about our cultural values. From the many war comics featuring a "red" threat that appeared during the Cold War to the comic books starring mutant superheroes that were published in the 1970s and 1980s, comics have expressed a great deal about our worst fears and our greatest hopes.

As a marginalized alternative art form, comic books are particularly intriguing because they often undermine the status quo and are capable of showing us a much darker, bleaker image of society than might ever appear in a more mainstream medium, such as television. As Ronald Schmitt writes in "Deconstructive Comics" (1992):

> Comic book characters reveal essential myths and ideologies of the cultures in which they are produced, but their popularity clearly stems from the fact that they offer alternatives to and escape from the ideology of the status quo. Far from being a watered-down, inferior substitute of "high" cultural art, they are distinct, alternative visions which reveal more about the fears, neuroses and power struggles of the [populace] than high art does. (154–55)

As Schmitt points out, the marginalized nature of comic books and their position as popular art allows them to inspect society from a different perspective than most mainstream art. Comic books are uniquely prepared to critique established norms:

> The medium of graphic narrative is where local, identifiable acts of resistance to the corporate/network narrative status quo may be observed. Drawing as it does from television, cinema, literature and the fine arts, graphic narrative, with its bastard lineage, exhibits a conspicuous range. Through this medium, combining both words *and* images, comic-book artists push the limits of conventional narrative practice and, in the process, provide new means of critical inquiry. (Nericcio 87)

In other words, the very form of comic books, with its conjunctive use of words and images, allows writers and artists to think about the nature of meaning in a different way than those who are constrained by the necessity of using either words or images. Comic books are also at the cutting edge of exploring new definitions of gender because of their marginalization, which allows them to be what Schmitt identifies as an "important deconstructive and revolutionary medium in the 20th century" (153). This deconstructive power is one of the reasons feminist theorists should be interested in comic books—texts that can create alternative worlds in which gender operates very differently than it does in our own real world.[7]

"Batman in a Bustier": Wonder Woman and Friends

It is partly the medium's potential to question, challenge, and subvert gender role norms that has led an increasing number of women to involve themselves with comic books and comic book art. Today, women are becoming a force to be reckoned with in the universe of comics. Margorie Ingall writes that "it is the best time ever for funky, weird, challenging girl cartoonists" (68).[8] Whether they are cartoonists or readers of cartoons, women are invading the formerly predominantly male sanctuary of the comic book, which is perhaps one of the reasons tough women in comic books are appearing with greater frequency than ever before. Such characters appeal to the growing number of women consumers. Without a doubt, the dictates of the marketplace strongly influence how women are represented in comic books. Comic book critic Roger Sabin writes, "the laws of the market rule" (234). Since the majority of comic book purchasers are boys and men, their tastes are catered to, resulting in many women characters who are still little more than overly endowed male fantasies who would be right at home in Hugh Hefner's mansion.

Another form of sexism in comic books is that women are not depicted in nearly the same numbers as men. As Thomas Young discovered in his 1991 study of Marvel Universe trading cards:

> Women are underrepresented among comic book super-heroes. . . . They generally do not play an important role in the morality drama of comic books, as illustrated by their fewer number of battles. . . . The fact that women super-heroes are less frequently called upon to restore Cosmic order, despite their equal effectiveness, might be an indication of sexism in the "Marvel Universe." (218)

Young is writing specifically about Marvel comics, but his words are equally germane to the comic books published by other companies, books in which women are almost always outnumbered by men. The overwhelming number of male heroes in comic books functions to assure readers that men are the only suitable subjects for action-adventure comics, affirming and naturalizing the centrality of men in the cosmos.

Although sexism operates to keep women in the margins of the comic-book universe, it is becoming more feasible for a tough woman to star in her own series of comic books. These women heroes, no matter where they might appear, are performing important cultural work. As Pamela S. Boker comments, "Between the covers of these action comics we encounter a group of extraordinary women characters, women who not only traverse the schizophrenic disparity between a woman's wielding of power and the acknowledgment of her innate sexuality, but in many ways eliminate completely the cultural divisiveness between genders" (108). I hold a less optimistic view than Boker does about the ability of women in comic books to eliminate the divisions between the genders because, as we shall discover, such books often emphasize the distinct *differences* between men and women, rather than the similarities. I am interested in what Boker terms the "schizophrenic quality" of the tough woman hero in action comics. How does a woman negotiate the he-man preserve of the action comic? How does she interact with her typically male comrades? What does her representation suggest about women's changing roles? Why does she appear at all?

This chapter focuses on the role of the tough hero (or anti-hero) because heroes, as critic Ian M. Taplin comments in his essay "Why We

Need Heroes to be Heroic" (1988), "enable us to externalize the inner contradictions of our lives. They are also a safety valve for our collective frustrations" (141). Some of the "inner contradictions" and "collective frustrations" are based on gender. The female hero can rescript stereotypes about what it means to be a woman. Just by *being,* she suggests that the male stranglehold on the heroic can be subverted. The woman hero serves as a bold, new role model for women and girls. Her appearance provides one visual clue to a culture that is gradually becoming more open to nonstereotypical gender roles and to women adopting tough roles. At the same time, her peripheral position in comic books, which are doubly marginalized as both popular literature and a genre marketed in the past principally to children, suggests the ways that tough women are still controversial in our society.

Before turning to more contemporary characters, we must look back at earlier comic strip women, who have been present since the beginning years of the comics.[9] In the first decades of the twentieth century, women were seldom presented as tough and independent. Instead, they were apt to require men to rescue them from all sorts of mishaps. Women in the early comics were commonly portrayed in a few stereotypically feminine roles. A number of female characters (Maggie, Minerva Gump, and Ma Feitelbaum) in the 1910s and 1920s were frumpy or domineering housewives. Other characters during this period (Nora, Polly, Winnie Winkle, Tillie the Toiler, Flapper Fanny, and Lillums Lovewell) were vamps. Some in the 1920s and 1930s were career girls, such as Jane Arden, Mississippi, and Connie—all reporters—and Myra North, a nurse. These career women led more active lives than many other women in comics, but even the girl reporters and nurses did not move far away from socially acceptable behavior for women. In a similar fashion, the evil women villains (such as Ardala Valmar, the Flame, and the Dragon-Lady) who were popular in the 1930s presented no major challenge to gender stereotypes; these women were slinky vamps who could not wait to get their clutches on a man.

Some female characters in the early comics did challenge gender stereotypes. A number who flew airplanes for a living appeared in the late 1920s and early 1930s. Betty Lou Barnes was featured in "Tailspin Tommy." She was a "daredevil aviatrix and the founder . . . of a shaky airline company named Three-Point Airlines" (Horn 71). Other women followed her lead, such as Peggy Mills in "Skyroads" and Jenny Dare, an aviatrix who was featured in her own strip, "Flyin' Jenny." Despite their independence, they were all stereotypical beauties and consequently did not offer a significant threat to the male domination of comics. Other heroic women followed, but none of them managed to grab the public imagination in the way that Superman and similar male superheroes did.

The first female character to attract a large following challenged the notion that women superheroes in comic books generally had to be subordinate to men; her name was Wonder Woman. The creation of William Moulton Marston (who also invented the lie detector), she made her first appearance in *All-Star Comics* in November 1941, and quickly became a hit. Writer Michael Harrington believes that the reason for her instant success lay in her "breathtaking fusion of feminism and patriotism and kinky sex" (9). Feminism helps to explain part of her appeal because Wonder Woman offered women a new and powerful role model. Lillian S. Robinson writes about her youthful fascination with Wonder Woman: "What enchanted me about Wonder Woman was her physical power. . . . She had developed her abilities to a . . . martial art" (101). I religiously watched the 1970s television show *Wonder Woman,* but I remember being dismayed that she was so infatuated with Captain Steve Trevor and that she appeared more interested in being his secretary than forging out on her own. In many ways, she was a schizophrenic character: she was tough and independent, but she still languished for a date with the handsome Steve. As media critic Susan Douglas writes, Wonder Woman "wasn't supposed to like or need men, but then she met one and kinda lost her resolve" (217). Although Wonder Woman was important because she possessed more autonomy and independence than most other comic book women, she still adhered to many traditional ideas about how women should look and behave.

Wonder Woman was far from alone as a wanna-be-tough female comic strip character. There were a number of others, including Batgirl, who appeared in 1966. Batgirl's handbag transformed into her weapons belt and her skirt became a cape; needless to say, her skintight bodysuit did not suggest that women should try to escape stereotypical notions of feminine dress. Batgirl was one of a plethora of women superheroes who appeared in the 1960s and 1970s. A character based on the Egyptian goddess Isis made her debut in 1976, starring in a comic book series about her adventures. But Isis was little more than Wonder Woman wearing a tennis skirt, which is what the Mighty Isis's crime-fighting outfit appeared to be. Like Wonder Woman, Isis flashed a lot of leg and would not have been out of place in the Rockettes. When Isis was not out fighting bad guys, she, like Wonder Woman, was engaged in a typical feminine job—she was a high school teacher. Isis was an Egyptian Wonder Woman (although, strangely enough, even though she was an Egyptian goddess, Isis appeared as Anglo and fair as Wonder Woman). In the same year as the Mighty Isis made her appearance, Ms. Marvel appeared. Ms. Marvel could compete against men, but her appearance, like that of the Mighty Isis, in no way challenged assumptions about feminine beauty. Another character similar to Ms. Marvel was the Dazzler, who starred in the early

1980s Marvel comics of the same name. She turned sound energy into dazzling light energy to blind her foes, allowing her to (believe it or not) make her getaway on the roller skates she always kept handy. In her non-super-hero life, she was an aspiring singer and a standard feminine beauty. Isis, Ms. Marvel, and the Dazzler failed to move far from traditionally female roles.

Tough women continue to be difficult to find in more recent comic books, which contain many supposedly tough women who actually are little more than overly endowed caricatures with large guns and skimpy costumes: " 'Bad girl' comics are booming. While American standards of literacy are dropping, college students still seem able to handle comics, especially when the cartoons show busty viragoes with names like Lady Death, Barb-Wire, and Avengelyne. [They resemble] Batman in a bustier; Captain America in a camisole" (Sullivan 37–38). Approximately fifty "bad girl" comic book series exist, some with very respectable sales (Sullivan 38). The Lady Death series from Chaos comics sells an impressive 160,000 copies every month (Sullivan 38). Scanning the racks of bad girl comics at the local comic store, one quickly discovers the reason for their popularity: sex. In book after book, female sexuality is emphasized, often with lurid pictures of women with enormous breasts and well-developed bodies, drawn in poses that feature spread legs or other sexually provocative poses.

One example of a typical bad girl comic book is Ricky Carralero's *Double Impact* series, featuring China and Jazz—better known as Double Impact—two extremely well-endowed women wearing matching skin-tight metallic silver outfits and toting huge guns. Although China and Jazz talk tough and sometimes act tough, men do the majority of the fighting in a number of the books. Another example of a bad girl comic is *Lethal Strike* by Everette Hartsoe. In this series, two sisters, Nicole and Jacklyn Mitchell, grow up to become a vigilante killer and an assassin, respectively. Both Nicole (Razor) and Jacklyn (Stryke) can take care of themselves, but the sisters are trapped in a fairly conventional world. For example, in "Lethal Strike #3," Stryke and Razor are fighting over the most traditional prize: a man. When Stryke learns that her lover, VonDrake, wants to leave her and take up with Razor, a fight breaks out between the two women. They are strong and independent but lack the physical strength of VonDrake, who manages to overpower both of them. Another bad girl is featured in John Arcudi's *Barb-Wire* series (1996). With her prominent breasts and barely-there attire, Barb-Wire could be a sister to Stryke and Razor. Barb-Wire is notably more physically active and independent than the other two, often single-handedly dealing with the villains who threaten her. Still, she is primarily a sex kitten. China, Jazz, Stryke, Razor, and Barb-Wire are just a few examples of the numerous women characters in comic books who have the superficial appearance of being tough but who clearly do not break free from the gender stereotype that women are chiefly sex objects designed for male gratification.

Yet in recent comic books tough women have appeared who are far more multidimensional than the overly endowed Stryke, Razor, and Barb-Wire. For instance, it has become de rigueur in the politically correct 1980s and 1990s to include at least one tough woman in a team of action-adventure fighters.[10] The G.I. Joe team includes a woman named Scarlett, a blackbelt at age fifteen and an expert with the power crossbow. However, she is outnumbered and out-gunned by her male compatriots, which is what generally happens to the female member of a comic book fighting team.

In recent years larger numbers of tough individual women have appeared in comic books. Jamie Hewlett and Alan Martin's Tank Girl springs to mind. A tank-driving, combat-boot-wearing, beer-swigging girl who flaunts a green and blue mohawk and has a boyfriend who is a mutant kangaroo, Tank Girl is no good girl. Loud, and ready to curse or hurl a beer can at her television, she is tough, rude, and in your face. She is everything that a girl is told not to be. Another tough girl is Inspector Maggie Sawyers, who leads the Special Crimes Unit of the Metropolis Police Force. Sawyers, Cindy Goff's artistic creation, who appeared in a special Superman series in the mid-1990s, is a gun-toting butch lesbian, one of a tiny group of openly lesbian characters in comics.[11] With her chiseled features, ice-blue eyes, short-cropped hair, and strong jaw line, Sawyers is a woman no one bosses around. She is a leader, and her forces jump to attention when she orders them into action.

Tough but Sensitive: Storm

When discussing tough women in comic books, one must mention the phenomenally popular X-Men, a group that has lasted since 1963 and that has spawned a number of closely related groups, including X-Force, X-Factor, and Excalibur. The X-Men consist of a bunch of fighters, all mutants, who have been trained by Charles Xavier at his School for Gifted Youngsters. The young mutants are taught to be protectors of humanity, even though they are often shunned by those they seek to help, who believe all mutants are evil. The X-Men team comprises Banshee, Nightcrawler, Wolverine, Colossus, Cyclops, and Storm. A number of other characters join the X-Men for brief periods, and former members of the X-Men (Jean Grey, Ice Man, the Beast, Cyclops, and the Angel) also make appearances.

Storm, who controls the natural elements and is the leader of the X-Men, is not the only tough woman in the X-Men, despite the name of the group, which reflects the typical male bias one finds in action-adventure comics. There is Kitty Pryde (also known as Shadow-Cat), for instance, who can walk through walls and other solid objects. She is the youngest of the group and seems immature in comparison with the rest of them; she often gets into trouble, resulting in the older X-Men coming to her rescue. The X-Men encounter a number of other tough women, such as Binary, Spiral, Mystique, Viper, and Dark Phoenix, but only Storm plays a dominant role in the series.

Storm is interesting as a tough female character because she begins her career in a more traditional female role. The daughter of an African princess, she lives as an animal-loving nature goddess on Mount Kilimanjaro until Xavier comes to spirit her away to join the X-Men. Of course, associations between nature and women go back to the dawn of humanity; these associations lessen Storm's power by showing that she is just a conduit for the much greater powers of nature. In many ways, she embodies femininity, which is evident from the description of her that appears in the 19 October 1986 volume of *Classic X-Men* entitled "First Friends": "Her true name is Ororo, which means 'Beauty'—which she is without a doubt, in spirit as in flesh." In this book, Storm and Jean are "normal" young women. One day, after hours of shopping for clothes, Storm sighs, "so much to wear—and so complicated." Jean reassures her friend, "You'll learn. Brace yourself, girl, we've only just begun." In this book, Storm and Jean are two girls who just happen to be superheroes, and being a superhero does not interfere with going shopping at the mall. It is wrong, however, to imagine Storm as too soft. After all, she is more than capable of taking care of herself. For example, in the volume entitled "Freedom Is a Four Letter Word" of *The Uncanny X-Men* (June 1986), Storm takes on a whole gang of thugs and remains unscathed.

Despite her show of strength, Storm's early representation helped to perpetuate gender stereotypes about the inherent femininity of women, until her creators began to portray her in a very different fashion. This change is depicted in Chris Claremont's graphic unpaginated novel *The Uncanny X-Men: From the Ashes* (1990), a compilation of a series of X-Men comics published in the 1980s. The main story concerns Jean Grey who, as Phoenix, was killed because she possessed too much power and turned evil. A new woman, Madelyne Pryor, is introduced, and she appears to be the identical twin of Jean Grey/Phoenix. Much of the book addresses the attempts by the X-Men to deal with this newcomer. For our purposes, however, one of the subordinate plots is more interesting: Ororo's (Storm's) transformation from earth goddess to punk tough girl. She literally grows into a new character, which leaves some of her teammates dismayed. For example, when they watch her fight an evil mutant who has threatened her, Ororo's friends assume she will lose because she has sworn never to kill a human. Instead, she is the victor and kills her opponent, something that Nightcrawler says he "never expected" of her. He is deeply disturbed by the transformation his friend and leader undergoes, reflecting, "Ororo is changing—before my eyes—but what truly terrifies me is that she doesn't seem to mind." The dismay Nightcrawler expresses is one sign that women's toughness is still not as acceptable as men's. Ororo is acceptable as an earth goddess but not as a tough punk.

Ororo herself recognizes the changes she is undergoing and is caught between her old and new selves, feeling "as though [she] stands at a crossroads," trapped between her identities as Ororo and Storm—identities that can be associated with her feminine, nurturing side and her masculine, tough side, respectively. The battle between her feminine and masculine self-representation continues when she meets Yukio, a devil-may-care female samurai in Japan. At first, Storm is baffled by Yukio's carefree attitude, but gradually Storm's interest grows. Finally, she welcomes Yukio's infectious attitude, commenting, "Whatever it means—this madness of yours that has infected me. I welcome it!" This marks the beginning of Storm's startling transformation. When she appears at Wolverine's wedding, she is no longer the same woman. She sports a mohawk rather than long hair and wears black leather, including a studded collar around her neck. Everyone at the wedding is stunned, Kitty perhaps most of all. She yells, "Your clothes! Your hair! What have you done?!! How could you?" Professor Xavier is also concerned about Storm's change in wardrobe, speculating as to whether it is "some whim . . . or indicative of a deeper, more serious metamorphosis." Storm's friends are disturbed, and her transformation is viewed with bewilderment and consternation. These feelings show that even in the alternative universe of the X-Men, toughness in women is regarded with uneasiness. Even as a leader, Storm has less access to a tough persona than do many of the male characters.[12] Women's toughness is viewed as abnormal in comic books, despite their explorations of alternative gender roles for both men and women.

Another intriguing plot line in *From the Ashes* is the transformation of the character Rogue, who tries to end her career as a villain and follower of the evil Mystique. Rogue's special talent (she absorbs people's powers and abilities through her touch) is driving her insane, causing her to seek a new path in life. She becomes a probationary member of the X-Men, but only Dr. Xavier endorses her membership. The other mutants are horrified at the thought of letting Rogue, their former enemy, become a member of the X-Men, and she must struggle for her place in the group, never quite allaying their fears that she is still treacherous. What is interesting about Rogue is that she is portrayed as very aggressive and tough, far more so than Storm. Rogue's rough, tough character is actually *too* extreme; her toughness must be reduced in order for the larger group to survive.

The comic book series makes numerous attempts to control and contain the threat of Rogue's toughness. For instance, in "The Morning After" (*The Uncanny X-Men,* October 1986), her physical appearance is of great importance to her. She catches a glimpse of her reflection in a mirrored window and thinks to herself that she looks as if she is an "[u]tter an' complete ragbag" (9). So, she does what many young women would do in a similar situation: she goes shopping, paying a visit to the nearby Bloomingdale's where she proceeds to try on a variety of different outfits. While there, she goes to the cosmetics counter where she asks a clerk, "Could you save this face?" (10). Rogue is as interested in the pursuit of beauty as any "normal" woman might be. Her toughness is contained by showing that she is just "one of the girls" after all.

Rogue is caught up in the pursuit of what feminist critic Naomi Wolf calls the PBQ: professional beauty qualification. In her best-selling book *The Beauty Myth* (1991), Wolf describes women as fixated on the endless search for beauty, as they try to imitate the impossibly beautiful figures found in the scores of women's magazines at grocery checkout lines across the country. The result is that women become obsessed by the PBQ, causing an ever greater number of women to pursue the appearance of a professional beauty in order to stay employed and earn promotions (27). Rogue and other comic book women are also obsessed with the PBQ. They might be able to stop flying bullets in their tracks with a precise flick of a bracelet (Wonder Woman) or control the powers of the weather (Storm), but many tough women in comic books, such as Rogue, still worry about their physical appearance. They are caught up in a search for beauty that can be dangerous, as theorist Susan Bordo points out: "In our own era, it is difficult to avoid the recognition that the contemporary preoccupation with appearance, which still affects women far more powerfully than men, even in our narcissistic and visually oriented culture, may function as a backlash phenomenon, reasserting existing gender configurations against any attempts to shift or transform power relations" (166). Bordo's words aptly describe the situation of many women in comic books, who are much more intent on maintaining a beautiful appearance than are the boys, reflecting a society in which a woman's beauty is still over-emphasized and often considered to be the sole measure of her worth.

Tough But Not Tough Enough: Elektra

Storm and Rogue are examples of strong women in comic books who are divided between different personalities, torn between their longing to be feminine (whether this entails nurturing others or purchasing makeup) and their desire to be tough and independent. They are split between traditionally feminine and masculine traits and are sometimes strongly ambivalent about this division, suggesting that being tough is not "normal" for women.

Another tough woman who experiences a similar tension between femininity and masculinity is Elektra, featured in Frank Miller's *Elektra, the Complete Saga* (1989). She is an assassin, a career track for women that is popular in comic books and science-fiction novels. Yukio in the X-Men, for example, is the Japanese woman assassin who goes gunning for Wolverine but ends up becoming infatuated with him. A series of comic books and an animated cartoon series also has been developed around the adventures of Aeon Flux, another female assassin. Because the ruthless assassin is one of the toughest characters in the popular media, an exploration of Elektra's tale is fruitful in order to demonstrate the ways that the media depict women as tough while simultaneously undermining their toughness. Often, toughness indicates that a character has been warped or twisted by some awful event in her life, conveying the message that a woman may be tough, but only if toughness is forced upon her. Sarah Connor, for example, becomes tough only because she must protect the world from nuclear annihilation.

Elektra, the Complete Saga does not begin with Elektra's story but with the super-hero Daredevil's. Readers are introduced to two college students, Franklin Nelson and Matthew Murdock, as they stroll across campus. Although blind, Matthew has no difficulty avoiding obstacles. Franklin and Matt meet important visitors, including the daughter of a Greek diplomat, who is accompanied by her guard and father. Immediately, Matt is smitten with the woman—Elektra—after hearing her "soft as velvet" voice (5) and breathing her "delicate French perfume" (4). At this point, Elektra appears to be a typically feminine college student. Although she comments that she is "well trained in martial arts" (6), she seems to be little different from her classmates. Matt and Elektra fall in love and have a traditional college romance, until she and her father are kidnapped by terrorists. Matt, who possesses super-powers that are later going to make him the champion "Daredevil," single-handedly frees Elektra and her father. She plays a minor role; Matt is the major actor. Elektra's father is accidentally killed later, which results in her leaving Matt, resolving never to allow the world to hurt her again. It is clear that she is embarking on the path that will eventually make her a highly trained assassin only because of the loss of her beloved father. The book presents this move as less than positive and portrays Elektra as running away from her grief, rather than addressing it. Because feelings are associated with women, Elektra is also running away from her femininity. The book makes it evident that her change to a more masculine-identified personality is something that most "normal" women would not consider.

Comic books are uneasy presenting a tough woman, such as Elektra, without reassuring the audience that she has been forced by circumstances to adopt traits that are usually seen as the prerogative of men.

After this introduction, the story flashes to a picture of a woman struggling through a blizzard in a bitter Arctic region. It is Elektra, who has gone there to climb "a wall that cannot be scaled" in order to join an elite group of warriors (13). She fails the climb, but the warrior group takes her in anyway. She trains, fights, and becomes a skilled warrior; yet she is rejected by the order's leader, a man named Stick, because she is filled with pain and rage. These two failures serve to show Elektra's weaknesses. While Daredevil has been depicted as infallible, Elektra is fallible. A hierarchy is established in which women inevitably rank second. This is a common tactic used by the popular media to deemphasize the threat posed by tough women. They are represented as far less tough than the men who surround them. Compared with the Terminator, for instance, Sarah Connor appears significantly less tough.

Elektra returns to her Sensei (or teacher) and informs him that she has planned to join the enemy—the Hand—but only to learn his secrets and use that knowledge against him. At this point, she is impetuous and foolish, lacking the wisdom of Stick. Again, this weakens her tough image and makes it apparent that she is no intellectual match for men. Despite her foolish actions, Elektra is unquestionably physically tough. This is evident when the Hand members attack her while she is sleeping in bed one evening; clad in a skimpy negligee, she manages to kill all the Hand's foot soldiers. She remains undisturbed when the group of masked and robed members of the Hand face her with drawn swords, asking them only to please hand over her clothes. Her physical prowess and her cool demeanor indicate that she is no one to tangle with, but her toughness is deflated by the emphasis on her femininity and her sexual desirability when the Hand's leader, Jonin, showers her with unwelcome affection. He is the active aggressor, while she plays a more passive role. He also has less interest in her fighting abilities than in her body. The emphasis on her physical attraction works to establish her as a "woman," despite her tough actions.

Leaving the Hand after being the object of Jonin's unwanted attention, Elektra goes on to become a hired mercenary. Though she is one of the best, it is obvious that this life is not what she desires. She is described as "a tortured soul. The killings, one after another, do not ease her pain. The profits do not make her richer" (37). She remains obsessed by her father's death. Her life, however, changes when she travels to New York and encounters Daredevil, failing to realize that he is actually Matt. He recognizes her and knows that she has become a bounty hunter, everything the straight-shooting Daredevil despises. Still, he reflects, "inside the ruthless bounty hunter is a woman—a woman who bandaged my arm and probably saved my life. She's a bitter, lonely woman who's striking back at the world that robbed her of her father. Yet she's still a woman—the first woman I ever loved" (40). Daredevil's speech reveals the general inability of comic books to move beyond stereotypical gender roles. According to him, Elektra became a Ninja warrior and a bounty hunter only because of the death of a family member. Even now, he believes, she has not entirely "gone bad." Despite his love for Elektra, the Daredevil resolves to "bring her to justice" (40). This, however, proves not to be an easy task.

Elektra is in the process of hunting down a man, and corners him as he tries to escape by plane. Her quarry urges his comrades to take her out, which confuses a muscle-bound hulk who protests to his boss, "She's just a *broad,* Mister Slaughter." The man attacks, even though he thinks it is "screwy" (44). She is more than a match for the three men who threaten her, defeating them with ease. Even after this display of muscular prowess, Elektra is in a bad situation when she is shot with a tranquilizer gun. Luckily, Daredevil saves her. Here, the same old story prevails: man rescues woman. After Matt rescues her, she rewards him with a kiss, just like any damsel-in-distress of bygone years. Despite her super strength and warrior skills, Elektra still needs to be protected by Matt. The message is clear: the man is the true tough figure. A woman, such as Elektra, cannot compete. This is a message that is so pervasive in the popular media that it has become entirely naturalized; many people assume that a woman cannot compete against a man, whatever the arena.

From this point on, Elektra's relationship with Matt shapes her actions, demonstrating that she is still driven principally by her emotions, despite her tough image. When she discovers that members of the Hand are pursuing Matt, she struggles with her new knowledge; she believes that Daredevil and she are enemies, but "[finds] herself on the next flight to New York" when she discovers he is endangered (53). She protects him from one of the Hand members who attacks him, but she does not reveal her presence. Acting as Matt's guardian angel becomes even more vital when he temporarily loses the radar power that makes it possible for the blind man to "see." Together they must fight the Ninjas, which causes Elektra's thoughts to return to the past she shared with Matt: "back to bright afternoons in a college gymnasium, where they trained and taught each other, where they danced together, as lovers and fellow warriors. . . . So little has changed about him, she thinks. How magnificent he is!" (63). Again, the attention is turned to the traditional romance of Elektra's past. This emphasis shows that her "unnatural" life has not changed her heart; she is still a woman concerned with primarily feminine issues, such as heterosexual romance.

As Elektra battles to save Daredevil's life and her own, she is torn between her former feelings for him and her new resolve that he is her enemy. Ultimately, she rescues Matt after he has passed out from a dangerous loss of blood, although she could have chosen to let him die. The rest of *Elektra, the Complete Saga* revolves around the pair battling the evildoers who attack them from every direction. Clearly, the real struggle is between Elektra and Matt, as he tries to end her criminal career. At one point, it looks as if she has squelched her old feelings for him when she buries him under a pile of bricks. Yet, when she has been seriously hurt by the assassin Bullseye, she staggers to Matt's home and dies in his arms. Here, it is evident that Elektra's love for Matt is an overwhelming emotion when she is confronted with the prospect of death. This story differs little from the millions of other popular texts that emphasize romantic love between a man and a woman as the primary passion of a woman's life.

The final episode of the series begins with Matt waking up from a nightmare, tortured by thoughts that Elektra is still alive. He even digs up her body, and discovers that she is dead—but not for long. The notorious members of the Hand are trying to resurrect her to make her do their bidding. Fortunately, Matt breaks into the temple where she is being brought back to life and destroys the Hand's members. In the ensuing chaos, Elektra's body vanishes. She has returned from the dead, and the epilogue shows her climbing the same impossible peak that she failed to climb in the beginning, with the following brief narrative: "He must never know. . . . She seeks a destiny of her own. She scales a wall that cannot be scaled" (187). She succeeds in climbing the peak. Her red Ninja outfit has turned pure white, identifying her as a renewed, purified character, but the scene of her climbing the mountain is so brief that it leaves readers wondering whether Elektra really will be able to locate the "destiny of her own" that she seeks.

Tough and Realistic: Martha Washington

Thus far, Storm, Elektra, and other tough girls in comic books are torn between being tough and adopting a more feminine persona. There are, however, a few female characters who present a tough image and are unconcerned with rules of decorum for women. One is Martha Washington, who stars in a series of futuristic comic books that focus on a universe that a reviewer labeled "a worst-case scenario of the violent fruits of right-wing extremism" (Kaganoff 52). In a grim, bleak world that makes even the worst contemporary slums look like model housing developments, Washington is one of the toughest and most realistic women to hit comic books. Her representation shows the potential of comic books to create truly strong women who do not fret about whether they are wearing eyeliner or whether they have a date for Saturday night. In addition, Washington's representation shows the ability of comic books and other alternative media forms to rethink gender roles and to expand the possible roles available to men and women.

Her adventures are collected in Frank Miller and Dave Gibbons's unpaginated graphic novel *Give Me Liberty: An American Dream* (1992). The first section focuses on Washington's youth, which she spent growing up in the mean streets of Cabrini Green, a low-income housing facility that is virtually a prison for its inhabitants: "Nobody ever gets out. Not even when they're dead." Growing up in the year 2000, she learns at an early age the harsh realities of life for her and other poor blacks living in the Green.

As she matures, Washington calls into question what it takes to be a woman and a tough hero and reflects on how social class and race influence both. At an early age, Washington displays her wizardry with computers, but Cabrini Green offers her no opportunity to further develop her skills. Her only hope for escape from the grim streets of the Green lies in her teacher, Donald, a man who has volunteered to teach in the Green. He befriends Washington, but his kindness ends abruptly when he is murdered. She is pursued by the killer, and, after a horrendous struggle, she manages to kill her attacker. The stress and horror of these events leaves her temporarily mentally unbalanced. She is taken to a mental facility, but, at this point, she is only pretending to be insane because she realizes this provides her with an opportunity to escape the Green. Here, her mental toughness is clear; Martha is not waiting for a man to rescue her, she is rescuing herself. She recognizes that no shining knight on a snow-white steed would risk the streets of the ghetto-prison where Martha lives to save her. She grows tough because she must in order to survive her daily life.

Martha's initiation as a warrior and fighter is far more grim than Elektra's. At first, it appears as if she might not even survive her incarceration in the mental institution. As a patient, she drifts with the tides of the bureaucracy by which she is trapped. Only when she ends up on the streets after she is released does she begin to awaken from her stupor. She fights back when white-uniformed men appear who pretend to help her but actually want to kill her. After she kills one of her attackers, she flees. As a fugitive, she cannot resist the allure of the PAX, an organization that is a "combination of the Marines and the Foreign Legion" and that guarantees to wipe clean the slate of anyone who joins (Kaganoff 52). Although just sixteen, she joins the PAX and journeys to the Amazon rain forest, where she engages in some fierce fighting and proves to be an outstanding soldier. After witnessing the deaths of all her comrades,

Martha sits down and cries, but she quickly stands up and brushes away her tears, saying, "This won't kill me. I won't die here. This won't kill me" (Figure 12). She is brushing away far more than her tears; like Elektra, Martha is brushing aside her femininity, too, with its connection to emotions. From here on, she emerges as one of the toughest women in the comic book universe. Her toughness is particularly intriguing because she does not possess the unrealistically pumped-up pecs of Superman or Batman, nor does she possess the huge breasts of many comic book women. She is not invincible, unlike many other heroes in comic books. On several occasions she is hurt seriously enough to require a trip to the hospital. Though she is not superhuman, she is still tougher than most women or men because she is aggressive, often violent, and able to take charge in even the most difficult situations.

Washington is not only tough but just and moral. For instance, when she discovers that her commanding officer, Lieutenant Moretti, is attempting to burn down the Amazon rain forest, she stabs him and manages to prevent the forest from being destroyed. She emerges as a war hero, like Moretti, who unexpectedly survives the stabbing. When Moretti warns her not to report his misdeeds, promising that they both will be heroes, she keeps her mouth shut; she knows that a poor black woman will not be believed, especially because Moretti is a well-to-do white man with friends in high places. For the rest of the saga, her conflict with Moretti plays a central role. Whereas Elektra's actions confirm that women, no matter how tough, will be ruled by their feelings, Martha's actions suggest that women can control their emotions.

Even someone as tough as Washington might find it difficult to survive in the world run amuck that she faces when she returns from war. The world she returns to is one where riots and battles are commonplace and various warring factions control different parts of the United States. Among these factions are the radical feminists, the Apaches, and the Surgeon General's troops—whose goal is to sterilize the population of the United States. It is a hypocritical place where both Washington and Moretti receive medals from the president, Howard Johnson Nissen, the former Acting Secretary of Agriculture, who assumed his position after a terrorist attack left the former president, Erwin Rexall—modeled after Ronald Reagan—in a deep coma.

In this chaotic world, Washington is able to survive because she is courageous, intelligent, and tough. She demonstrates her bravery numerous times during a war against the Aryan Thrust, a gay Nazi group that is trying to take over the United States. Martha is very much the leader and is far more intelligent than her followers or the members of the Aryan Thrust, whom she travels to meet in their spaceship. Her extraordinary presence of mind is evident when a member of the Aryan

Figure 12. Martha Washington brushes aside tears (*Give Me Liberty,* copyright Frank Miller and Dave Gibbons, published by Dark Horse Comics, Inc.).

Figure 13. Martha Washington takes control (*Give Me Liberty,* copyright Frank Miller and Dave Gibbons, published by Dark Horse Comics, Inc.).

Thrust points a machine gun at her and she informs him, "You know you can't fire that thing. Not in here." She is calm and rational; her opposition is rattled and irrational (Figure 13). When a battle erupts between Martha and four Aryan Thrust members, she defeats all four. Her resourcefulness is again displayed when the members of the Thrust shoot at her and blast a hole in the ship, resulting in its destruction and the end of the Aryan Thrust members. Martha is made of more durable stuff. She manages to survive and flees with Raggyann, a psychic schizophrenic who has been literally wired into the ship's command system. At this point, Martha is a female version of the tough guy hero, someone who always manages to destroy the tremendous opposition that she confronts. But as a black woman, she changes the whole scenario because she is not supposed to be able to defeat a group of large, burly white men. Nevertheless, she does. In this fashion, the book turns all the conventions of the typical boy-rescues-girl adventure story upside down. What is left is a subversive narrative that suggests women can be more capable of leading than men are.

Martha repeatedly shows her ability to take charge as the story continues, and as I pointed out in Chapter 1, the ability to be taken seriously as a leader is a primary characteristic of toughness. After leaving the ship, Martha finds her problems have only begun. She crash-lands in an Apache-controlled area and barely misses being blown up when her shuttle explodes. The Apaches then capture her and Raggyann. Although she escapes, she is held captive by the surgeon general and his minions and is given an entirely new personality. It is now up to Raggyann and Baby's Breath Wasserstein, the Apache who has befriended Martha, to rescue their friend and restore her memory. She shoots the surgeon general, and Washington escapes, along with Raggyann, Wasserstein, and the First Lady, who carries the president's brain in a specially designed container. At this point, Washington is still the group's leader, a complete reversal from most action comic books that feature a group with only one or two subordinate women. Again, it is apparent that the Martha Washington series subverts more traditional comic book narratives.

She remains in charge as the group escapes to the rain forest, attempting to hide from Moretti. A dozen men attack Martha and Wasserstein. The soldiers are decimated by her well-planned attack, but Wasserstein is so seriously hurt that Martha must leave him and pursue Moretti and his five remaining men. Even against these odds, she destroys her enemies and finally has Moretti at her mercy. She does not kill him, however. He ends up in prison where he will soon face a firing squad for treason; there, Washington visits him and compassionately offers him a belt so that he may hang himself. The complexity of her character is evident. She is tough enough to defeat six men, but she also possesses a sense of law and justice, which is important because women's actions are often portrayed by the media as ruled by their emotions. Washington shows that morality and toughness coexist in women.[13]

Her adventures, more clearly than those of Storm or Elektra, suggest that women can be tough and confident and not have to worry about whether they are presenting a feminine image. Martha shows that toughness does not mean that a woman will be denied respect. She is esteemed by her comrades for her ability to take charge and to survive. She demonstrates that comic books *can* present heroic women who challenge society's expectations about how women are supposed to act. But characters such as Washington are a minority, largely outnumbered by buxom women wearing clinging garments that expose a great deal of cleavage. Comic books have been and still are ambivalent about how to portray toughness in women and how to reconcile it with the other qualities that have been traditionally associated with women.

New Images

Comic books offer women a variety of non-traditional tough roles. Whether Martha Washington, Elektra, Storm, or one of the other numerous tough characters in comic books from the 1980s and 1990s, tough women are appearing in greater numbers than ever before. The increasing prevalence of tough women in comic books and other media forms, however, does not suggest that cultural definitions of femininity and masculinity are changing dramatically. The tough girl in comic books is vastly outnumbered by her male cohorts, and the comic book woman is still more likely to be a chesty, blonde-haired sex toy than a brave commander like Martha Washington. Because of the overwhelming prevalence of heavily stereotyped male and female characters in their pages, comic books continue to reinforce traditional notions about what it means to be a man or woman, although, as this chapter has shown, such roles are more open to change today.

To gain a better understanding of how tough women's roles are being rescripted, I examine the television show *Xena: Warrior Princess* in the next chapter, exploring how this popular show creates a surprisingly no-nonsense heroine. In many ways, *Xena* offers viewers a new vision of toughness.

Chapter 9
A Tough Girl for a New Century
Xena, Warrior Princess

> We don't need another hero, except for Xena, Warrior Princess. Like something out of Russ Meyer combined with Betty Page and projected onto the walls of the Clit Club, Xena is full-tilt, strap-on, Greco-medieval realness, as much superfreak as superhero in her leather minidress and breastplates, her thigh-high lace-up leather boots, her coal black hair, her piercing blue eyes, her fetching way with a spear.
> —Stacey D'Erasmo (47)

A nearly six-foot-tall warrior woman, dressed in a leather outfit, whose sword-fighting talent would make the Three Musketeers envious is difficult to overlook, especially when she also has a piercing battle cry and is capable of defeating an army of the most brawny males. Unfortunately, this warrior exists only in the imaginary realm of television, where New Zealander Lucy Lawless portrays Xena in the highly successful television show *Xena: Warrior Princess.* In this series Lawless dispatches "insane numbers of bad guys with her kicks, her spear, or her sword" (D'Erasmo 47). Some critics have understood Xena as nothing more than a pseudo-superhero who—with her short costume and long legs—appeals primarily to men, not women. But is there more to Xena than merely being a sex object for men and prepubescent boys? This chapter explores Xena's popularity in the 1990s, suggesting that her depiction represents an important shift from earlier media images of tough women. Although I argue that Xena marks a move toward a more self-reflexive vision of toughness, I also explore the ways that tough women, including Xena, help to perpetuate stereotypical notions about what it means to be a hero, especially a tough female one.

I have chosen to conclude this book with a chapter on Xena because she provides an intriguing example of what happens when a very tough woman is featured in the mainstream media. Unlike Storm, Elektra, and Martha Washington, who find their homes in the more narrow realm of alternative comic books, Xena has found her place in the most widely distributed media form in the United States: television. More interestingly, her toughness is not diminished as it is for many other female characters examined in this book. Nor is Xena's maternal side emphasized, as is true for Ripley. Xena breaks many of the rules of feminine decorum, but her show remains extremely successful. This chapter examines the reasons for *Xena*'s popularity, suggesting that it is popular in part because it calls into question what is required of a tough hero.

When I first watched *Xena,* I was disappointed because I thought the show's star seemed to be little more than a voluptuous babe in a leather costume with a cheerleader yell. Only after I studied the show more carefully did I recognize that it was accomplishing something new with its leather-clad heroine. My initial reaction to *Xena* is common. When I told a friend of mine that the show had surprisingly strong women characters and was worth watching, her only answer was an incredulous "*That* show?" She has yet to turn on *Xena: Warrior Princess* and is unlikely to agree with Lawless's assessment that, "For my money, [playing Xena is] the best part for a woman in 30 years of television" (qtd. in Richmond 39).

Watching *Xena* for the first time, viewers often assume that its star is a modern-day Wonder Woman who affirms that women are more concerned about maintaining a meticulous manicure than winning a sword fight. One critic describes the warrior as "a Wonder Woman for our times" (O'Connor 18). Another writer also notes a connection between the two superheroes: "With her blue eyes, dark hair, alabaster skin, and impressive array of breast-plates, series star Lucy Lawless hails from the same gene pool that spawned Wonder Woman Lynda Carter" (Stewart 24). Xena, however, is not merely an updated version of Wonder Woman. Substantial differences exist between the two, differences that make Xena tougher and more independent than her predecessor.

It is a mistake to view Xena primarily as a sex symbol. Although she appeals to men and boys, she is not just another of the busty vixens who stride through the pages of comic books and fantasy novels. Xena is tougher and more complicated than most other female characters. "Xena doesn't apologize for being a better fighter than almost every man on earth. And she doesn't smile at men unless she really, really likes them—which is seldom," one writer comments (Minkowitz 74). Watching *Xena: Warrior Princess,* a viewer finds it difficult not to be struck by how independent its hero is. She is never dependent on Hercules, her male counterpart, who has his own show but occasionally makes guest appearances on *Xena.* Depicting Xena as a heroic woman who does not rely on a man to save her when trouble occurs makes her tougher than virtually all women in similar action-adventure shows. Not only is Xena self-sufficient (excluding the occasional assistance she receives from her sidekick, Gabrielle, who accompanies the warrior princess on adventures), she also seems to be physically stronger than most of the tough women I have examined in this book. Xena is a new version of the superhero. Wonder Woman relied primarily on her magic lasso; she did not often tangle physically with the bad guys. Xena frequently kicks or punches the evildoers who dare confront her as she "defends the powerless [and] chastens the wicked" (Stockwell 81). Although she sometimes depends on a weapon called a chakram—similar to a circular boomerang—to dispatch the human predators who risk life and limb by challenging her, she is more likely to have a sword fight with her adversaries. She is often involved in very physical fights from which she always emerges the victor. Athletic, super-powerful, Xena is more closely aligned with heroic tough guys like the Terminator, Rocky, or Rambo than with Charlie's Angels or the Bionic Woman. Writing about Xena's unique appeal, Donna Minkowitz aptly describes the warrior's tough image: "The Bionic Woman smiled too much. Even Cagney and Lacey worried about looking 'overmasculine.' No woman television character has exhibited the confidence and strength of the male heroes of archetype and fantasy—or if she did, she was a one-episode fluke, and her anomalous presence could reassure viewers that next week all the regular women characters would be back, nervous and self-questioning as ever" (74).

In Xena, the producers of the television program have created a superhero who attracts a wide audience: "Lucy/Xena's appeal cuts across all age, gender and sexual preference lines" (Dickinson 55). Even little girls sometimes model their play on Xena's exploits, and one writer thinks the fighter is "a great role model for little girls who feel less than empowered by Barbie" (Ostrow G1). Xena's appeal is particularly interesting because her show—and television in general—possesses the power to change how we construct and understand gender in real life. In *Women Watching Television: Gender, Class, and Generation in the American Television Experience* (1991), Andrea L. Press writes, "Television is one of our most powerful cultural institutions. In a society in which more people have television sets than indoor plumbing, where children spend more time in front of the television set than in any other activity, few would deny television's symbolic power" (8). Given television's power to alter how we perceive the world, what *Xena* conveys about desirable roles for women has the ability to change how women understand their gendered identities. Karal Ann Marling in *As Seen on TV: The Visual Culture of Everyday Life in the 1950s* (1994) argues that television images influence real life. She suggests that our collective cultural aesthetic in the 1950s was changed by the increasingly important role of television. In a similar way, watching a tough woman like Xena on television alters our collective sensibility about toughness and gender. Xena can change how her viewers perceive gender in a way that a "real" woman rarely can. Although Xena lives in a mythical universe, how she is depicted suggests a great deal about actual women and their changing relationship to the heroic, tough roles that previously have been assumed by men.

"The Chick in a Brass Bra": Xena and the Warrior Woman Tradition

Despite Xena's current popularity, her show, which first aired in September 1995, initially had difficulty getting programming slots. Many local television stations refused to air *Xena* because they assumed people would not be interested in a tough female hero who was clearly superior to the men she battled (Minkowitz 75).[1] But *Xena*'s executive producers, Robert Tapert and Sam Raimi, managed to find stations to air *Xena,* in part because of their success with *Hercules: The Legendary Journeys,* an action-adventure television series that stars Kevin Sorbo as a New Age version of Hercules.[2] *Xena* has since become wildly popular in its own right, attracting a broad international audience that includes everyone from young girls to grown women and men.[3] Fans cannot seem to watch enough of Xena's adventures, and they idolize their hero. One fan comments, "No one can conquer her—not evil kings, not fickle gods, not filthy hordes of gnarly barbarians. On foot or on horseback, swinging on ropes or flipping through the air, she is the ruler of my TV universe" (Dickinson 55). Xena's popularity is such that it is now possible to buy comic books, action figures, and novels featuring her adventures.[4] Numerous websites established by zealous Xenites—as her fans call themselves—feature the warrior woman and her exploits. If browsing a website does not offer a Xenite enough of her favorite hero, the fan can attend the monthly Xena Night at the Meow Mix, a lesbian bar in New York City (Dolby 6). The most zealous Xenite can join a Xena cruise, like the one offered by Olivia Cruises and Resorts for female Xena fans (Stockwell 81).[5] Young Xenites might wish to purchase some of the Xena picture books or action figures that are available.[6]

The show that inspires this kind of ardent fan interest has a fairly simple plot: "Xena, played by Lucy Lawless, is a downright-surly female warlord with a short temper and a shorter toga who first appeared on *Hercules* as a blood-thirsty villain. Now, as star of her own series, Xena roams her mythical land determined to atone for her sins" (Stockwell 81). Xena and Gabrielle (Renee O'Connor) wander the countryside of a mythical land that appears vaguely Greek or Roman, although the producers feel free to throw in references to any culture without concern for historical accuracy. As Xena and Gabrielle journey, accompanied by Xena's horse, Argo, they solve the problems of a countryside that is

Figure 14. Xena (Lucy Lawless), Gabrielle (Renee O'Connor), and Argo (*Xena: Warrior Princess*).

constantly ravaged by the depredations of warlords, giants, and gods (Figure 14).[7] Never does a week pass during which the dynamic duo fail to set right some evil, usually depending on what one critic calls Xena's "lethal cheerleader kicks" (Stewart 24). Although pretty handy with a fighting staff herself, Gabrielle often requires rescuing by Xena, who is so tough that she makes hardened male warriors, who tower over her and are far more muscular than she is, beg for mercy.

Xena is not the first woman warrior to appear in the popular media (Figure 15). We need to position Xena in relation to her predecessors, for, as John Fiske argues, no text can be understood without analyzing how it fits into a vast universe of other works. Thus, Xena cannot be understood fully without acknowledging the long line of similar female characters who appeared earlier in the century. As Elizabeth Kastor observes, "Post-feminist though she may be, Xena is also retro, the latest incarnation of what science fiction writer and critic Gregory Feeley calls 'the chick in a brass bra.' The archetype was created in 1916, when Edgar Rice Burroughs published his first story about Thuvia, Maid of Mars, in

Figure 15. Xena (Lucy Lawless) as a warrior princess (*Xena: Warrior Princess*).

All-Story Magazine, and fearsome, well-endowed women warriors have populated magazines, pulp novels, and comic books ever since" (C5). Numerous swords and sorcery films also have featured warrior women, including Valaria, Queen of Thieves, in *Conan the Barbarian* (1981), Zula in *Conan the Destroyer* (1984), and Sonya Blade in *Mortal Kombat* (1995).

The warrior woman also appears occasionally in today's video games, such as the Huntress in Blades of Vengeance and (Sofia in) Battle Arena Toshinden II.

While it is important to acknowledge the influence of the "chick in a brass bra" tradition and how it operates to depict women as sexually alluring objects for men, we also need to recognize that Xena does not comfortably fit this mold. The chick in a brass bra often appeared in earlier texts only to justify the super-virility of a male hero. The warrior woman might have started out appearing tough and invincible, but she typically was defeated by the tougher and stronger man, with whom the formerly unconquerable woman then fell in love. This happened to the title character in *Red Sonja* (1985)—a swaggering barbarian sword fighter—when she met a warrior played by Arnold Schwarzenegger. In contrast to this traditional capitulation of warrior women in early texts, Xena remains an independent, tough loner—except for her friendship with Gabrielle. In this fashion, *Xena: Warrior Princess* looks back at the old tradition of the chick in a brass bra and, relying on much of the imagery associated with this character, rewrites her in a fashion appropriate for the postmodern 1990s.

More than Just Another Superhero

> Don't you ever touch my horse again!
> —Xena speaking to Gabrielle in "The Titans"

If we are to understand how Xena represents a new and different image of toughness for the 1990s and beyond, we need also to recognize how she questions and changes what it means to be a hero. Reshaping notions of the heroic is important because being a hero has long been considered an almost exclusively male preserve. Xena represents one of the strongest 1990s challenges to the dominance of the male hero.[8]

Xena destabilizes many traditional notions of what constitutes a hero. As I have mentioned, the overwhelming majority of action-adventure films star men. Most arcade games feature overmuscled males defeating the (male) minions of evil and darkness, and the vast number of action-figure heroes are male. Of course, tough women *are* a presence in films and video games and among action figures. They represent, however, such a minuscule minority that they do little to alter the belief that a hero should be male. One female action figure out of a gang of ten or twelve convinces people that a woman is a rare oddity in the land of superheroes. Xena questions the notion that the "natural" hero is a man. She demonstrates that the woman superhero does not require five or six men as reinforcements, which is often the case in the action-figure aisle of the toystore or on Saturday morning cartoons.

Another way that Xena changes traditional notions of the heroic is by being physically stronger and tougher than the men who surround her. She is "the sort of woman who can grab an arrow in mid-flight, who can hurl grown men through the air" (Kastor C1). No man (except Hercules) is a match for the warrior princess. For instance, Joxer, the unwanted tagalong and a frequent character on the show, is nothing more than a warrior-wanna-be. And real warriors—hulking, muscle-bound men in pursuit of plunder and booty—quiver in fear when Xena strides onto the scene. She destroys them with ease, if they do not flee first. When she is in dire straits, no muscular man comes to the rescue. Week after week, she is shown calculating her escapes from seemingly hopeless predicaments and executing them with superheroic finesse—something seldom done by other similar female characters. This ability to escape danger is reminiscent of the Bionic Woman's escapades. However, Jaime Sommers could always count on the Six Million Dollar Man when a spy mission became too difficult to handle. Xena seldom depends on anyone but herself (and sometimes Gabrielle and Argo). Portraying Xena as tougher than the men around her and showing her rescuing herself rather than relying on men subverts the notion that women "naturally" must be rescued by men.

The program emphasizes the physical toughness of not only Xena but women in general by having many tough women characters on the show. This is antithetical to most heroic sagas, which rarely feature more than a single strong female character. The most intriguing example of another tough woman is Callisto, who is as good a fighter as Xena, and maybe better; in one episode ("Callisto") the evil warrior actually manages to cut Xena's arm when the two are fighting. Like Xena, Callisto is tougher than any man. Although no match for Callisto, Gabrielle is also tougher than many of the men who surround her. In "Callisto," for example, Gabrielle easily beats up Joxer, who is trying to capture her. Although he says, "She must be threatened by my masculine prowess and all," it is evident that Gabrielle has no fear of him or other men and is more than capable of taking care of herself. Compared with Gabrielle, Joxer is as tough as Jell-O. By representing Callisto, Gabrielle, and other women as tough and physically capable of taking care of themselves, the television show creates a world where the notion that heroic action is reserved for men is ludicrous.

Xena makes another change in the hero role: she calls into question the idea that the chick in a brass bra is created mainly for the voyeuristic pleasure of men. Xena repeatedly scorns the men who ogle her. She is more likely to punch out than offer sexual favors to men who get too close. For example, in the episode "Ten Little Warlords," she works with the god Ares. Although he is attracted to her, she rolls her eyes at his ardor, visibly bored. In "The Royal Couple of Thieves," her rebuff is more aggressive. When the Prince of Thieves suggests that they sleep in the same bed in the room they share at a warlord's castle, Xena's only reply to his overtures is to flip him over her shoulder and against a wall. The next time he propositions her, she responds with a bone-cracking head-butt. At the episode's end, the Prince of Thieves attempts to kiss Xena. She ignores him and thrusts her hand forward to receive a handshake. Her evident lack of interest in the men who lust after her shatters the myth of the chick in the brass bra. In earlier episodes she is tough only until the "right" man comes along, demonstrating the potency of the male hero and the inability of any woman, no matter how tough, to resist the allure of a man. But Xena's character undergoes a transformation. She is no longer content to be the passive subject of the desiring male gaze, and she quickly makes clear that she does not want such attention—a radical notion in the popular media where bathing suit calendars, men's magazine centerfolds, and many other media sources portray the female body as something women wish to have admired by men.

Xena also reconceptualizes what it means to be a tough hero by depicting the close friendship between Xena and Gabrielle. "You are part of my heart," Xena says to Gabrielle in the episode "Ulysses." Although this relationship is clearly very important to the warrior princess, it does not detract from her tough image. Nor is the friendship something fleeting; it is an integral part of the series. What is unusual about this friendship is that tough women in the popular media rarely have close female friends. Scully appears to have no friends except for Mulder. Captain Janeway is distanced from her female crew members. Martha Washington and Elektra have no close women friends. Friendships are rare for tough women because such relationships can undermine the cool, aloof attitude of the tough hero. *Xena* shows that toughness in women does not have to be antithetical to friendship. The result is a new vision of the tough woman hero that emphasizes both her physical toughness and her connection to other women.

Another way that the television show shakes up notions about the female superhero is by its lack of emphasis on Xena's heterosexuality. Think about Wonder Woman and her relationship with Captain Steve Trevor. Remember Elektra and her love for Daredevil. Consider the unrequited love of Jaime Sommers for Steve Austin. Typically, popular media genres go out of their way to emphasize the heterosexuality of the tough, heroic woman. Emphasizing a woman hero's heterosexuality reassures the audience that she has not departed too far from a woman's "normal" sexual orientation, despite the other ways that she might call into question gender stereotypes. Unlike Wonder Woman, Xena is not portrayed as reassuringly heterosexual. She has no regular love interest and does not avail herself of the many sexual propositions she receives. She is evidently bored by male lust. Further, she travels with a woman companion, and the two are especially close friends. For example, in the episode "A Day in the Life," they take a bath together and scrub each other's backs. At the episode's conclusion, the last images are of the two women lying side by side in bed and staring up at the stars, looking very much like a pair of lovers. In "Return of Callisto," Xena appears distraught when Gabrielle agrees to marry the man to whom she was betrothed before meeting Xena. The morning after the wedding, however, Gabrielle's husband is conveniently killed by Callisto, leaving Gabrielle free to return to Xena. Xena cares so much about Gabrielle that she repeatedly risks her life rescuing Gabrielle from the most deadly dangers. In the episode "The Titans," Xena saves Gabrielle from a titan who towers over the women. In "A Necessary Evil," Xena risks falling into a pit of molten lava to save her friend. In "A Fistful of Dinars," Xena again saves Gabrielle, who is hanging on to the remnants of a broken bridge. These are only a few of many episodes that emphasize the closeness between Xena and Gabrielle. It is difficult to avoid thinking about the possibility that Xena and Gabrielle are a lesbian couple, which explains the popularity of *Xena* among lesbians. This interpretation is encouraged by the show's co-producer, Liz Friedman, a lesbian herself, who admits that some episodes of the show contain "sapphic double entendres" (Stockwell 81).

It would be wrong, however, to understand the show as being entirely comfortable about presenting Xena as a lesbian. As Fiske comments, television is open to interpretation, but there are always meanings that are preferred: "The fact that *Dallas* has more meanings than Hollywood can control or any one audience group can activate, does not negate television's struggle to control its meanings, and prefer some over others" (*Television* 126). In a similar fashion, *Xena* might be considered a queer show by its queer viewers, but that does not prevent the network from discouraging those readings by making efforts to suggest Xena's heterosexuality. Although the program repeatedly toys with lesbianism and the possible lesbianism of the two lead characters, the show stops short of saying the taboo L word and drops frequent hints about Xena's past heterosexual relationships. In "A Fistful of Dinars," for instance, we meet a warlord whom Xena once almost married. Hints are also made that Xena might have had a sexual relationship with Hercules. An even more blatant display of her possible heterosexuality occurs in the episode "Ulysses" in which Xena seems smitten with Ulysses, until she discovers that his wife is still alive.

These suggestions of Xena's heterosexuality allow the show to remain uncommitted about its star's sexual orientation. The producers of *Xena* are keenly aware that their show appeals to different audiences and wish to attract all potential viewers. Rather than interpret this obfuscation as a failure, we need to recognize that this marketing ploy allows the program to play with lesbian iconography more explicitly than perhaps any mainstream television show other than *Ellen.*[9] *Xena* is the first program aimed at a mass audience to show a superhero whose sexual orientation remains ambiguous, calling into question the notion that a superhero must be heterosexual.

Although *Xena* is designed to earn a profit for its producers, networks, and anyone connected to making the show, the producers cannot entirely control how the program is interpreted by its audience. As Lynne Joyrich points out in *Re-Viewing Reception: Television, Gender, and Postmodern Culture* (1996): "Even if television's postmodern construction of split and/or multiple subject positions is promoted solely for its profit-making potential, its discourses (and the discourses around it) may nonetheless reformulate our notions of identity and difference, both extending and negating conventional terms" (17). In other words, television exploits not just one subject position for the viewer and the character but many. Her thoughts apply aptly to *Xena,* in which the two leading women do reformulate notions about gendered identity, even though they also ensure a larger profit for the show's network and producers.

One of the most interesting ways that *Xena* challenges traditional notions of what it means to be a hero is through the show's heavily self-reflexive nature. This puts *Xena* at odds with more traditional television shows, which cultural critic Larry Gross views as typically not self-reflexive: "The dominant conventions of our mass media are those of 'realism' and psychologically grounded naturalism. Despite a limited degree of reflexivity which occasionally crops up, mainstream film and television are nearly always presented as transparent mediators of reality which can and do show us how people and places look, how institutions operate; in short, the way it is" (131). This is not true for *Xena,* which uses self-reflexivity and a lack of realism to question what it means to be heroic.

In "A Day in the Life," for example, the self-reflexive criticism of the whole action-adventure genre and typical female roles in that genre is clear. A peasant man has fallen in love with Xena, causing Gabrielle and Xena to muse about why men fall for the warrior princess so frequently:

> "Why does this always happen?" Xena remarks.
> "The blue eyes, the leather," Gabrielle replies. "Some guys just love leather."
> "I think a wardrobe change is in order."
> "You could wear chain mail."
> "Yeah, but I think that would just attract a kinkier group," Xena sighs.

This interchange reveals the show's ability to examine and often satirize the conventional iconography of the hero and the chick in a brass bra—conventions on which the show itself is built. This self-reflexive inspection is particularly noteworthy because it is so different from earlier depictions of the heroic tough woman. Storm and Elektra are serious characters, as is Wonder Woman; these superheroes accept the conventions of the superhero world without question. Xena, however, questions the rules that structure her universe, creating a very different environment for the superhero. The environment she creates is important because it allows her to question the heroic conventions that long have helped to ensure the male superhero's dominance.

Another way the show alters traditional concepts of the hero is by creating a "troubled, flawed, even melancholic" heroine (Weinstein F18). She is haunted by her past and always travels to places where people fear her because of what she has done. People fear that her violent, aggressive nature will be directed at them. Not only does her conscience have to bear the murder of Callisto's parents, Xena also must remember that she and her army were responsible for the deaths of hundreds if not thousands of people before she changed her ways. She is a flawed heroine; even after becoming a friend and protector of the people upon whom she once preyed, she has not undergone a complete transformation. She still takes savage delight in fighting her foes. In "The Titans," Xena laughs gleefully when she encounters the titans, who are many times her size and easily able to destroy her. She admits at one point that she might again decimate the countryside to exact revenge if anything happened to Gabrielle. And rather than rescue her longtime foe in "Return of Callisto," Xena allows Callisto to sink in quicksand and die. Yet, in an earlier episode ("Callisto"), Xena did save Callisto from death. In these examples, we can see the hero's struggle to maintain a balance between her past and present. In a later episode ("Intimate Stranger") Xena is haunted by her foe's death and feels that she did not give Callisto a chance to redeem herself, an opportunity that Xena was offered by Hercules. Clearly, she is a troubled hero who possesses a far more complex soul than Wonder Woman or Superman. Emphasizing this aspect of Xena's character is one way that *Xena: Warrior Princess* shows that toughness has a more sinister side.

Xena is not the only character in the show who is morally ambiguous. Looking like a *Baywatch* beach blonde gone bad, Callisto is the personification of all that is evil—yet in many ways, she is the mirror image of Xena. The two have many things in common, including similar fighting styles, battle cries, and costumes (Figure 16). But Callisto is a Valley Girl run amok who does not hesitate to kill anyone who stands in her way. She is a vamp and a siren. Oozing sexuality, the evil Callisto fol-

Figure 16. Callisto (Hudson Leick)—a Valley Girl run amok (*Xena: Warrior Princess*).

lows in the footsteps of a long line of similar women characters from comic books and pulp novels. Typically, these evil harpies are depicted as insane because they dare to usurp men's power and authority. Such women meet nasty fates or end up falling in love with the male hero and changing their villainous ways. At first I thought Callisto fit the stereotype that power drives a woman mad, and that she deserved to meet with a horrid end. But Callisto is different from her predecessors because of her origins, which she mentions repeatedly. She was "created" after Xena's army torched Callisto's village and killed her family, when Callisto was just a small child. This episode of violence, which was at least partly Xena's fault, makes it far more difficult to claim Callisto as purely evil or Xena as purely good. Instead, the show reveals that each of them has an identity that is closely bound up with the identity of the other. In this fashion, the program destabilizes the notion that hero and villain are opposites and, instead, shows the mutual relationship between the two. The nature of a hero (or villain) always remains ambiguous in *Xena*.

What it means to be a hero is also made more complex through the show's use of camp—an over-the-top, tongue-in-cheek attitude toward the world, which pokes fun at social conventions and questions social norms. Camp reveals the artificiality of things we accept as the norm (such as gender roles). Whether we are viewing Xena's wildly improbable stunts, the silliness of some of the acting, or Xena's hyperbolic toughness—the show is high camp; one critic calls it "a delightfully cheesy schlock drama that often looks like *Spartacus, American Gladiators,* and *Mad Max* rolled into one" (Minkowitz 76). This campy attitude makes Xena appear less of a threat to tough heroes like the ones played by Stallone and Schwarzenegger, who often inhabit a serious, grim world in which camp is a rarity. Xena's campiness allows viewers to recognize that they do not need to take her and her exploits too seriously. We see the *deus ex machina* and realize that Xena's tough character is only a performance.

Although the show's campy nature diminishes the threat posed by a tough woman, Xena remains a very tough character. Camp creates a safe space in which the producers of the show can develop a tough woman who is clearly identified as make-believe. The campy quality of the show also enables such a character to be shown on mainstream television and to become phenomenally popular. Camp opens a space in the hero world, allowing Xena to exist. If she were serious, she would never have been so successful. She helps people get used to the idea of women who are tough, paving the way for the eventual acceptance of more serious female heroes.

Although I have described some of the ways that Xena represents a rescripting of the tough woman hero, she also helps to affirm traditional stereotypes about what is desirable for a hero. The seemingly contradictory image of Xena is only to be expected given the nature of television's ideology. As critic Mimi White observes, "Within individual programs, between programs and commercials, and across a variety of programs, television is highly fragmented and heterogeneous, allowing for the orchestration of a variety of issues, voices, positions, and messages" (161). She suggests that "within a single episode, evening, or season of television, the ideology of particular programs may emerge as variable, slippery, or even contradictory" (153). It is also true that different audiences emerge with different understandings of a particular television show because, as Fiske points out: "Culture is a process of making meanings that people actively participate in; it is not a set of preformed meanings handed down to and imposed upon the people" ("British" 285). It is impossible to receive a monolithic message from *Xena* because different people bring different cultural backgrounds to their viewing of the show and carry away different messages, ranging from the conservative to the radical.

Because of the often paradoxical nature of the ideology conveyed by television, it is not surprising to discover that Xena breaks some gender conventions but also helps support others. As a long-legged, raven-haired beauty, for example, Xena does not challenge the idea that a heroine should be gorgeous.[10] When she needs to drag herself out of quicksand after fighting Callisto or must fight an entire army single-handedly, Xena still looks stunning. She never seems to suffer a bad hair day. Xena's frequent acrobatic flips do little to interfere with her coiffure. Her indestructible beauty suggests not only that a heroic woman (or any woman) should be stunning but also that her appearance must be maintained despite the perils she confronts. The show further stresses that women should be beautiful by depicting women who are homely as buffoons. The fat, dowdy matron supervising the beauty pageant contestants in "Here She Comes . . . Miss Amphipolis" is obviously included for comic interest. Similarly, Minya in "A Day in the Life" is a hefty peasant woman who wishes to emulate Xena. When Minya dresses up in a Xena-lookalike costume, it is obvious that she cannot match the physical charms of the warrior princess. Minya is a comic character whose presence only highlights Xena's desirability.

While stressing Xena's beauty, the program also highlights her sexual desirability, which, amazingly, the show manages to do without compromising her toughness. In "Warrior . . . Princess . . . Tramp" Lawless plays three characters of widely different temperaments who all look alike and at one point or another, impersonate the other two. In this episode, the familiar image of the warrior princess is appropriated by a feminine, maternal, naive princess and by a lusty "tramp" who wants nothing more than to jump bumbler Joxer's bones. But because the three characters are distinct from each other, Xena's reputation and tough image remain unscathed while the show allows viewers (especially males) a fantasy of other more sexually approachable and traditionally feminine Xenas. Xena's femininity and sexuality are also explored in several episodes during which she actually changes bodies. For instance, in "Intimate Stranger" Callisto and Xena exchange bodies. Xena ends up in Callisto's body while Callisto returns to the underworld in Xena's body. This gives the show an opportunity to depict Xena's personality wearing Callisto's smaller, more feminine body. And because Callisto is in Xena's body, we see that body being sexual, as, for instance, when Callisto has an affair with Ares in "Intimate Strangers."

Another way the program emphasizes Xena's sexual appeal without reducing her toughness is by employing masquerade. In the episode "Here She Comes . . . Miss Amphipolis," Xena disguises herself as a contestant in a beauty pageant and appears much more feminine than she usually does. In "The Royal Couple of Thieves," she pretends to be a concubine. To distract a group of thieves and murderers, the disguised warrior woman gives an erotic belly dance performance. Similarly, in "Cradle of Hope," she pretends to be a dancing girl and attracts the attention of every male in the room. But when Xena goes undercover—whether as a beauty contestant, concubine, or dancing girl—a tension exists that is not found in the masquerades of earlier television tough women. Xena constantly asserts her strength and independence, knocking out warlords who approach too closely during the dance of three veils, for instance, or rolling her eyes at the shenanigans of the lust-infused males she cons with her feminine wiles. This comic subtext destabilizes the disguise and asserts the existence of an "authentic identity" behind the performance. In contrast, disguise in *The Avengers, Charlie's Angels,* and *The Bionic Woman* served to destabilize the identity and, hence, the toughness of the main characters.

A heroic convention that the producers of *Xena* fail to destabilize is the notion that a hero should be white. Xena and Gabrielle are white, as were Tarzan, Conan the Warrior, the Lone Ranger (Tonto was always a secondary character), Superman, Flash Gordon, and Batman. Although the whiteness of the hero or superhero has become less of a necessity during the last few decades, the realm of the heroic is still largely lily white, reflecting a culture in which whiteness has long been equated with goodness. *Xena* fails to disturb this assumption because not only the two stars but also the vast majority of positively portrayed people they encounter are white. Blacks and Asians are rare in Xena's world, and the only darker people to appear are usually swarthy enemy warriors, like Draco or Bacchus, whom she quickly dispatches. In some ways, the program seems to reinforce the idea that white people are "good guys" and people with darker skin are "bad guys."

Beyond 2000

> Xena inhabits a prelapsarian world in which it is possible for a woman in thigh-high boots to win every battle, all the time, always fighting fair.
>
> —Stacey D'Erasmo (47)

What parting thoughts does *Xena* leave with us about the changing characterization of the female hero at the start of a new century? The show does reveal the growing potential for the hero to be reflective about her actions and what it means to be a hero. The self-reflexivity that is evident in *Xena* is one way the show examines and reimagines what it means to be a hero. The increasingly self-reflexive quality of the popular media when it comes to the creation of heroes (think of the recent adventures of Batman, the Dark Knight) is a sign that notions of the heroic are in flux. *Xena* is part of this change and, I hope, will help pave the way for women to adopt the heroic roles that have long been the province of men, while simultaneously questioning what those roles entail.

Xena is also involved in broadening the definition of who can be a hero. She shows her audience that it is possible for a woman to be strong and heroic and not need a man to rescue her. Even today, this is an unusual message for the mainstream media to convey. More controversially, Xena cares a great deal more about her horse and Gabrielle than about any man. When men are provoked by her sexual charms, she is disinterested, and she and Gabrielle are easily interpreted as a lesbian couple. In these ways, the show challenges the belief that a woman should be heterosexual or at least appear actively interested in men.

Despite the ways that *Xena* creates a new tough woman for the 90s, offering women a female character with authority and autonomy, the show also adheres to some stereotypes about the nature of the tough hero, because any television program is apt to convey "multiple and sometimes contending constructions" (Van Zoonen 51). For example, Xena is a beautiful woman who upholds the convention that women superheroes should always be attractive. Xena also supports the long-standing tradition in American culture that the tough hero, with rare exceptions, should be white. But perhaps it is too much to expect one television program to revolutionize the entire action-adventure genre. Despite its shortcomings, *Xena: Warrior Princess* still shows a hero who makes viewers recognize that women can be just as tough as the boys, while questioning what it means to be tough.

Epilogue

> Dare me. I've killed a grizzly, raced in minus 62 degrees, given birth without painkillers. What of it?
>
> —Kathy Swenson, Iditarod racer

Swenson is one of many women who have taken part in the Iditarod, which must be the toughest organized sporting event ever created. The Iditarod is a 1,049-mile dog-sled race between Anchorage and Nome, Alaska, and the conditions the racers face are almost impossible to imagine. Temperatures can dip to sixty degrees below zero; racers are lucky if they catch a few hours of sleep a night. They need to stand up in their sleds for nearly two weeks, a difficult feat for even the most athletic. Yet a number of women have participated in this brutal race, including Lolly Medley, Kate Persons, Mary Shields, Libby Riddles, Verona Thompson, Kathy Swenson, Dee Dee Jonrowe, and Pat Danly. But the most famous woman associated with the race and the one who has received the most press coverage is Susan Butcher. Once described as "tough as a dog harness," she has displayed amazing grit and determination as an Iditarod racer (qtd. in "Butcher" 99).[1] In 1985 she was attacked by a moose, which killed two of her dogs, forcing her to withdraw from the race. During another race, she was thrown into the frigid waters of the Norton Sounds, forcing her to run alongside her dogs for miles to keep from freezing to death. Despite these setbacks and other mishaps, from 1978 to 1992 she was among the top ten Iditarod finishers an amazing twelve times, winning four times and coming in second on four occasions.

The women who race in the Iditarod are far from the only tough women who compete in sports. Toughness is frequently associated with women and girls who participate in sports typically dominated by men. For example, when eleven-year-old Rachel Richardson decided that she wanted to be an ice hockey goalie and play with a boys' team, her mother commented that Rachel's father always "[knew] that [his daughter was] tough" (qtd. in Anderson 10). Seventeen-year-old boxer Lakiea Coffen was described in one article as "tough enough" to deal with any amount of discrimination that she might face in a male-dominated sport (Hammonds A11). The friends of eleven-year-old Shauna St. Pierre also emphasized her toughness after she informed them that she wanted to play football with a boys' team. Her coach described Shauna as "rough and tough" (qtd. in Wambsgans 1). He claimed that Shauna could "be just as tough as any guy on the team" (qtd. in Wambsgans 3). Unlike Shauna, teenager Tiffany Moss was not allowed to play basketball in Washington's all-male Urban Coalition, despite the fact that "many of her teammates felt that she was tough enough to stand the competition" (Wright A1). These young women are examples of the growing number of girls and women in the 1990s who, even at the risk of being labeled unfeminine or unwomanly, pursue tough exploits that have long been considered solely for men.

These women who pursue male-dominated sports are only a few examples of real contemporary women who openly challenge the societal convention that women are not tough enough to compete with men. Although I picked examples from sport, I could have chosen examples of women from many other fields. It is partly because of the increased presence of real tough women that the media are changing their images of women, creating tougher characters such as Martha Washington and Xena.[2] In turn, these images influence how real women perceive the acceptability (or lack of acceptability) of female toughness. The media influence the "real" world and the "real" world influences the media. It is impossible to determine with precision whether the media or the world outside the media is responsible for beginning a trend. What is certain is that both real women like Susan Butcher and fictional women like Xena are helping to change how society perceives the relationship between women and toughness. There is an on-going cultural battle about whether or not women should be allowed to possess the same tough attributes as men—a battle in which Butcher and Xena are foot soldiers.

There is no single answer about who will emerge as the victor in this struggle. As I have shown, toughness has become more accessible to women during the past three decades, and women appearing in the media seem progressively more tough. Sarah Connor is tougher than any of Charlie's Angels. Martha Washington is tougher than Emma Peel. Xena is tougher than the Bionic Woman. Alex from *Nemesis 2* is far tougher than any of them. At first inspection, the popular media seem to suggest that there is increasingly little difference between the tough man and the tough woman, but such is not the case. Throughout this book I have demonstrated how the toughness of even the toughest women is limited, confined, reduced, and regulated in a number of ways. In some cases, the femininity or maternity of a tough woman is emphasized, suggesting that toughness does not significantly change what is considered to be a woman's essential nature. In other cases, the sexuality of a tough woman is stressed. In a society where a woman's sexuality is often associated with her subordination, this emphasis reduces the threat of her toughness. In yet other situations, tough women are not as tough as their male cohorts, often needing to be rescued by men. If the tough woman is the physical equal of a man (or is his superior), often it is only because, like the Bionic Woman or Alex, she has undergone a physical modification that has made her stronger and faster than a typical woman; this ploy suggests that unmodified women are no match for men. Finally, the tough woman sometimes appears in a futuristic science-fiction world or in the distant past of mythology, where she is safely distanced from our present time.

As I have argued, however, the containment of women's toughness is never absolute. The sexuality of Mrs. Peel and the Angels might be emphasized, the maternal nature of Ripley and Captain Janeway played up, or the underlying femininity of the Bionic Woman, Scully, and Elektra stressed—it matters little how the popular media reduce the transgressive nature of tough women—but such figures still offer visions of female power and independence that help to challenge the gender status quo. Whether watching the Bionic Woman or reading about the adventures of Martha Washington, women can form and carry away from these experiences a desire to be tough, even if men or other women feel intimidated or threatened by such behavior. Thus, it becomes clear how impossible it is to perceive the depiction of the tough girl in the popular media as entirely positive or negative; instead, like most popular culture characters, she is a multivalent representation that can be read in numerous and even paradoxical ways. Much more work remains to be done by cultural critics regarding how viewers perceive and use the images of tough women that they see in the media. How do women audience members utilize images of tough women? Are the new images of tough women changing how viewers understand their own relationship to toughness? These are intriguing and important questions that need to be addressed in order to understand how the media help constitute gender roles.

It is apparent that women's toughness will continue to be controversial into the foreseeable future. As I have argued throughout this book, representations of toughness significantly affect how gender is fashioned and performed in our society. Tough women challenge the assumption that toughness is an attribute associated with men. Tough women also show that masculine characteristics, such as toughness, are not biologically defined but are instead a carefully choreographed performance that either a man or a woman might engage in. This is disturbing because it suggests that gender roles might not be as inflexible as Americans assume, an idea that throws into question the whole foundation upon which our culture is based. If masculine attributes, such as toughness, and feminine attributes, too, are conceived as free-floating signifiers that refer to either a male or female body, our whole culture is destabilized because it is based on what are perceived as the essential differences between men and women. Because of the threat tough women pose to the whole gender system, conflict about their depiction will continue.

It is also clear that toughness and its relationship to women *is* changing. Xena, for instance, is a far tougher image of womanhood than we would have seen on television even ten years ago. Martha Washington is far different from the female characters who appeared in comics just a few decades earlier; independent, courageous, and heroic, she breaks many stereotypes that suggest that women are passive victims. Xena and Washington prove that the relation between women and toughness is changing. The new images of tough women in the popular media will have an impact on how our society constructs women and men outside the media. The depiction of tough women on television can challenge and even change the assumption that toughness is primarily a male attribute, which could potentially lead to more social power for women. As I have previously argued, as long as men are primarily associated with toughness, they will be the predominate power-holders in a culture where toughness is strongly aligned with leadership, authority, and power.

What must be considered, however, is whether it is desirable for women—either in the popular media or reality—to ascribe to the same tough images as men. Do we want female characters who are as brutal as the Terminator? Are we hoping to see women who are as merciless as Dirty Harry? Are we secretly longing to cheer for women who are as violent as Rambo? These are disturbing questions with no simple answers. The tough woman is sometimes guilty of the worst excesses of her male cohorts, but she also suggests that women can be strong heroes and leaders, roles that have long been considered the province of men. The tough woman demonstrates that it is acceptable, and even desirable, for women to be physically strong—a positive message in a society that is still ambivalent about women developing physical power equal to that of men. Finally, the tough girl shows the ability of women to be strong, autonomous individuals who are not dependent on men. We need to recognize the positive messages that the tough girl embodies, but, at the same time, recognize that her increased popularity might have negative impact.

The depiction of the tough woman is changing. Writers and artists are actively engaged in challenging and re-creating the mainstream depiction of the tough woman. Whether in underground comic books, lesbian detective novels, alternative films, or feminist-influenced 'zines, a wide variety of alternative sources are creating their own images of tough girls, which often are far more radical than those presented by the mainstream. The depictions of tough women in these alternative genres have the power to influence mainstream depictions of tough women. Thus, the image of the tough woman in the twenty-first century is apt to come from a conglomeration of different sources and to look very different from the images we are familiar with today.

Regardless of the many ways the tough girl may change in the future, we must recognize that the mainstream media are still conservative when it comes to challenging traditional depictions of women and femininity. The tough girl is still not tolerated or accepted in our culture nearly as much as the more conventionally feminine, non-tough woman. Tough women are still perceived as societally suspect, and are liable to be identified as lesbians, which is why their depiction in the mass media always carries a certain amount of risk. American culture's conservative ideology about traditional gender roles will continue to exert tremendous pressure on the ways that women and men behave. Thus, the tough girl might help to radicalize how women view femininity, but she is still very much an outsider in a culture that assumes that the smiling model on the cover of *Ladies' Home Journal* is somehow a more "normal" woman than Xena or Ripley, an assumption that binds women to the cult of femininity and separates them from authority and power.

Notes

Introduction

1. The role of economics in determining the gender of action figures is huge. Toy manufacturers want to make money. They figure that girls do not play with action figures. They also assume that boys do not want to play with female action figures, so manufacturers only put one female in a group of seven. Toy stores, too, want to make money. For the reasons just mentioned, they determine that female actions figures will not sell; therefore, stores do not stock them.

2. Film critic Elayne Rapping also has noted the overwhelming prominence of men: "Anyone searching for a Saturday night movie knows full well that mindless macho blockbusters have virtually dominated the cineplex screen and box offices for lo these many years, reducing us all to choosing between Arnold Schwarzenegger and Leonardo the Ninja Turtle" (43).

3. The association between men and action-adventure films was made clearer to me while watching Jean-Claude Van Damme's *Bloodsport* (1987) on television. It was advertised by the station, TBS, as one of a special series of "movies for guys who like movies."

4. Other males I saw on video cartridge boxes included Pierce Brosnan (*Detonator*), Harrison Ford (*Blade Runner, Raiders of the Lost Ark*, and *Indiana Jones and the Temple of Doom*), Roger Moore (*For Your Eyes Only*), Chuck Norris (*Code of Silence* and *Delta Force 2*), Keanu Reeves (*Speed*), Burt Reynolds (*Heat*), and Bruce Willis (*Die Hard*).

5. For another article that discusses the prevalence of the 1990s tough girl in films, see Mandy Johnson, "Women as Action Heroes." An article that discusses the prevalence of strong but not necessarily tough women in films is Richard Corliss's "The Ladies Who Lounge." A woman can be strong without necessarily being tough. Toughness suggests being as aggressive as men are supposed to be. Toughness suggests a threat: The tough person is dangerous and might strike back. Toughness is also associated with masculinity. Strength does not necessarily share the same associations. For a more in-depth discussion of the many meanings of toughness, see Chapter 1.

6. A notable example of the ambivalence with which the media looks at women's toughness appears in the 1995 television movie *Generation X* (Fox Television). The stars of the show are all mutant teenagers, struggling to survive in a world that despises them. One of the young women, Buff (Suzanne Davis), stands out

because of her tremendous strength and musculature. Instead of being happy with bulging muscles, she is ashamed and will not undress in front of her friends. For Buff and countless other women, looking too tough and muscular is something to avoid at all costs because it might make them unattractive to men.

7. In the 1980s and 1990s, a number of books and essays were written about individual tough women, such as Ripley in the Alien films and Sarah Connor in the Terminator movies, and about tough girls in specific genres such as the detective novel. What was missing was a more comprehensive study of the representation of women's toughness that seeks to bring together a wide variety of genres, as does this book. This more comprehensive approach is important to show the multitude of ways that women's toughness has been constituted in the popular media.

8. Additional studies of the depiction of the tough guy include Steve Neale, "Masculinity as Spectacle: Reflections on Men and Mainstream Cinema"; James Robert Parish, *The Tough Guys;* Richard Sparks, "Masculinity and Heroism in the Hollywood 'Blockbuster': The Culture Industry and Contemporary Images of Crime and Law Enforcement"; and Rupert Wilkinson, *American Tough: The Tough-Guy Tradition and American Character.* Other studies that address the representation of male toughness (but do not focus solely on it) include Maurice Berger, Brian Wallis, and Simon Watson, eds., *Constructing Masculinity;* Dennis Bingham, *Acting Male: Masculinities in the Films of James Stewart, Jack Nicholson, and Clint Eastwood;* Steven Cohan and Ina Rae Hark, eds., *Screening the Male: Exploring Masculinities in Hollywood Cinema;* Susan Jeffords, *The Remasculinization of America: Gender and the Vietnam War;* Pat Kirkham and Janet Thumin's two edited volumes, *You Tarzan: Masculinity, Movies and Men* and *Me Jane: Masculinity, Movies and Women;* and Richard Slotkin, *Gunfighter Nation: The Myth of the Frontier in Twentieth-Century America.*

9. Tasker's book is of particular interest because it provides a fairly detailed discussion of tough women. This work, however, discusses only the tough woman in films, without trying to explore how she appears in many different genres.

10. The toughness bandwagon is not limited to women. Male actors have also discovered that toughness sells. John Travolta is one actor who has moved from being a sensitive guy to a tough guy, a move that helped to renew a floundering career.

11. Of course, many scholarly works address how popular culture helps to constitute our lives. A few of the studies that have influenced this book include John Fiske, *Television Culture;* Tania Modleski, *Loving with a Vengeance: Mass-Produced Fantasies for Women;* Chandra Mukerji and Michael Schudson, eds., *Rethinking Popular Culture: Contemporary Perspectives in Cultural Studies;* Andrew Ross, *No Respect: Intellectuals and Popular Culture;* and Susan Willis, *A Primer for Daily Life.*

12. A few of the many writers who analyze women's roles in popular culture include Rosemary Betterton, ed., *Looking on: Images of Femininity in the Visual Arts and Media;* Lorraine Gamman and Margaret Marshment, eds., *The Female Gaze: Women as Viewers of Popular Culture;* Janice A. Radway, *Reading the Romance: Women, Patriarchy, and Popular Literature;* Elayne Rapping, *Media-tions: Forays into the Culture and Gender Wars;* June Sochen, *Enduring Values: Women in Popular Culture;* Lynn Spigel and Denise Mann, eds., *Private Screenings: Television and the Female Consumer;* and Judith Williamson, *Consuming Passions: The Dynamics of Popular Culture.*

13. See Sherrie A. Inness, *Delinquents and Debutantes: Twentieth-Century American Girls' Cultures; Intimate Communities: Representation and Social Transformation in Women's College Fiction, 1895–1910; The Lesbian Menace: Ideology, Identity, and the*

Representation of Lesbian Life; and *Nancy Drew and Company: Culture, Gender, and Girls' Series.*

14. My choice of sources has been influenced by my desire to show the prevalence of the tough girl in a multitude of areas. Thus, I have tried to pick sources that reflect her appearance in many genres. Within one book, of course, I am able to mention only a few of the sources where the tough girl appears. I feel, however, that the films, television shows, and comic books I have picked are representative of how other media sources represent the tough girl.

15. My work has been influenced by studies such as John Fiske's *Understanding Popular Culture* (1989), George Lipsitz's *Time Passages: Collective Memory and American Popular Culture* (1990), Karal Ann Marling's *As Seen on TV: The Visual Culture of Everyday Life in the 1950s* (1994), Myra Macdonald's *Representing Women: Myths of Femininity in the Popular Media* (1995), Patricia Mellencamp's *High Anxiety: Catastrophe, Scandal, Age, and Comedy* (1992), and Susan J. Douglas's *Where the Girls Are: Growing Up Female with the Mass Media* (1994), which all use a wide variety of popular source materials to support their arguments.

Chapter 1. Beyond Muscles

1. In "The Wimp Factor," Bruce Curtis provides a thoughtful reflection on the relationship between toughness and Bush and other political leaders. Curtis argues that toughness and masculinity frequently are used to assert the leadership skills of a candidate: "According to the masculine logic of sexual politics, all women and all men are relatively 'womanized,' except the hardest, toughest, most powerful, most masculine" (50). I concur, and believe that displaying toughness is one way that men affirm their presumed ability to lead. The assumption that women are not tough prevents them from having political power, as well as power in other areas.

2. Extensive work exists on the construction of masculinity. See Gail Bederman, *Manliness and Civilization: A Cultural History of Gender and Race in the United States, 1880–1917;* Michael Kimmel, *Manhood in America: A Cultural History;* and R. W. Connell, *Masculinities.*

3. Other examples of tough men in fiction include Destry in Max Brand's *Destry Rides Again* (1930), a Western about the exploits of a hard-bitten cowboy who has spent six years in prison for a crime that he did not commit. Specializing in fist fights, Destry can beat up any man in town and is gunning for the men who sent him away. In another Western, Jack Schaefer's *Shane* (1949), a larger-than-life hero is nearly invincible. Shane is a "solid, compact" (61) man who is "plenty rugged" (61). Lithuanian Jurgis Rudkus in Upton Sinclair's novel *The Jungle* (1906), with his "mighty shoulders and . . . giant hands," is also tough (4). When confronted by the horrendous working conditions of the Chicago stockyards, Rudkus replies only, "I will work harder" (20). Hemingway's stoic heroes, such as Lieutenant Frederic Henry in *A Farewell to Arms* (1929) and Robert Jordan in *For Whom the Bell Tolls* (1940), are also notable. Of course, this is only the beginning of a list that could continue for hundreds of pages.

4. Beach's novel contains a woman who appears tough but is actually only pseudo-tough. Cherry Malotte lives in the Alaskan Klondike, is stunningly beautiful, deals cards like a champion, and handles a gun with ease, even when confronted by a rabid dog. She is cool and collected under stress. However, her Achilles' heel is that she is in love with a man who does not love her, and she is

willing to sacrifice anything to gain his love one day. In this fashion, her toughness loses its edge. She is tough, but only until a man comes along.

5. Numerous men who have appeared on television shows over the last few decades make no pretenses to being tough: Jack Tripper on *Three's Company,* Private Gomer Pyle on *Gomer Pyle, U.S.M.C.,* Darrin Stephens on *Bewitched,* Gilligan on *Gilligan's Island,* Ward Cleaver on *Leave It to Beaver,* Captain Tony Nelson on *I Dream of Jeannie,* Lenny and Squiggy on *Laverne & Shirley,* and Andy Taylor on *The Andy Griffith Show* are only a few examples. These men, however, are buffoons, not heroes. Tough men are the ones who are depicted as heroes and men to emulate.

6. I am not suggesting that it *is* more difficult to be a police officer than a school teacher. I am merely pointing out how the larger culture perceives these jobs and labels them with respect to their toughness quotient.

7. Tough women in literature include Janie Crawford in Zora Neale Hurston's novel *Their Eyes Were Watching God* (1937). Although not tough physically, Janie endures the hardships of being an African-American woman in a society that views blacks as second-class citizens. Another tough woman is the central character of Mary Austin's story "The Walking Woman" (1909). The Walking Woman is "a sort of whom men speak respectfully" (255). She is courageous enough to walk alone through the broad stretches of the desert West: "She had been set on her way by teamsters who lifted her out of white, hot desertness and put her down at the crossing of unnamed ways, days distant from anywhere" (256). Ibsen's impetuous title character in his play *Hedda Gabler* (1890) is yet another woman with unusual stamina and nerves of steel. She toys with a brace of pistols left to her by her father, even shooting at one of her visitors, remarking that she is "just killing time. Shooting up into the blue" (371). Eventually, she shoots herself rather than continue on in a loveless and stifling marriage.

8. The same working-class rage is displayed by Dolly Hawkins in Myra Page's novel *Daughter of the Hills* (1950). Growing up in the Cumberland Mountains of Tennessee, Dolly is the daughter and wife of a coal miner. Not only is she physically strong, she overcomes great hardships as she struggles to support her family with her husband's meager wages. Although her parents and her husband all die, she endures.

9. For further information about this tradition, see Paula Rabinowitz, *Labor and Desire: Women's Revolutionary Fiction in Depression America.*

10. For additional information on the complex ritual of drag, see Judith Butler, *Gender Trouble.*

11. Being tough is supposedly such a challenging task for women that a number of women's magazines have published articles that focus on what toughness entails for a woman. In October 1983 *Vogue* published an article by Kay Larson entitled "Tough Women" that discusses how confusing it is that there are "no prototypes to suggest how to be feminine and tough all at once" (222). Larson writes about the men who are fearful of tough women and why it is necessary for women to be tough, without regard for whether they are "offending anybody—any man" (222). In April 1995, the *Ladies' Home Journal* published "The Nice Woman's Guide to Being Tough." In this essay, Andrew Higbie presents five "tough but nice tactics" for the woman who wants to take charge of her life (117). This article presents the idea that toughness is not a "natural" response for women; it must be learned. Men, presumably, know exactly how to be tough and require no similar guide. For more on the construction of toughness in women's magazines, see Chapter 3.

12. For studies that address the perceived connection between masculinity, toughness, and lesbianism, see Sue-Ellen Case, "Towards a Butch-Femme Aesthetic"; Judith Halberstam, "Techno-homo: On Bathrooms, Butches, and Sex with Furniture"; Sherrie A. Inness and Michele E. Lloyd, "G.I. Joes in Barbie Land: Recontextualizing Butch in Twentieth-Century Lesbian Culture"; Esther Newton, "The Mythic Mannish Lesbian: Radclyffe Hall and the New Woman"; and Alisa Solomon, "Not Just a Passing Fancy: Notes on Butch." Much more work needs to be done on the complex ways in which masculinity and toughness are associated with lesbianism.

13. The image of the physically tough woman is not something new. She has always been a reality in fiction and real life. In Carson McCullers's novella "The Ballad of the Sad Café" (1951), the owner of the café, Miss Amelia, is as tough as they come. Six feet two inches tall, Miss Amelia is described as "a dark, tall woman with bones and muscles like a man" (4). She is ornery and more than able to hold her own in a fist fight with a man. What is changing is that such a character is becoming more common and mainstream. For example, Xena in the television show *Xena: Warrior Princess* is more than capable physically of taking care of herself and is surprisingly independent of men. She is discussed in greater depth in Chapter 9.

14. Numerous scholars have studied the importance of style as a method of forming identities, including Fred Davis, *Fashion, Culture, and Identity;* Stuart Ewen, *All Consuming Images: The Politics of Style in Contemporary Culture;* Dick Hebdige, *Subculture: The Meaning of Style;* and Claudia Brush Kidwell and Valerie Steele, eds., *Men and Women: Dressing the Part.*

Chapter 2. Semi-Tough

1. For information about the popularity of the Angels, see Charles Champlin, "Jaclyn Smith: The Cool 'Angel' "; Cutler Durkee, "When Angels Were the Rage"; Carolyn See, "I'm Not the Difficult One"; and "TV's Super Women."

2. For additional sources about *The Avengers,* see Steven Chibnall, "Avenging the Past"; Peter Dean, "Wind Up"; " 'Good-Chap Sexuality' "; Dave Rogers, *The Avengers, The Avengers Anew,* and *The Complete Avengers;* and Cathi Unsworth, "Suave Central."

3. Scholarly work on the three shows has been limited. David Buxton discusses *The Avengers* in *From the Avengers to Miami Vice: Form and Ideology in Television Series.* Susan J. Douglas writes about both *Charlie's Angels* and *The Bionic Women* in *Where the Girls Are: Growing Up Female with the Mass Media.*

4. Similar to Fiske, Christine Gledhill writes, "The viewing or reading situation affects the meanings and pleasures of a work by introducing into the cultural exchange a range of determinations, potentially resistant or contradictory, arising from the differential social and cultural constitution of readers or viewers—by class, gender, race, age, personal history, and so on. This is potentially the most radical moment of negotiation, because the most variable and unpredictable" (70).

5. Additional recent studies that analyze the connections between women and television include Camille Bacon-Smith, *Enterprising Women: Television Fandom and the Creation of Popular Myth;* Helen Baehr and Gillian Dyers, eds., *Boxed In: Women and Television;* Mary Ellen Brown, ed., *Television and Women's Culture: The Politics of the Popular;* Bonnie J. Dow, *Prime-Time Feminism: Television, Media Culture, and the*

Women's Movement Since 1970; Laura Stempel Mumford, *Love and Ideology in the Afternoon: Soap Opera, Women, and Television Genre;* Martha Nochimson, *No End to Her: Soap Opera and the Female Subject;* Andrea L. Press, *Women Watching Television: Gender, Class, and Generation in the American Television Experience;* Jane M. Shattuc, *The Talking Cure: TV Talk Shows and Women;* and Lynn Spigel, *Make Room for TV: Television and the Family Ideal in Postwar America.* A number of essays in Helen Baehr and Ann Gray's edited collection, *Turning It On: A Reader in Women and Media,* also address the complex relationship between television and women.

6. For background information on Aaron Spelling, see Mimi Swartz, "Aaron Spelling."

7. The sequel touted itself as a new and improved *Charlie's Angels,* in which the women had to think as well as look gorgeous. The new Angels, however, were little different from the old ones. *Self* magazine had a fashion spread featuring the New Angels with the following caption: "Here . . . the guns are put away and the gowns come out as the Angels—dressed to seduce, not sleuth—do the town: on Rodeo Drive or lighting up the Beverly Hills Hotel" (Linden Gross 77). This is just Hollywood as usual: the Angels are beautiful starlets, with more curves than cunning. They are a far cry from tough women such as Elektra, Martha Washington, or Xena. For more information about *Angels '88,* see D. Keith Mano, "So You Want to Be an Angel."

8. Because little scholarship exists on the Bionic Woman, I have had to depend on Internet sources for information about the bionic accessories that were available to accompany the Bionic Man or Bionic Woman action figures. The best online source for information on the bionic duo is Rod Rehn's Bionic FAQ.

9. A *Six Million Dollar Man* fan could also buy all kinds of booty, including a Six Million Dollar Man action-figure, complete with a bionic eye and "bionic grip," the Six Million Dollar Man view-master, an AM wrist radio, bionic mission vehicle, bionic video center, mission control center, and a porta-communicator. You could set up a complete bionic command post in the comfort of your own home.

10. Additional information about the success of the two bionic television shows can be found in "The $500,000 Timex"; Joel H. Cohen, *The Six Million Dollar Man and the Bionic Woman: Lee Majors and Lindsay Wagner;* Bill Davidson, "The 'Bionic Woman' Flexed Her Financial Muscles"; David Houston, *Lindsay Wagner: Superstar of the Bionic Woman;* and Dwight Whitney, "Tigress or Pussycat?"

Chapter 3. Pretty Tough

1. For additional critical work on magazines for women and girls, see Ros Ballaster, Margaret Beetham, Elizabeth Frazer, and Sandra Hebron, *Women's Worlds: Ideology, Femininity and the Woman's Magazine;* Shelley Budgeon, "Fashion Magazine Advertising: Constructing Femininity in the 'Postfeminist' Era"; Kerry Carrington and Anna Bennett, " 'Girls' Mags' and the Pedagogical Formation of the Girl"; Kalia Doner, "Women's Magazines: Slouching Towards Feminism"; Margaret Duffy and J. Michael Gotcher, "Crucial Advice on How to Get the Guy: The Rhetorical Vision of Power and Seduction in the Teen Magazine *YM*"; Gigi Durham, "The Taming of the Shrew: Women's Magazines and the Regulation of Desire"; Marjorie Ferguson, *Forever Feminine: Women's Magazines and the Cult of Femininity;* Elizabeth Frazer, "Teenage Girls Reading *Jackie*"; Ellen McCracken, *Decoding Women's Magazines from Mademoiselle to Ms.* and "Demystifying *Cosmopolitan:* Five Critical Methods"; Kathryn McMahon, "The *Cosmopolitan* Ideology

and the Management of Desire"; Angela McRobbie, *Feminism and Youth Culture: From "Jackie" to "Just Seventeen";* Kate Peirce, "A Feminist Theoretical Perspective on the Socialization of Teenage Girls Through *Seventeen* Magazine"; Jennifer Scanlon, *Inarticulate Longings: The Ladies' Home Journal, Gender, and the Promises of Consumer Culture;* and Janice Winship, *Inside Women's Magazines.*

2. Other studies of advertising and its influence include Diane Barthel, *Putting on Appearances: Gender and Advertising;* Stuart Ewen, *All Consuming Images: The Politics of Style in Contemporary Culture* and *Captains of Consciousness: Advertising and the Social Roots of the Consumer Culture;* and Judith Williamson, *Decoding Advertisements: Ideology and Meaning in Advertising.*

3. Additional articles on leather fashions in popular women's magazines include "The Leather Forecast" and Nell Scovell, "Leather Perfect."

4. Leather is so potentially dangerous for women to wear because of its association with masculinity that articles in women's magazines spend a great deal of time discussing exactly how and when women should wear leather attire. See "Do's and Don'ts."

5. Combining a feminine style with a more masculine one is not the only way to limit the tough image of masculine clothing. Another tactic appears in an advertisement for Calvin Klein jeans in which a woman wears clothing associated with toughness and masculinity—ripped jeans, hiking boots, and a worn denim shirt. She has short hair and is standing in a rugged outdoor setting, but her tough image is reduced because her shirt is completely unbuttoned, revealing a glimpse of her breasts (Calvin Klein Jeans 3). As previously mentioned, emphasizing a woman's sexuality reduces her tough image.

6. Studies on the social anxieties aroused by cross-dressing include Marjorie Garber, *Vested Interests: Cross-Dressing and Cultural Anxiety;* Corinne Holt Sawyer, "Men in Skirts and Women in Trousers, from Achilles to Victoria Grant: One Explanation of a Comedic Paradox"; and Julie Wheelwright, *Amazons and Military Maids: Women Who Dressed as Men in the Pursuit of Life, Liberty, and Happiness.*

Chapter 4. Lady Killers

1. Other discussions of the increased prevalence in the 1980s and 1990s of women who kill in films and books include Mitchell Fink, "Actresses Tough It Out"; Charles Fleming, "That's Why the Lady Is a Champ"; Krin Gabbard and Glen O. Gabbard, "Phallic Women in the Contemporary Cinema"; Richard Grenier, "Killer Bimbos"; Brook Hersey, "Word on Movies: Women Fight Back"; Christine Holmlund, "A Decade of Deadly Dolls: Hollywood and the Woman Killer"; Kathi Maio, "Film: Women Who Murder for the Man"; Sonia Murray, "Bad Babes at the Box Office"; Karen Thomas, "Female Roles Are Packing a New Punch"; and Virginia Tiger, "Alice and Charlie and Vida and Sophy—A Terrorist's Work Is Never Done."

2. Other works address women who kill in real life. Eileen MacDonald discusses women who kill for political reasons in *Shoot the Women First,* and Coramae Richey Mann explores the socioeconomic reasons American women kill in *When Women Kill.* Also, see Ann Jones, *Women Who Kill,* and Mark MacNamara, "Can a Woman Kill Like a Man?"

3. The representation of the woman killer is by no means confined to recent decades. Women who kill have been represented for centuries. For instance, Frances E. Dolan discusses women murderers from the 1600s who were written

about in numerous "legal treatises, pamphlets, scaffold speeches . . . ballads, and plays" (25). Perhaps one of the reasons for society's long-standing fascination with the killer woman is that she is representative of a culture turned upside down, since "normal" women in Western cultures have long been assumed to be maternal, not murderous. Describing the killer woman's punishment, whether in a seventh-century ballad or a twentieth-century film, is one way to demonstrate to the audience that social order will not be long unbalanced.

4. For more information about the depiction of women who kill, see the collection edited by Helen Birch, *Moving Targets: Women, Murder and Representation.* Also see Rhoda Estep, "Women's Roles in Crime as Depicted by Television and Newspapers."

5. Why is an action-adventure team never composed of more women than men? The few women are always greatly outnumbered by their male counterparts. The relatively rare women who appear in such teams uphold the ideology that tough women are something of an oddity, whether in films, comic books, cartoons, or action figure sets.

6. A film that takes the idea of the insane killer woman to its ludicrous extreme is *Serial Mom* (1994, director John Waters), which stars Kathleen Turner as suburban housewife Beverly Sutphin, a woman who seems to have it all—a loving husband, a lovely suburban home, and two happy children—until she is revealed to be a psychotic killer.

7. For an article that discusses the life of Hilary Henkin, the screenwriter of *Romeo Is Bleeding* and one of the few women who write action-adventure films, see James Greenberg, "One Tough Cookie."

8. The deadly woman terrorist or assassin has become a staple of popular culture. For example, Friday, the main character of Robert Heinlein's science-fiction novel *Friday* (1982), is a highly trained killer with a "hair-trigger kill reflex" (27). But Friday is more sex kitten than killer, and her sexual exploits take up more of the book than her killing pursuits. Also see Deborah Christian, *Mainline;* William Gibson, *Neuromancer;* and John Le Carré, *The Little Drummer Girl.*

Chapter 5. A Tough Girl as One of the Boys

1. Anderson is the subject of a number of Internet web sites set up by her admirers, including those by the Gillian Anderson Testosterone Brigade, the Gillian Anderson NeuroTransmitter Association, and the Gillian Anderson British Association. Numerous fan sites on the Internet also focus solely on Jodie Foster. Anderson's and Foster's significant presences on the Internet points out the sometimes obsessive levels of interest that the women attract.

2. Biographical descriptions of Foster's life and her meteoric rise to fame are plentiful, including "Foster, Jodie"; Melina Gerosa, "Jodie Loses Her Cool"; Gerri Hirshey, "Jodie Foster"; Fred Schruers, "A Kind of Redemption"; Michael Segell, "What's Driving Miss Jodie?"; Guy Trebay, "A Voice of Her Own"; and Tracy Young, "Vogue Arts."

3. See "The Objects of Beauty."

4. Reviews of *The Silence of the Lambs* include Richard Alleva, "What's for Dinner? 'Silence' & 'Sleeping' "; Stanley Kauffmann, "Gluttons for Punishment"; Stuart Klawans, "Films: *The Silence of the Lambs*"; Terrence Rafferty, "The Current Cinema: Moth and Flame"; John Simon, "Horror, Domestic and Imported"; and "Writers on the Lamb."

5. Other critical studies of *The Silence of the Lambs* include James Conlon, "Silencing Lambs and Educating Women"; Greg Garrett, "Objecting to Objectification: Re-Viewing the Feminine in *The Silence of the Lambs*"; Judith Halberstam, "Skinflick: Posthuman Gender in Jonathan Demme's *The Silence of the Lambs*"; Jeanne Silverthorne, "The Cave"; Janet Staiger, "Taboos and Totems: Cultural Meanings of *The Silence of the Lambs*"; Carol Watts, "From Looking to Coveting: The 'American Girl' in *The Silence of the Lambs*"; and Elizabeth Young, "*The Silence of the Lambs* and the Flaying of Feminist Theory."

6. Books addressed to *X-File* fans include Ted Edwards, *X-Files Confidential: The Unauthorized X-Philes Compendium;* N. E. Genge, *The Unofficial X-Files Companion: An X-Phile's Guide to the Mysteries, Conspiracies, and Really Strange Truths Behind the Show;* Frank Lovece, *The X-Files Declassified: The Unauthorized Guide;* and Brian Lowry, *The Truth Is Out There: The Official Guide to the X-Files.*

7. Articles that discuss the international success of the *X-Files* include Steve Clarke, "U.K. Requires 'X' Ray Vision"; John Hopewell, "Home-Grown TV, Brand 'X' Fare Best"; Edith Hill Updike, "X-Files' Supernatural Hold on Japan"; and Mark Woods, "Youth TV Sizzles."

8. Articles about the appeal of the *X-Files* include Gretchen Atwood, "Extreme X-Filers"; David Bischoff, "Opening the *X-Files:* Behind the Scenes of TV's Hottest Show"; John Blake, "X-Files Attracts Devoted Following"; C. Eugene Emery, Jr., "Paranormal and Paranoia Intermingle on Fox TV's 'X-Files' "; Tom Gliatto, "X-Ellence"; Barbara Kantrowitz and Adam Rogers, "The Truth Is X-ed Out There"; Michael Kaplan, "Invasion of the X-Philes"; James Martin, "X-Appeal"; Mark Nollinger, "Twenty Things You Need to Know about *The X-Files*"; Jonathan Ross, "Talking with Aliens"; Rick Schindler and Stephanie Williams, "An X-Files Encyclopedia from A to X"; and James Swallow, "X-aminations."

9. Popular articles that focus on David Duchovny and give little or no attention to Gillian Anderson include Maureen Dowd, "Looking for Space Aliens (and Denying Yale)"; James Grant, "Red Hot Right Now: David Duchovny"; Jack Hitt, "X-Factor Actor"; Mark Nollinger, "The David Duchovny X-perience"; and Steve Pond, "Secret Agent Man." Compare the smaller number of articles that focus on Anderson: Tom Gliatto, "Occult Leader"; and Stephanie Mansfield, "Gillian Looks Like a Million." Chris Mundy discusses both actors in "David Duchovny and Gillian Anderson."

Chapter 6. Tough Women in Outer Space

1. Other examples of tough women pilots or commanders in contemporary science fiction include senior pilot Reverdy Jian in Melissa Scott's novel *Dreamships;* Dee Steinway in Suzy McKee Charnas's story "Scorched Supper on New Niger"; Captain Isoura "Izzie" Antopolous in Sydney Long's "For the Right Reason"; and commander "Mel" in P. J. Beese's "White Wings."

2. Feminist-influenced studies of science fiction include Nadya Aisenberg, *Ordinary Heroines: Transforming the Male Myth;* Lucie Armitt, ed., *Where No Man Has Gone Before: Women and Science Fiction;* Marleen S. Barr, ed., *Future Females: A Critical Anthology;* Marleen S. Barr, *Lost in Space: Probing Feminist Science Fiction and Beyond;* Elyce Rae Helford, "Reading Space Fictions: Representations of Gender, Race, and Species in Popular Culture"; Sarah Lefanu, *In the Chinks of the World Machine: Feminism and Science Fiction;* Constance Penley et al., eds., *Close Encounters: Film, Feminism, and Science Fiction;* Robin Roberts, *A New Species: Gender and Science in*

Fiction; Joanna Russ, *To Write Like a Woman: Essays in Feminism and Science Fiction;* and Jenny Wolmark, *Aliens and Others: Science Fiction, Feminism and Postmodernism.*

3. Perhaps one of the reasons for Ripley's unusual toughness is that the film script was originally designed for either a man or a woman to play the starring role (Penley, "Time Travel" 73).

4. Reviews of *Aliens* include David Edelstein, "Movies: Mother of the Year"; Derek Elley, "*Aliens*"; Pauline Kael, "The Current Cinema"; and Ari Korpivaara, "Roll Over Rambo."

Reviews of *Alien 3* include Anne Billson, "Back into the Closet"; Jayne Blanchard, "At the Movies: *Alien 3*"; and Jewelle Gomez, "The Hero of Us All."

5. Other feminist studies of one or more of the films in the *Aliens* trilogy include Barbara Creed, "*Alien* and the Monstrous-Feminine"; Susan Jeffords, " 'The Battle of the Big Mamas': Feminism and the Alienation of Women"; James H. Kavanagh, "Feminism, Humanism and Science in *Alien*"; Kathleen Murphy, "The Last Temptation of Sigourney Weaver"; Janice Hocker Rushing, "Evolution of 'The New Frontier' in *Alien* and *Aliens:* Patriarchal Co-optation of the Feminine Archetype"; and Amy Taubin, "Invading Bodies: *Aliens 3* and the Trilogy."

6. My thanks to Michele Lloyd for this idea.

7. A similar parent-child relationship is featured in *Commando* (1985, director Mark L. Lester), an action-adventure film starring Arnold Schwarzenegger and focusing on the relationship between single father John Matrix (Schwarzenegger) and his daughter, Jenny (Alyssa Milano). When his daughter is kidnapped by terrorists, Matrix's one goal becomes rescuing his daughter; as he says, "All that matters for me now is Jenny." The relationship between Matrix and his daughter, however, is not nearly as important to the film as Ripley's relationship to Newt; because Matrix does not spend the majority of the film in the company of his daughter, he is free to work unimpeded. Although Matrix is constituted as the ultimate avenging father who thinks nothing of mowing down a small army of men to rescue his daughter, it is still difficult to watch *Commando* and assume that Jenny has the same significance for Matrix that Newt has for Ripley.

8. In her study of twenty reviews of *Aliens,* critic Christine Holmlund points out that half of them focused on motherhood (144). Essays that focus on the dynamics of motherhood in the *Aliens* films include Lynda Bundtzen, "Monstrous Mothers: Medusa, Grendel, and Now Alien"; Mary Ann Doane, "Technophilia: Technology, Representation, and the Feminine"; Jane R. Goodhall, "Aliens"; Robin Roberts, "Adoptive Versus Biological Mothering in *Aliens*"; Dennis Patrick Slattery, "Demeter-Persephone and the *Alien*(s) Cultural Body"; and Lynda Zwinger, "Blood Relations: Feminist Theory Meets the Uncanny Alien Bug Mother."

9. Women with shaved heads are prevalent in science fiction. Examples include Illia in *Star Trek, the Movie* and Sharrow in *Against a Dark Background.* Ripley's bald head has been compared to rock star Sinead O'Connor's. For both women, the absence of hair signifies their outsider status, because hair (and the more the better) is often considered the supreme signifier of a woman's femininity. This is why many critics have been disturbed and even outraged by Ripley's shorn head, and why the directors of the show were uneasy about depicting her without hair.

10. Articles that focus on Kate Mulgrew's ascent into the captain's seat include Betsy Israel, "Where No Ma'am Has Gone"; John Leonard, "The Next Next Generation"; Michael Logan, "Voyager: A 'Star Trek' Is Born"; "Mulgrew"; and Alan W. Petrucelli, "On Our Cover."

11. Articles that address women's roles in earlier Star Trek television shows and

films include Karin Blair, "Sex and *Star Trek*"; Anne Cranny-Francis, "Sexuality and Sex-Role Stereotyping in *Star Trek*"; and Rhoda V. Wilcox, "Shifting Roles and Synthetic Women in *Star Trek: The Next Generation.*"

Chapter 7. Post-Apocalyptic Tough Girls

1. In this chapter I use "post-apocalyptic" to refer to a future world that has suffered a catastrophe, such as a nuclear war, which has resulted in an earth far different from the one we know today.

2. The *Terminator* films are not post-apocalyptic works in the same way that *Tank Girl, Nemesis 2,* or *APEX* are, since they are largely set in a pre-apocalyptic world. The *Terminator* films, however, will be included in this chapter because they share many similarities with the other works. Most importantly, Sarah Connor becomes tough because of the impending apocalypse; in a similar fashion, the women in the other films need to be tough to survive in the post-apocalypse world. In each film, the end of society as we know it is impending or has already come about, demonstrating that tough women are only allowed to exist under the most unusual of circumstances. One cannot help but wonder whether Sarah Connor would have continued to be the somewhat ditzy waitress she was at the beginning of *The Terminator* if she had not discovered that the world was going to end in a nuclear holocaust.

3. Other studies of apocalyptic thought include Richard Dellamora, ed., *Postmodern Apocalypse: Theory and Cultural Practice at the End;* Saul Friedländer, Gerald Holton, Leo Marx, and Eugene Skolnikoff, eds., *Visions of Apocalypse: End or Rebirth?;* Joann James and William J. Cloonan, eds., *Apocalyptic Visions Past and Present;* Dietmar Kamper and Christoph Wulf, eds., *Looking Back on the End of the World;* David Ketterer, *New Worlds for Old: The Apocalyptic Imagination, Science Fiction, and American Literature;* Zbigniew Lewicki, *The Bang and the Whimper: Apocalypse and Entropy in American Literature;* John R. May, *Toward a New Earth: Apocalypse in the American Novel;* Eric S. Rabkin, Martin H. Greenberg, and Joseph D. Olander, eds., *The End of the World;* Douglas Robinson, *American Apocalypses: The Image of the End of the World in American Literature;* Christopher Sharrett, ed., *Crisis Cinema: The Apocalyptic Idea in Postmodern Narrative Film;* Charles B. Strozier, *Apocalypse: On the Psychology of Fundamentalism in America;* and W. Warren Wagar, *Terminal Visions: The Literature of Last Things.*

4. For further information about Schwarzenegger's depiction in the *Terminator* films, see Jonathan Goldberg, "Recalling Totalities: The Mirrored Stages of Arnold Schwarzenegger"; and Albert Liu, "The Last Days of Arnold Schwarzenegger."

5. Other critical studies of the *Terminator* saga include Joe Abbott, "They Came from Beyond the Center: Ideology and Political Textuality in the Radical Science Fiction Films of James Cameron"; Thomas B. Byers, "Terminating the Postmodern: Masculinity and Pomophobia"; Norman L. Friedman, "*The Terminator:* Changes in Critical Evaluations of Cultural Productions"; Susan Jeffords, *Hard Bodies: Hollywood Masculinity in the Reagan Era;* Kevin Pask, "Cyborg Economies: Desire and Labor in the *Terminator* Films"; and Constance Penley, "Time Travel, Primal Scene, and the Critical Dystopia."

6. Film reviews of *Terminator 2* include John Podhoretz, "The Good, the Bad and the Funny," and Kenneth Turan, "He *Said* He'd Be Back."

7. For articles that discuss Hamilton's muscular physique, see George Leonard, "Body Double"; Mark Morrison, "She's Back"; and Ann Trebbe, "Beauty and the Biceps."

8. Even though the film softened Linda Hamilton's tough image, she was still too tough for the mainstream, and for years after her role in *Terminator 2* was identified as too strong to co-star with Hollywood's leading men (Longsdorf 8). While Hamilton found it more difficult to find starring roles after her appearance, Schwarzenegger found it easier.

9. Knowledge of guns is often used in films and books to show a woman's toughness. For instance, in Iain M. Banks's *Against a Dark Background* (1993), the main character, Sharrow, is patronized by a gun dealer when she requests a FrintArms HandCannon. He questions her choice, remarking, "that's an awfully big gun for such a lovely lady" (182). She shows her expertise when she orders "a HandCannon, with the eighty-mill silencer, five GP clips, three six-five AP/wire-fléchettes clips, two bipropellant HE clips, two incendiary clips and a Special Projectile Pack" (183). In this novel and other texts, a knowledge of guns implies toughness. The size of a hero's gun is also important. Sharrow's choice of an "awfully big gun" is common among tough heroes.

10. Natasha's toughness is reduced in other ways, too. The danger she embodies is eliminated when she is killed by a robot at the film's conclusion. The parallel universe in which she lives is also eradicated, which eliminates the threat of women assuming men's roles. As if this were not enough to convince viewers that tough girls do not last long, the message is again hammered in when the film concludes with a scene between the hero and his wife in their real universe. Not only is she a stereotypically feminine, beautiful woman with not a hint of toughness, but she is also noticeably pregnant, assuring the audience that gender roles have not been challenged by the film.

11. Other reviews of *Blood of Heroes* include Manohla Dargis, "Joust Between Friends"; Gregory P. Fagan, "Cheap Thrills: *Blood of Heroes*"; Ralph Novak, "Picks & Pans: *The Blood of Heroes*"; and Merrill Shindler, "Short Takes: *Blood of Heroes.*"

12. Film reviews of *Tank Girl* include Gary Dauphin, "Reel to Reel: *Tank Girl*"; Leslie Felperin, "Reviews: *Tank Girl*"; Leonard Klady, "Film Review: *Tank Girl*"; Andrew Mueller, "Film: *Tank Girl*"; Ralph Novak, "Picks and Pans: *Tank Girl*"; Steve Pond, "21st Century Fox"; and Jonathan Romney, "Tanked Up on Attitude."

Chapter 8. Tough Girls in Comic Books

1. For more on the construction of Wonder Woman, see Molly Rae Rhodes's dissertation, "Doctoring Culture: Literary Intellectuals, Psychology and Mass Culture in the Twentieth-Century United States."

2. For a detailed discussion of some of these heroines and others, see Trina Robbins, *The Great Women Superheroes,* which provides one of the most in-depth discussions of the development of the female superhero.

3. Another source on the dominance of tough males in comics is Jeffrey S. Lang and Patrick Trimble, "Whatever Happened to the Man of Tomorrow? An Examination of the American Monomyth and the Comic Book Superhero."

4. Essays that focus on the increasing prevalence of comic books and graphic novels aimed at an adult audience include Mikal Gilmore, "Comic Genius";

Peter S. Prescott, "The Comic Book (Gulp!) Grows Up"; and Lloyd Rose, "Comic Books for Grown-Ups."

5. Not everyone in the 1940s and 1950s was equally scandalized about comic books. See, for instance, Frederic M. Thrasher, "The Comics and Delinquency: Cause or Scapegoat?"

6. Historical and critical studies of comic books include Martin Barker, *Comics: Ideology, Power and the Critics;* Ariel Dorfman and Armand Mattelart, *How to Read Donald Duck: Imperialist Ideology in the Disney Comics;* Robert C. Harvey, *The Art of the Funnies: An Aesthetic History;* M. Thomas Inge, *Comics as Culture;* Greg S. McCue and Clive Bloom, *Dark Knights: The New Comics in Context;* Russel Nye, *The Unembarrassed Muse: The Popular Arts in America;* Maria Reidelbach, *Completely Mad: A History of the Comic Book and Magazine;* Roger Sabin, *Adult Comics: An Introduction;* and William W. Savage, Jr., *Comic Books and America, 1945–1954.*

7. For another feminist-influenced critical essay about comic books, see Linda Baughman, "A Psychoanalytic Reading of a Female Comic Book Hero."

8. For more information on contemporary women cartoonists, see Terri Sutton, "Media Kids: Terri Sutton on Bad-Girl Cartoonists."

9. Much of the information in the following paragraphs about women in the early comics comes from Maurice Horn's *Women in the Comics.*

10. Of course, women made their appearance in fighting teams long before the 1980s. The Invisible Girl was the female member of the Fantastic Four when the team first appeared in 1961. She was, however, notably less important than her male comrades. She also married the group's leader, Reed Richards, which tended to further diminish her pseudo-tough image.

11. For an article about the increasing numbers of gays and lesbians in comic books, see Andy Mangels, "Lavender Crusaders."

12. It comes as little surprise that Storm's toughness is repeatedly undermined. For instance, during one extended period, she loses her superhero powers, making it impossible for her to manipulate the weather. And in another incident, in "The Last Run" (*The Uncanny X-Men,* December 1986), she suffers a spiritual and mental breakdown, which results in her saying, "I have no right to lead the X-Men" (21). Storm is a strong leader, but her leadership skills are open to question. The impact of Storm's tough character is reduced by showing her fallibility.

13. Martha's moral but tough character continues to be evident in her later adventures. See her depiction in *Martha Washington Stranded in Space* and *Martha Washington Goes to War.*

Chapter 9. A Tough Girl for a New Century

1. For more on the first appearance of *Xena: Warrior Princess,* see Mike Duffy, "Xena Is Brash, Can-Do Heroine to Rival All Mythological Babes," and David Tobenkin, "MCA Hopes Xena Has Strength of Hercules."

2. Other articles on the success of *Hercules: The Legendary Journeys* include Jim Benson, " 'ET' Makes Syndie Gains: 'Hercules' Finishes Strong" and " 'Hercules' Muscles in on 'Trek' "; Jamie Bufalino, "Coming on Strong"; Tom Gliatto, "Sorbo the Greek"; Glenn Kenny, "Coming on Strong"; Rick Marin, "A Caring Demigod Kicks Butt"; Rita Street, "Hercules Lifts Genre"; David Tobenkin, "Hercules Muscles in on Competition," and "MCA Muscles in on Action Hours."

3. By 1996, the show had already been licensed to run until 1998 in fifteen countries (Ostrow G1). For additional information on the international success of the two shows, see Bill Carter, "Pow! Thwack! Bam! No Dubbing Needed."

4. The novels that have been written about Xena's adventures include Ru Emerson, *The Empty Throne, The Huntress and the Sphinx,* and *The Thief of Hermes.*

5. For more information about the Xena craze, see Glenn Kenny, "*Xena*-phobia? No, We Love Her"; David Rensin, "Lucy Lawless: The Woman Behind the Warrior"; Peter Richmond, "Mything Links"; Karen S. Schneider, "Xena-Phile"; and Frederick C. Szebin, "Lucy Lawless, Xena: Warrior Princess."

6. For example, see Kerry Milliron's picture books, *Princess in Peril* and *Queen of the Amazons.*

7. For more information on Gabrielle and the actress who plays her, see Allan Johnson, "What a (Side)kick!"

8. The continuing assumption that even in the 1990s heroes need to be male was brought home to me when I was watching a recent Paramount Pictures video that had a trailer of film clips to accompany the song "I Need a Hero." Every one of over a dozen action-adventure films that were shown featured a male hero. Just two clips bothered to portray a woman at all; in one of those cases she was hugging the male hero, who had presumably rescued her, and in the other she was the hero's love interest. Clearly, the assumption that the hero must be male is still alive and thriving as we approach a new century.

9. One of the episodes in which the lesbian overtones are unmistakable is "Girls Just Want to Have Fun," in which Gabrielle is endangered by baccae (female followers of the God Bacchus who look remarkably like modern vampires). They kill men and transform other women into baccae. Some of the baccae look strikingly like the women you might find at a trendy dance spot that caters to lesbians, and Gabrielle is transformed into a baccha after a suggestively sexual dance with them, leaving Xena to rescue her friend. Another episode with unavoidable lesbian overtones is "The Quest," in which Xena has presumably died, and Gabrielle is taking her body to be buried. When asked what she would have told Xena if she were still alive, Gabrielle reflects, "I would have told her how empty my life was before she came. . . . And that I love her." At another point, Gabrielle laments over Xena's body, "We'll be together again. One day." When Gabrielle visits Xena in a strange land between life and death, the two share what appears to be a kiss on the lips, but the second before the kiss occurs, the mythical landscape fades into Gabrielle's real life, where Gabrielle is shown kissing the King of Thieves, whose body is being inhabited by Xena's soul. These episodes show the way the program plays openly with lesbianism and the idea that the two women are lovers.

10. Although Xena adheres to the tradition that the woman superhero needs to be a beauty and reveal a lot of leg, there are also ways that her body fails to conform to such traditions. For instance, she is a big woman, standing 5'10" (Schneider 93). She is no Twiggy, and her costume is not as skimpy as most costumes for female superheroes. It is not skintight, as are most superhero costumes, which cling to a woman's every curve. The costume also does not reveal Xena's abdomen, which makes her appear tougher and less feminine.

Epilogue

Note to epigraph: Qtd. in Liz Brody, "A Shaggy-Dog Story from Alaska," 124.

1. For additional sources about Butcher's career, see "Butcher Extends Iditarod

Reign to 3 Years"; Larry Eldridge, "Urbanite Answers Call of Wild and Becomes Top Dog Sled Racer"; "Mush Mother"; John Skow, "Here's One Musher Who Is No Lazy Susan"; and Candice Szirak, "An Intense Drive."

2. Another notable new tough girl in popular culture is the female 82nd Airborne Division helicopter pilot who is part of the 1997 G.I. Joe Classic Collection—the first female action character for the G.I. Joe line since 1967, when the collection included a nurse.

Works Cited

Abbot, Joe. "They Came from Beyond the Center: Ideology and Political Textuality in the Radical Science Fiction Films of James Cameron." *Literature/Film Quarterly* 22.1 (1994): 21–27.

Abramowitz, Rachel. "Loving a Lie." *Premiere* Mar. 1993: 58–60.

Aisenberg, Nadya. *Ordinary Heroines: Transforming the Male Myth.* New York: Continuum, 1994.

Alien. Dir. Ridley Scott. Perf. Sigourney Weaver. 1979. Videocassette. Fox Video, 1992.

Alien 3. Dir. David Fincher. Perf. Sigourney Weaver. 1992. Videocassette. Fox Video, 1992.

Aliens. Dir. James Cameron. Perf. Sigourney Weaver. 1986. Videocassette. Fox Video, 1992.

Allen, Robert C., ed. *Channels of Discourse: Television and Contemporary Criticism.* Chapel Hill: University of North Carolina Press, 1987.

Alleva, Richard. "What's for Dinner? 'Silence' and 'Sleeping.'" *Commonweal* 5 Apr. 1991: 226–27.

Allison, Dorothy. *Bastard Out of Carolina.* New York: Dutton, 1992.

Anderson, Harry M., Jr. "Girl Plays Hockey with the Boys for 'Fun.'" *Detroit News* 16 Dec. 1993: 10.

APEX: Advanced Prototype EX-termination Unit. Dir. Phillip J. Roth. Perf. Lisa Ann Russell. Videocassette. Republic Pictures, 1993.

Arcudi, John. *Barb-Wire.* Milwaukie, Ore.: Dark Horse Comics, 1996.

Armitage, Shelley. "Rawhide Heroines: The Evolution of the Cowgirl and the Myth of America." *The American Self: Myth, Ideology, and Popular Culture.* Ed. Sam B. Girgus. Albuquerque: University of New Mexico Press, 1981. 166–81.

Armitt, Lucie, ed. *Where No Man Has Gone Before: Women and Science Fiction.* London: Routledge, 1991.

Atwood, Gretchen. "Extreme X-Filers." *10 Percent* July 1995: 12.

Austin, Mary. "The Walking Woman." *Stories from the Country of Lost Borders.* Ed. Marjorie Pryse. New Brunswick: Rutgers University Press, 1987. 255–62.

Bacon-Smith, Camille. *Enterprising Women: Television Fandom and the Creation of Popular Myth.* Philadelphia: University of Pennsylvania Press, 1992.

Baehr, Helen, and Gillian Dyer, eds. *Boxed In: Women and Television.* New York: Pandora, 1987.

Baehr, Helen, and Ann Gray, eds. *Turning It On: A Reader in Women and Media.* London: Arnold, 1996.

Ballaster, Ros, Margaret Beetham, Elizabeth Frazer, and Sandra Hebron. *Women's Worlds: Ideology, Femininity and the Woman's Magazine.* New York: Macmillan, 1991.

Banks, Iain M. *Against a Dark Background.* New York: Bantam, 1993.

Barbarella—Queen of the Galaxy. Dir. Roger Vadim. Perf. Jane Fonda. 1968. Videocassette. Paramount Home Video, 1980.

Barker, Martin. *Comics: Ideology, Power, and the Critics.* New York: Manchester University Press, 1989.

Barr, Marleen S., ed. *Future Females: A Critical Anthology.* Bowling Green: Bowling Green State University Popular Press, 1981.

——. *Lost in Space: Probing Feminist Science Fiction and Beyond.* Chapel Hill: University of North Carolina Press, 1993.

Barthel, Diane. *Putting on Appearances: Gender and Advertising.* Philadelphia: Temple University Press, 1988.

Barthes, Roland. *Mythologies.* 1957. New York: Hill and Wang, 1986.

Bartky, Sandra Lee. *Femininity and Domination: Studies in the Phenomenology of Oppression.* New York: Routledge, 1990.

Basic Instinct. Dir. Paul Verhoeven. Perf. Michael Douglas and Sharon Stone. Carolco/Le Studio Canal, 1992.

Baudrillard, Jean. "The Anorexic Ruins." *Looking Back on the End of the World.* Ed. Dietmar Kamper and Christoph Wulf. New York: Semiotext(e), 1989. 29–45.

Baughman, Linda. "A Psychoanalytic Reading of a Female Comic Book Hero: *Elektra: Assassin.*" *Women and Language* 13.1 (1990): 27–30.

Baumgold, Julie. "Killer Women." *New York* 29 July 1991: 24+.

Beach, Rex. *The Spoilers.* 1906. Upper Saddle River: Gregg Press, 1969.

Bederman, Gail. *Manliness and Civilization: A Cultural History of Gender and Race in the United States, 1880–1917.* Chicago: University of Chicago Press, 1995.

Beese, P. J. "White Wings." *Women at War.* Ed. Lois McMaster Bujold and Roland J. Green. New York: Tor, 1995. 247–65.

Benson, Jim. "'ET' Makes Syndie Gains: 'Hercules' Finishes Strong." *Variety* 4 Sept. 1995: 29.

——. "'Hercules' Muscles in on 'Trek.'" *Variety* 15 Apr. 1996: 84.

Ben-Tov, Sharona. *The Artificial Paradise: Science Fiction and American Reality.* Ann Arbor: University of Michigan Press, 1995.

Berger, Arion. "Wunderkind." *Harper's Bazaar* Nov. 1991: 124+.

Berger, John. *Ways of Seeing.* London: Penguin, 1972.

Berger, Maurice, Brian Wallis, and Simon Watson, eds. *Constructing Masculinity.* New York: Routledge, 1995.

"The Best and the Worst Looks of the '90s." *Vogue* Jan. 1996: 122–31.

Betterton, Rosemary, ed. *Looking on: Images of Femininity in the Visual Arts and Media.* London: Pandora, 1987.

Bijan. Advertisement. *Vanity Fair* Jan. 1993: 17.

Billson, Anne. "Back into the Closet." *New Statesman and Society* 5.216 (21 Aug. 1992): 35.

Bingham, Dennis. *Acting Male: Masculinities in the Films of James Stewart, Jack Nicholson, and Clint Eastwood.* New Brunswick: Rutgers University Press, 1994.

Birch, Helen, ed. *Moving Targets: Women, Murder and Representation.* Berkeley: University of California Press, 1994.

Bischoff, David. "Opening the X-Files: Behind the Scenes of TV's Hottest Show." *Omni* Dec. 1994: 42+.

Black Widow. Dir. Bob Rafelson. Perf. Theresa Russell and Debra Winger. Twentieth-Century Fox, 1987.

Blair, Karin. "Sex and *Star Trek.*" *Science-Fiction Studies* 10.3 (1983): 292–97.

Blake, John. " 'X-Files' Attracts Devoted Following." *Cincinnati Enquirer* 20 May 1996: C5.

Blanchard, Jayne. "At the Movies: *Alien 3.*" *Washingtonian* July 1992: 22.

The Blood of Heroes. Dir. David Peoples. Perf. Joan Chen and Rutger Hauer. 1989. Videocassette. HBO Video, 1990.

Bloodsport. Dir. Newt Arnold. Perf. Jean-Claude Van Damme. 1987. TBS, 10 Oct. 1996.

Boker, Pamela S. "America's Women Superheroes: Power, Gender, and the Comics." *Mid-Atlantic Almanac* 2 (1993): 106–18.

Bonnie and Clyde. Dir. Arthur Penn. Perf. Warren Beatty and Faye Dunaway. Warner Brothers, 1967.

Bordo, Susan. *Unbearable Weight: Feminism, Western Culture, and the Body.* Berkeley: University of California Press, 1993.

Brand, Max. *Destry Rides Again.* 1930. Roslyn: Black's Readers Service, 1958.

Brody, Liz. "A Shaggy-Dog Story from Alaska." *Shape* Feb. 1994: 110+.

Brooks, Tim, and Earle Marsh. *The Complete Directory of Prime Time Network TV Shows, 1946–Present.* New York: Ballantine Books, 1979.

Brown, Mary Ellen, ed. *Television and Women's Culture: The Politics of the Popular.* London: Sage, 1990.

Brown, Terry. "The Butch Femme Fatale." *The Lesbian Postmodern.* New York: Columbia University Press, 1994. 229–43.

Bruning, Fred. "Tough, Smart and a Presidential Bedmate." *Maclean's* 21 Dec. 1992: 9.

Budgeon, Shelley. "Fashion Magazine Advertising: Constructing Femininity in the 'Postfeminist' Era." *Gender and Utopia in Advertising: A Critical Reader.* Ed. Luigi and Alessandra Manca. Lisle, Ill.: Procopian Press, 1994.

Bufalino, Jamie. "Coming on Strong." *TV Guide* 15 July 1995: 16–18.

Bundtzen, Lynda K. "Monstrous Mothers: Medusa, Grendel and Now Alien." *Film Quarterly* 40.3 (1987): 11–17.

Burroughs, Edgar Rice. *The Gods of Mars.* 1912. Garden City: Nelson Doubleday, 1971.

——. *Tarzan of the Apes.* 1914. New York: Ballantine Books, 1973.

"Butcher Extends Iditarod Reign to Three Years." *Sporting News* 28 Mar. 1988: 50.

"Butcher, Susan." *Current Biography* 52.6 (1991): 96–99.

Butler, Judith. *Gender Trouble: Feminism and the Subversion of Identity.* New York: Routledge, 1990.

Buxton, David. *From the Avengers to Miami Vice: Form and Ideology in Television Series.* Manchester: Manchester University Press, 1990.

Byers, Thomas B. "Terminating the Postmodern: Masculinity and Pomophobia." *Modern Fiction Studies* 41.1 (1995): 5–33.

Calvin Klein. Advertisement. *Vanity Fair* Sept. 1992: 16–17.

Calvin Klein Jeans. Advertisement. *Vanity Fair* Aug. 1984: 3.

Carralero, Ricky. *Double Impact.* Issue 4. Miami: High Impact Studios, 1995.

Carrington, Kerry, and Anna Bennett. " 'Girls' Mags' and the Pedagogical Formation of the Girl." *Feminisms and Pedagogies of Everyday Life.* Ed. Carmen Luke. Albany: State University of New York Press, 1996. 147–66.

Carter, Bill. "Pow! Thwack! Bam! No Dubbing Needed." *New York Times* 3 Nov. 1996, sec. 4:6.
Case, Sue-Ellen. "Towards a Butch-Femme Aesthetic." *Discourse* 11 (1988–89): 55–73.
Castle, Terry. *Masquerade and Civilization: The Carnivalesque in Eighteenth-Century English Culture and Fiction.* Stanford: Stanford University Press, 1986.
Champlin, Charles. "Jaclyn Smith: The Cool 'Angel.'" *McCall's* July 1977: 36+.
Charnas, Suzy McKee. "Scorched Supper on New Niger." *Women of Wonder: The Contemporary Years.* Ed. Pamela Sargent. San Diego: Harcourt Brace, 1995. 47–80.
Cherryh, C. J. *Downbelow Station.* New York: Daw Books, 1981.
Chibnall, Steven. "Avenging the Past." *New Society* 28 Mar. 1985: 476–77.
Christian, Deborah. *Mainline.* New York: Tor, 1996.
Claremont, Chris. "First Friends." *Classic X-Men* 1.2 (19 Oct. 1986). New York: Marvel Comics.
——. "Freedom Is a Four Letter Word." *Uncanny X-Men* 1.206 (June 1986). New York: Marvel Comics.
——. *The Uncanny X-Men: From the Ashes.* New York: Marvel Comics, 1990.
——. "The Last Run." *Uncanny X-Men* 1.212 (Dec. 1986). New York: Marvel Comics.
——. "The Morning After." *Uncanny X-Men* 1.210 (Oct. 1986). New York: Marvel Comics.
Clark, Danae. "Commodity Lesbianism." *Camera Obscura* 25–26 (1991): 181–201.
Clarke, Steve. "U.K. Requires 'X' Ray Vision." *Variety* 29 May 1995: 36.
Cohan, Steven, and Ina Rae Hark, eds. *Screening the Male: Exploring Masculinities in Hollywood Cinema.* London: Routledge, 1993.
Cohen, Joel H. *The Six Million Dollar Man and the Bionic Woman: Lee Majors and Lindsay Wagner.* New York: Scholastic, 1976.
Commando. Dir. Mark L. Lester. Perf. Arnold Schwarzenegger. 1985. Videocassette. CBS Fox Video, 1986.
Committee on the Judiciary. *Comic Books and Juvenile Delinquency.* Washington, D.C.: U.S. Government Printing Office, 1955.
Conlon, James. "Silencing Lambs and Educating Women." *Post Script* 12.1 (1992): 3–12.
Connell, R. W. *Masculinities.* Berkeley: University of California Press, 1995.
Constigan, Kelly. "Marathon Medic." *Savvy Woman* May 1989: 66+.
Corliss, Richard. "The Ladies Who Lounge." *Time* 7 Oct. 1996: 86–87.
——. "A Screen Gem Turns Director." *Time* 14 Oct. 1991: 68–72.
Cranny-Francis, Anne. "Sexuality and Sex-Role Stereotyping in *Star Trek.*" *Science Fiction Studies* 12.3 (1985): 274–84.
Creed, Barbara. "*Alien* and the Monstrous-Feminine." *Alien Zone: Cultural Theory and Contemporary Science Fiction Cinema.* Ed. Annette Kuhn. New York: Verso, 1990. 128–41.
Cunningham, Kim. "Captain's Courageous." *People Weekly* 16 Oct. 1994: 116.
Curtis, Bruce. "The Wimp Factor." *American Heritage* Nov. 1989: 40+.
D'Acci, Julie. "Defining Women: The Case of *Cagney and Lacey.*" *Private Screenings: Television and the Female Consumer.* Ed. Lynn Spiegel and Denise Mann. Minneapolis: University of Minnesota Press, 1992. 169–201.
Dargis, Manohla. "Joust Between Friends." *Village Voice* 27 Feb. 1990: 66.
Dauphin, Gary. "Reel to Reel: Tank Girl." *Village Voice* 11 Apr. 1995: 64.

Davidson, Bill. "The 'Bionic Woman' Flexed Her Financial Muscles . . ." *TV Guide* 8 May 1976: 21+.

Davis, Erik. "Earth's Most Wanted." *Village Voice* 26 Oct. 1993: 49–50.

Davis, Fred. *Fashion, Culture, and Identity.* Chicago: University of Chicago Press, 1992.

Davis, Rebecca Harding. *Life in the Iron Mills.* 1861. Old Westbury, N.Y.: Feminist, 1985.

Dean, Peter. "Wind Up." *Sight & Sound* Nov. 1993: 62.

Dellamora, Richard, ed. *Postmodern Apocalypse: Theory and Cultural Practice at the End.* Philadelphia: University of Pennsylvania Press, 1995.

The Demolitionist. Dir. Robert Kurtzman. Perf. Bruce Abbott and Nicole Eggert. Videocassette. A-Pix Entertainment, 1996.

D'Erasmo, Stacey. "Xenaphilia." *Village Voice* 26 Dec. 1995: 47.

Dickinson, Chris. "For the Love of Lucy," *St. Louis Post-Dispatch* 5 Sept. 1996, sec. GO: 55.

Doane, Mary Ann. *Femmes Fatales: Feminism, Film Theory, Psychoanalysis.* New York: Routledge, 1991.

——. "Technophilia: Technology, Representation, and the Feminine." *Body/Politics: Women and the Discourse of Science.* Ed. Mary Jacobus, Evelyn Fox Keller, and Sally Shuttleworth. London: Routledge, 1990. 163–76.

Dolan, Frances E. *Dangerous Familiars: Representations of Domestic Crime in England, 1550–1700.* Ithaca: Cornell University Press, 1994.

Dolby, Tom. "Making the Xena." *Village Voice* 3 Sept. 1996: 6.

Doner, Kalia. "Women's Magazines: Slouching Towards Feminism." *Social Policy* 23 (1993): 37–43.

Dorfman, Ariel, and Armand Mattelart. *How to Read Donald Duck: Imperialist Ideology in the Disney Comic.* 1975. New York: International General, 1984.

"Do's and Don'ts." *Glamour* Sept. 1992: 344.

Doty, Alexander. *Making Things Perfectly Queer: Interpreting Mass Culture.* Minneapolis: University of Minnesota Press, 1993.

Double Impact. Dir. Sheldon Lettrich. Perf. Jean-Claude Van Damme. Columbia Pictures, 1991.

Double Indemnity. Dir. Billy Wilder. Perf. Fred MacMurray, Barbara Stanwyck, and Edward G. Robinson. Paramount, 1944.

Douglas, Susan J. *Where the Girls Are: Growing Up Female with the Mass Media.* New York: Random House, 1994.

Dow, Bonnie J. *Prime-Time Feminism: Television, Media Culture, and the Women's Movement Since 1970.* Philadelphia: University of Pennsylvania Press, 1996.

Dowd, Maureen. "Looking for Space Aliens (and Denying Yale)." *New York Times* 26 Mar. 1995: 37+.

Duffy, Margaret, and J. Michael Gotcher. "Crucial Advice on How to Get the Guy: The Rhetorical Vision of Power and Seduction in the Teen Magazine *YM.*" *Journal of Communication Inquiry* 20.1 (1996): 32–48.

Duffy, Martha. "Take this Job and Love it." *Time* 6 Aug. 1990: 70–72.

Duffy, Mike. "Xena Is Brash, Can-Do Heroine to Rival All Mythological Babes." *Detroit News and Free Press* 8 Sept. 1995: E3.

Durham, Gigi. "The Taming of the Shrew: Women's Magazines and the Regulation of Desire." *Journal of Communication Inquiry* 20.1 (1996): 18–31.

Durkee, Cutler. "When Angels Were the Rage." *People Weekly* 20 Oct. 1986: 112–21.

Dyer, Gillian. "Women and Television: An Overview." *Boxed In: Women and Television.* Ed. Helen Baehr and Gillian Dyer. New York: Pandora, 1987. 6–16.
Easthope, Antony. *What a Man's Gotta Do: The Masculine Myth in Popular Culture.* Boston: Unwin Hyman, 1990.
Edelstein, David. "Movies: Mother of the Year." *Rolling Stone* 28 Aug. 1986: 41–42.
Edwards, Ted. *X-Files Confidential: The Unauthorized X-Philes Compendium.* Boston: Little, Brown, 1996.
Eldridge, Larry. "Urbanite Answers Call of Wild and Becomes Top Dog Sled Racer." *Christian Science Monitor* 4 Mar. 1988: 18.
Eller, Daryn. "Fighting Fit." *Harper's Bazaar* Aug. 1992: 122–25.
Elley, Derek. "Aliens." *Films and Filming* 383 (Aug. 1986): 34–35.
Emerson, Ru. *The Empty Throne.* New York: Boulevard Books, 1996.
———. *The Huntress and the Sphinx.* New York: Boulevard Books, 1997.
———. *The Thief of Hermes.* New York: Boulevard Books, 1997.
Emery, C. Eugene, Jr. "Paranormal and Paranoia Intermingle on Fox T.V.'s 'X-Files.'" *Skeptical Inquirer* 19.2 (Mar.–Apr. 1995): 18–19.
Engelhardt, Tom. "The Shortcake Strategy." *Watching Television: A Pantheon Guide to Popular Culture.* Ed. Todd Gitlin. New York: Pantheon Books, 1986. 68–110.
Estep, Rhoda. "Women's Roles in Crime as Depicted by Television and Newspapers." *Journal of Popular Culture* 16.3 (1982): 151–56.
Evans, Caroline, and Minna Thornton. *Women and Fashion: A New Look.* New York: Quartet Books, 1989.
Evolution. Advertisement. *Vogue* Mar. 1996: 343.
Ewen, Stuart. *All Consuming Images: The Politics of Style in Contemporary Culture.* New York: Basic, 1988.
———. *Captains of Consciousness: Advertising and the Social Roots of the Consumer Culture.* New York: McGraw-Hill, 1976.
Fagan, Gregory P. "Cheap Thrills: *Blood of Heroes.*" *Video Review* Oct. 1990: 119.
Fatal Attraction. Dir. Adrian Lyne. Perf. Glenn Close and Michael Douglas. Paramount Pictures, 1987.
Felperin, Leslie. "Reviews: Tank Girl." *Sight & Sound* 5.7 (July 1995): 54–55.
"Feminine Denim." *Cosmopolitan* Aug. 1996: 156–67.
Ferguson, Marjorie. *Forever Feminine: Women's Magazines and the Cult of Femininity.* London: Heinemann, 1983.
Fink, Mitchell. "Actresses Tough It Out." *People Weekly* 7 June 1993: 37.
Fiske, John. "British Cultural Studies." In Allen, ed., *Channels of Discourse,* 254–89.
———. *Television Culture.* London: Methuen, 1987.
———. *Understanding Popular Culture.* Boston: Unwin Hyman, 1989.
"The $500,000 Timex." *Time* 26 Apr. 1976: 85.
Flagg, Fannie. *Fried Green Tomatoes at the Whistle Stop Cafe.* New York: Random House, 1987.
Fleming, Charles. "That's Why the Lady Is a Champ." *Newsweek* 7 June 1993: 66.
For Your Eyes Only. Dir. John Glen. Perf. Roger Moore and Carole Bouquet. Videocassette. MGM/UA Home Entertainment, 1981.
"Foster, Jodie." *Current Biography* 53.8 (1992): 200–04.
Frazer, Elizabeth. "Teenage Girls Reading *Jackie.*" *Media, Culture and Society* 9 (1987): 407–25.
Friedländer, Saul, Gerald Holton, Leo Marx, and Eugene Skolnikoff, eds. *Visions of Apocalypse: End or Rebirth?* New York: Holmes & Meier, 1985.
Friedman, Norman L. "*The Terminator:* Changes in Critical Evaluations of Cultural Productions." *Journal of Popular Culture* 28.1 (1994): 73–80.

"Full Pants Ahead!" *Mademoiselle* July 1988: 102–07.

"Funny Face." *Vanity Fair* July 1987, 90–93.

Gabbard, Krin, and Glen O. Gabbard. "Phallic Women in the Contemporary Cinema." *American Imago* 50.4 (1993): 421–39.

Galaxis. Dir. William Mesa. Perf. Richard Moll and Brigitte Nielson. Videocassette. Interlight/Osmosis Productions, 1995.

Gamman, Lorraine, and Margaret Marshment, eds. *The Female Gaze: Women as Viewers of Popular Culture*. Seattle: Real Comet Press, 1989.

Garber, Marjorie. *Vested Interests: Cross-Dressing and Cultural Anxiety*. New York: Routledge, 1992.

Garrett, Greg. "Objecting to Objectification: Re-Viewing the Feminine in *The Silence of the Lambs*." *Journal of Popular Culture* 27.4 (1994): 1–12.

Generation X. Fox Television. 20 Feb. 1996.

Genge, N. E. *The Unofficial X-Files Companion to the Mysteries, Conspiracies and Really Strange Truths Behind the Show*. New York: Crown, 1995.

Gerosa, Melina. "Jodie Loses Her Cool." *Ladies' Home Journal* Feb. 1995: 152+.

Gibson, William. *Neuromancer*. New York: Ace Books, 1984.

Gilda. Dir. Charles Vidor. Perf. Rita Hayworth, Glenn Ford, and George Macready. Columbia, 1946.

Gilmore, Mikal. "Comic Genius." *Rolling Stone* 27 Mar. 1986: 56+.

Gledhill, Christine. "Pleasurable Negotiations." *Female Spectators: Looking at Film and Television*. Ed. E. Deidre Pribram. London: Verso, 1988. 64–89.

Gliatto, Tom. "Occult Leader." *People Weekly* 13 Mar. 1995: 97–98.

———. "Sorbo the Greek." *People Weekly* 3 July 1995: 81–83.

———. "X-ellence." *People Weekly* 9 Oct. 1995: 72+.

Gloeckner, Phoebe. "Comic Books: A Medium Deserving Another Look." *ETC: A Review of General Semantics* 46.3 (1989): 246–47.

Goldberg, Jonathan. "Recalling Totalities: The Mirrored Stages of Arnold Schwarzenegger." *differences* 4.1 (1992): 172–204.

GoldenEye. Dir. Martin Campbell. Perf. Pierce Brosnan, Izabella Scorupco, and Famke Janssen. United Artists, 1995.

Goldsmith, Steven. *Unbuilding Jerusalem: Apocalypse and Romantic Representation*. Ithaca: Cornell University Press, 1993.

Gomez, Jewelle. "The Hero of Us All." *Village Voice* 2 June 1992: S5.

" 'Good-Chap Sexuality.' " *Newsweek* 4 Apr. 1966: 94.

Goodhall, Jane R. "Aliens." *Southern Review* 23.1 (1990): 73–82.

Goodwin, Andrew, and Garry Whannel, eds. *Understanding Television*. London: Routledge, 1990.

Goscilo, Margaret. "Deconstructing *The Terminator*." *Film Criticism* 12.2 (1987–1988): 37–52.

Grant, James. "Red Hot Right Now: David Duchovny." *Cosmopolitan* 1 Oct. 1995: 144.

"The Great Suit Caper." *Essence* Nov. 1988: 84–91.

Greenberg, Harvey R. "Fembo: *Aliens'* Intentions." *Journal of Popular Film and Television* 15.4 (1988): 165–71.

———. "Reimagining the Gargoyle: Psychoanalytic Notes on *Alien*." *Close Encounters: Film, Feminism and Science Fiction*. Ed. Constance Penley, et al. Minneapolis: University of Minnesota Press, 1991. 83–104.

Greenberg, James. "One Tough Cookie." *Harper's Bazaar* Aug. 1993: 92+.

Grenier, Richard. "Killer Bimbos." *Commentary* 92.3 (1991): 50–52.

Griffin, P. M. "Lizard." *Women at War.* Ed. Lois McMaster Bujold and Roland J. Green. New York: Tor, 1995. 341–67.

Griffith, Nicola. *Ammonite.* New York: Ballantine Books, 1992.

Griggers, Cathy. "A Certain Tension in the Visual/Cultural Field: Helmut Newton, Deborah Turbeville and the *VOGUE* Fashion Layout." *differences* 2.2 (1990): 76–104.

Grizzard, Lewis. "Just Think of Hillary as First Tough Cookie." *Atlanta Journal Constitution* 22 Nov. 1992: C1.

Gross, Larry. "Out of the Mainstream: Sexual Minorities and the Mass Media." *Remote Control: Television, Audiences, and Cultural Power.* Ed. Ellen Seiter, Hans Borchers, Gabriele Kreutzner, and Eva-Maria Warth. New York: Routledge, 1989. 130–49.

Gross, Linden. "Casting Call." *Self* Dec. 1988: 76–81.

Halberstam, Judith. "F2M: The Making of Female Masculinity." *The Lesbian Postmodern.* Ed. Laura Doan. New York: Columbia University Press, 1994. 210–28.

———. "Skinflick: Posthuman Gender in Jonathan Demme's *The Silence of the Lambs.*" *Camera Obscura* 27 (Sept. 1991): 37–52.

———. "Techno-homo: On Bathrooms, Butches, and Sex with Furniture." *Processed Lives: Gender and Technology in Everyday Lives.* Ed. Jennifer Terry and Melodie Calvert. New York: Routledge, 1997. 184–93.

Hammonds, Karl. "Lakiea Coffen Is Tough Enough." *Afro-American* 19 Aug. 1995: A11.

Harrington, Michael. "It's a Bird, It's a Plane, It's . . ." *Spectator* 4 Nov. 1995: 8–9.

Hart, Lynda. *Fatal Women: Lesbian Sexuality and the Mark of Aggression.* Princeton: Princeton University Press, 1994.

Hartsoe, Everette. *Lethal Strike.* Issue 3. Hickory, N.C.: London Night Studios, 1995.

Harvey, Robert C. *The Art of the Funnies: An Aesthetic History.* Jackson: University Press of Mississippi, 1994.

Haug, Frigga, ed. *Female Sexualization: A Collective Work of Memory.* 1983. London: Verso, 1987.

Haywood, Richette L. "Secretary Hazel O'Leary: Bright, Charming, Tough." *Ebony* Feb. 1995: 94–100.

Heath, Stephen. "Representing Television." *Logics of Television: Essays in Cultural Criticism.* Ed. Patricia Mellencamp. Bloomington: Indiana University Press, 1990. 267–302.

Hebdige, Dick. *Subculture: The Meaning of Style.* New York: Methuen, 1979.

Heinlein, Robert. *Friday.* New York: Holt, Rinehart, 1982.

Helford, Elyce Rae. "Reading Space Fictions: Representations of Gender, Race, and Species in Popular Culture." Ph.D. diss., University of Iowa, 1992.

Hemingway, Ernest. *A Farewell to Arms.* 1929. New York: Scribner's, 1957.

———. *For Whom the Bell Tolls.* New York: Scribner's, 1940.

Hersey, Brook. "Word on Movies: Women Fight Back." *Glamour* May 1991: 174.

Higbie, Andrea. "The Nice Woman's Guide to Being Tough." *Ladies' Home Journal* Apr. 1995: 114+.

Hirshey, Gerri. "Jodie Foster." *Rolling Stone* 21 Mar. 1991: 34+.

Hitt, Jack. "X-Factor Actor." *Playboy* Nov. 1995: 92+.

Holmlund, Christine. "A Decade of Deadly Dolls: Hollywood and the Woman Killer." *Moving Targets: Women, Murder and Representation.* Ed. Helen Birch. Berkeley: University of California Press, 1994. 127–51.

Hopewell, John. "Home-grown TV, Brand 'X' Fare Best." *Variety* 25 Sept. 1995: 84+.

Horn, Maurice. *Women in the Comics.* New York: Chelsea House, 1980.

Hossent, Harry. *Gangster Movies: Gangsters, Hoodlums and Tough Guys of the Screen.* London: Octopus Books, 1974.

Houston, David. *Lindsay Wagner: Superstar of the Bionic Woman.* New York: Belmont Tower Books, 1976.

Hurston, Zora Neale. *Their Eyes Were Watching God.* 1937. New York: Harper & Row, 1990.

Ibsen, Henrik. *Hedda Gabler.* 1890. *Six Plays by Henrik Ibsen.* Trans. Eva Le Gallienne. New York: Modern Library, 1957. 341–428.

Ingall, Margorie. "Supergirls." *Sassy* Nov. 1994: 68+.

Inge, M. Thomas. *Comics as Culture.* Jackson: University Press of Mississippi, 1990.

Inness, Sherrie A. *Intimate Communities: Representation and Social Transformation in Women's College Fiction, 1895–1910.* Bowling Green: Bowling Green State University Popular Press, 1995.

——. *The Lesbian Menace: Ideology, Identity, and the Representation of Lesbian Life.* Amherst: University of Massachusetts Press, 1997.

Inness, Sherrie A., ed. *Delinquents and Debutantes: Twentieth-Century American Girls' Cultures.* New York: New York University Press, 1998.

——. *Nancy Drew and Company: Culture, Gender, and Girls' Series.* Bowling Green: Bowling Green Popular Press, 1997.

Inness, Sherrie A., and Michele E. Lloyd. "G.I. Joes in Barbie Land: Recontextualizing Butch in Twentieth-Century Lesbian Culture." *Queer Studies: A Lesbian, Gay, Bisexual, and Transgender Anthology.* Ed. Brett Beemyn and Mickey Eliason. New York: New York University Press, 1996. 9–34.

Israel, Betsy. "Where No Ma'am Has Gone." *People Weekly* 30 Jan. 1995: 45–46.

James, JoAnn, and William J. Cloonan, eds. *Apocalyptic Visions Past and Present.* Tallahassee: University Presses of Florida, 1988.

Jeffords, Susan. " 'The Battle of the Big Mamas': Feminism and the Alienation of Women." *Journal of American Culture* 10.3 (1987): 73–84.

——. *Hard Bodies: Hollywood Masculinity in the Reagan Era.* New Brunswick: Rutgers University Press, 1994.

——. *The Remasculinization of America: Gender and the Vietnam War.* Bloomington: Indiana University Press, 1989.

Johnson, Allan. "Real Partners." *Chicago Tribune* 24 Nov. 1995, sec. 5: 3.

——. "What a (Side)kick!" *Chicago Tribune* 28 May 1996, sec. 7: 7.

Johnson, Mandy. "Women as Action Heroes." *Glamour* Mar. 1994: 153.

Jones, Amelia. " 'She Was Bad News': Male Paranoia and the Contemporary New Woman." *Camera Obscura* 25–26 (Jan.–May 1991): 297–320.

Jones, Ann. *Women Who Kill.* New York: Holt, Rinehart and Winston, 1980.

Jordan, Catherine. "Go Ahead, Make Her Day." *Los Angeles Times* 26 Apr. 1994: D1+.

Joyrich, Lynne. *Re-Viewing Reception: Television, Gender, and Postmodern Culture.* Bloomington: Indiana University Press, 1996.

Kael, Pauline. "The Current Cinema." *New Yorker* 11 Aug. 1986: 74+.

Kaganoff, Penny. "Trade Comics: *Give Me Liberty: An American Dream.*" *Publisher's Weekly* 13 Dec. 1991: 52.

Kamper, Dietmar, and Christoph Wulf, eds. *Looking Back on the End of the World.* Trans. David Antal. New York: Semiotext(e), 1989.

Kantrowitz, Barbara, and Adam Rogers. "The Truth Is X-ed Out There." *Newsweek* 5 Dec. 1994: 66.

Kaplan, Michael. "Invasion of the X-Philes." *TV Guide* 20 Jan. 1996: 32–34.

Kastor, Elizabeth. "Woman of Steel." *Washington Post* 21 Sept. 1996: C1+.

Kauffmann, Stanley. "Gluttons for Punishment." *New Republic* 18 Feb. 1991: 48–49.

Kavanagh, James H. "Feminism, Humanism and Science in *Alien*." *Alien Zone: Cultural Theory and Contemporary Science Fiction Cinema*. Ed. Annette Kuhn. New York: Verso, 1990. 73–81.

Kelley, Edith Summers. *Weeds*. 1923. Old Westbury: Feminist, 1982.

Kenny, Glenn. "Coming on Strong." *TV Guide* 19 Nov. 1994: 42.

——. "*Xena*-phobia? No, We Love Her." *TV Guide* 30 Sept. 1995: 37.

Ketterer, David. *New Worlds for Old: The Apocalyptic Imagination, Science Fiction, and American Literature*. Bloomington: Indiana University Press, 1974.

Kidwell, Claudia Brush, and Valerie Steele, eds. *Men and Women: Dressing the Part*. Washington, D.C.: Smithsonian Institution Press, 1989.

Kimmel, Michael. *Manhood in America: A Cultural History*. New York: Free Press, 1996.

Kingston, Maxine Hong. *The Woman Warrior: Memoirs of a Girlhood Among Ghosts*. 1976. New York: Vintage Books, 1977.

Kipling, Rudyard. *Captains Courageous: A Story of the Grand Banks*. New York: Century, 1897.

Kirkham, Pat, and Janet Thumin, eds. *Me Jane: Masculinity, Movies and Women*. New York: St. Martin's, 1995.

——. *You Tarzan: Masculinity, Movies and Men*. London: Lawrence and Wishart, 1993.

Klady, Leonard. "Film Review: *Tank Girl*." *Variety* 3 Apr. 1995: 142.

Klawans, Stuart. "Films: *The Silence of the Lambs*." *Nation* 25 Feb. 1991: 246–48.

Korpivaara, Ari. "Role Over, Rambo." *Ms.* Sept. 1986: 14.

Krupp, Charla. "She's Bald and She's Back!" *Glamour* June 1992: 163.

La Femme Nikita. Dir. Luc Besson. Perf. Anne Parillaud. 1990. Videocassette. Vidmark Entertainment, 1991.

Lane, Christina. "The Liminal Iconography of Jodie Foster." *Journal of Popular Films and Television* 22.4 (1995): 149–53.

Lang, Jeffrey S. "Whatever Happened to the Man of Tomorrow? An Examination of the American Monomyth and the Comic Book Superhero." *Journal of Popular Culture* 22.3 (1988): 157–73.

Larson, Kay. "Tough Women." *Vogue* Oct. 1983: 222.

"The Leather Forecast." *Vogue* Oct. 1994: 386–91.

"Leather or Not." *Glamour* Sept. 1995: 254–59.

"The Leather Report." *Seventeen* Nov. 1995: 136–41.

Lebowitz, Lisa. "Genteel Dapper Dandy Appeal." *Harper's Bazaar* Apr. 1988: 208–11.

Le Carré, John. *The Little Drummer Girl*. New York: Knopf, 1983.

Lefanu, Sarah. *In The Chinks of the World Machine: Feminism and Science Fiction*. London: Women's Press, 1988.

Leonard, George. "Body Double." *Self* July 1992: 86–93.

Leonard, John. "The Next Next Generation." *New York* 30 Jan. 1995: 82.

Lewicki, Zbigniew. *The Bang and the Whimper: Apocalypse and Entropy in American Literature*. Westport: Greenwood, 1984.

Lipsitz, George. *Time Passages: Collective Memory and American Popular Culture.* Minneapolis: University of Minnesota Press, 1990.

Liu, Albert. "The Last Days of Arnold Schwarzenegger." *Genders* 18 (1993): 102–12.

Logan, Michael. "Voyager: A 'Star Trek' Is Born." *TV Guide* 8 Oct. 1994: 14–20.

Long, Sydney. "For the Right Reason." *Women at War.* Ed. Lois McMaster Bujold and Roland J. Green. New York: Tor, 1995. 135–53.

Longsdorf, Amy. "Peak Condition." *Everybody's News* 21 Feb. 1997: 8.

Lottman, Eileen. *The Bionic Woman: Extracurricular Activities.* New York: Berkley, 1977.

Lovece, Frank. *The X-Files Declassified: The Unauthorized Guide.* Secaucus: Carol, 1996.

Lowry, Brian. *The Truth Is Out There: The Official Guide to the X-Files.* New York: HarperPrism, 1995.

Lynn, Elizabeth A. *The Northern Girl.* New York: Berkley Books, 1980.

Ma Barker's Killer Brood. Dir. Bill Karn. Perf. Lurene Tuttle, Tristram Coffin, Paul Dubov, and Nelson Leigh. Filmservice, 1960.

MacDonald, Eileen. *Shoot the Women First.* New York: Random House, 1991.

Macdonald, Myra. *Representing Women: Myths of Femininity in the Popular Media.* London: Arnold, 1995.

MacNamara, Mark. "Can a Woman Kill Like a Man?" *Los Angeles Magazine* Aug. 1991: 72–80.

Madden, David, ed. *Tough Guy Writers of the Thirties.* Carbondale: Southern Illinois University Press, 1968.

Maio, Kathi. "Film: Women Who Murder for the Man." *Ms.* Nov. 1991: 82–84.

Mangels, Andy. "Lavender Crusaders." *Advocate* 1 Aug. 1989: 54–60.

Mann, Coramae Richey. *When Women Kill.* Albany: State University of New York Press, 1996.

Mano, D. Keith. "So You Want to Be an Angel." *Life* May 1988: 144–46.

Mansfield, Stephanie. "Gillian Looks Like a Million." *TV Guide* 6–12 July 1996: 6–14.

Marin, Rick. "A Caring Demigod Kicks Butt." *Newsweek* 5 June 1995: 65.

Marling, Karal Ann. *As Seen on TV: the Visual Culture of Everyday Life in the 1950s.* Cambridge: Harvard University Press, 1994.

Martin, James. "X-Appeal." *America* 21 Oct. 1995: 22.

"Masculine Tailoring and Feminine Touches." *Elle* Mar. 1997: 352–61.

May, John R. *Toward a New Earth: Apocalypse in the American Novel.* Notre Dame: University of Notre Dame Press, 1972.

McConnell, Frank. "Comic Relief." *Commonweal* 28 Feb. 1992: 21–22.

McCracken, Ellen. *Decoding Women's Magazines from Mademoiselle to Ms.* New York: St. Martin's, 1993.

——. "Demystifying *Cosmopolitan:* Five Critical Methods." *Journal of Popular Culture* 16.2 (1982): 30–42.

McCue, Greg S., and Clive Bloom. *Dark Knights: The New Comics in Context.* Boulder, Colo.: Pluto, 1993.

McCullers, Carson. *The Ballad of the Sad Café and Other Stories.* New York: Bantam Books, 1991.

McGrath, Ellie. "Tough Enough to Win the West." *Savvy Woman* May 1990: 12.

McMahon, Kathryn. "The *Cosmopolitan* Ideology and the Management of Desire." *Journal of Sex Research* 27.3 (1990): 381–96.

McRobbie, Angela. *Feminism and Youth Culture: From "Jackie" to "Just Seventeen."* Boston: Unwin Hyman, 1991.
Meehan, Diana M. *Ladies of the Evening: Women Characters of Prime-Time Television.* Metuchen: Scarecrow, 1983.
Mellen, Joan. *Big Bad Wolves: Masculinity in the American Film.* New York: Pantheon, 1977.
Mellencamp, Patricia. *A Fine Romance . . . Five Ages of Film Feminism.* Philadelphia: Temple University Press, 1995.
——. *High Anxiety: Catastrophe, Scandal, Age and Comedy.* Bloomington: Indiana University Press, 1992.
Meluch, R. M. "Traitor." *Women at War.* Ed. Lois McMaster Bujold and Roland J. Green. New York: Tor, 1995. 18–56.
"Men's Department." *New Woman* Nov. 1995: 106–10.
Miller, Frank. *Stan Lee Presents: Elektra, the Complete Saga.* New York: Marvel, 1989.
Miller, Frank, and Dave Gibbons. *Give Me Liberty: An American Dream.* Milwaukie, Ore.: Dark Horse Comics, 1992.
——. *Martha Washington Goes to War.* Milwaukie, Ore.: Dark Horse Comics, 1995.
——. *Martha Washington Stranded in Space.* Milwaukie, Ore.: Dark Horse Comics, 1995.
Milliron, Kerry. *Princess in Peril.* New York: Random House, 1996.
——. *Queen of the Amazons.* New York: Random House, 1996.
Minkowitz, Donna. "Xena: She's Big, Tall, Strong—and Popular." *Ms.* July 1996: 74–77.
Modleski, Tania. *Loving with a Vengeance: Mass-Produced Fantasies for Women.* Hamden: Archon Books, 1982.
Moore, Alan, and Dave Gibbons. *Watchmen.* New York: D.C. Comics, 1986.
Morrison, Mark. "She's Back." *US* Aug. 1991: 70–73.
Mortal Kombat. Dir. Paul Anderson. Perf. Bridgette Wilson, Robin Shou, and Linden Ashby. Videocassette. New Line Home Video, 1995.
Mueller, Andrew. "Film: *Tank Girl.*" *Melody Maker* 24 June 1995: 43.
Mukerji, Chandra, and Michael Schudson, eds. *Rethinking Popular Culture: Contemporary Perspectives in Cultural Studies.* Berkeley: University of California Press, 1991.
"Mulgrew." *Off Our Backs* Mar. 1995: 4.
Mulvey, Laura. "Visual Pleasure and Narrative Cinema." *Screen* 16.3 (1975): 6–18.
Mumford, Laura Stempel. *Love and Ideology in the Afternoon: Soap Opera, Women, and Television Genre.* Bloomington: Indiana University Press, 1995.
Mundy, Chris. "David Duchovny and Gillian Anderson." *US* May 1997: 44+.
Murphy, Kathleen. "The Last Temptation of Sigourney Weaver." *Film Comment* 28.4 (1992): 17–20.
Murray, Sonia. "Bad Babes at the Box Office." *Atlanta Journal-Constitution* 6 Nov. 1996: E1.
"Mush Mother." *U.S. News and World Report* 28 Mar. 1988: 11.
"My Style." *Essence* Nov. 1996: 142.
Neale, Steve. "Masculinity as Spectacle: Reflections on Men and Mainstream Cinema." *Screen* 24.6 (1983): 2–16.
Neibaur, James L. *Tough Guy: The American Movie Macho.* Jefferson: McFarland, 1989.
Nemesis 2: Nebula. Dir. Albert Pyun. Perf. Sue Price. Videocassette. WarnerVision Films, 1995.

Nericcio, William Anthony. "Artif(r)acture: Virulent Pictures, Graphic Narrative and the Ideology of the Visual." *Mosaic* 28.4 (1995): 79–109.

Never Say Never Again. Dir. Irvin Kershner. Perf. Sean Connery, Barbara Carrera. 1983. Videocassette. Warner Home Video, 1995.

Newton, Esther. "The Mythic Mannish Lesbian: Radclyffe Hall and the New Woman." *Signs* 9 (1984): 558–75.

Newton, Judith. "Feminism and Anxiety in *Alien*." *Alien Zone: Cultural Theory and Contemporary Science Fiction Cinema*. Ed. Annette Kuhn. New York: Verso, 1990. 82–87.

Nochimson, Martha. *No End to Her: Soap Opera and the Female Subject*. Berkeley: University of California Press, 1992.

No Contest. Dir. Paul Lynch. Perf. Shannon Tweed. Norstar Productions, 1994.

Nollinger, Mark. "The David Duchovny X-perience." *TV Guide* 21 Dec. 1996: 18+.

——. "Twenty Things You Need to Know About *The X-Files*." *TV Guide* 6 Apr. 1996: 18+.

Novak, Ralph. "Picks & Pans: *The Blood of Heroes*." *People Weekly* 12 Mar. 1990: 22–23.

——. "Picks & Pans: *Tank Girl*." *People Weekly* 17 Apr. 1995: 64.

Nye, Russel. *The Unembarrassed Muse: The Popular Arts in America*. New York: Dial, 1970.

"The Objects of Beauty." *US* 16 May 1991: 40+.

O'Connor, John J. "Syndication Gravy Train Adds Cars." *New York Times* 12 Sept. 1995: C18.

On Deadly Ground. Dir. Steven Seagal. Perf. Steven Seagal. 1994. Videocassette. Warner Brothers, 1994.

Ostrow, Joanne. "It's No Wonder This Woman Has Become Xena: Worldwide Cult Queen." *Denver Post* 20 Nov. 1996: G1.

Page, Myra. *Daughter of the Hills: A Woman's Part in the Coal Miners' Struggle*. 1950. New York: Feminist, 1986.

"Pale Fire." *Vogue* Apr. 1996: 312–17.

Parish, James Robert. *The Tough Guys*. New Rochelle: Arlington House, 1976.

Pask, Kevin. "Cyborg Economies: Desire and Labor in the *Terminator* Films." Postmodern Apocalypse: Theory and Cultural Practice at the End. Ed. Richard Dellamora. Philadelphia: University of Pennsylvania Press, 1995. 182–98.

Peirce, Kate. "A Feminist Theoretical Perspective on the Socialization of Teenage Girls Through *Seventeen* Magazine." *Sex Roles* 23.9–10 (1990): 491–500.

Penley, Constance. "Time Travel, Primal Scene, and the Critical Dystopia." *Close Encounters: Film, Feminism, and Science Fiction*. Ed. Constance Penley et al. Minneapolis: University of Minnesota Press, 1991. 63–80.

Penley, Constance, et al., eds. *Close Encounters: Film, Feminism, and Science Fiction*. Minneapolis: University of Minnesota Press, 1991.

Petrucelli, Alan W. "On Our Cover." *Working Mother* Sept. 1995: 24–28.

Phillips, Mark, and Frank Garcia. *Science Fiction Television Series: Episode Guides*. Jefferson: McFarland, 1996.

Podhoretz, John. "The Good, the Bad and the Funny." *Insight* 22 July 1991: 41.

Polsgrove, Carol. "Feminine and Tough." *Progressive* Mar. 1988: 34.

Pond, Steve. "21st Century Fox." *US* Apr. 1995: 27+.

——. "Secret Agent Man." *US* May 1995: 80+.

Portis, Charles. *True Grit*. New York: Simon and Schuster, 1968.

Prescott, Peter S. "The Comic Book (Gulp!) Grows Up." *Newsweek* 18 Jan. 1988: 70–71.

Press, Andrea L. *Women Watching Television: Gender, Class, and Generation in the American Television Experience.* Philadelphia: University of Pennsylvania Press, 1991.
"Pretty, Powerful: The New Sexy Is Strong." *Mademoiselle* Mar. 1991: 168–71.
"Pretty Tough." *Seventeen* May 1988: 168–71.
Price, Richard. "Madonna Flexes Her Muscles." *Ladies' Home Journal* Nov. 1990: 198+.
Price, Simon. "Tape That: 'The X-Files.' " *Melody Maker* 2 Sept. 1995: 13.
Prizzi's Honor. 1985. Dir. John Huston. Perf. Jack Nicholson, Kathleen Turner, Anjelica Huston. Videocassette. Summa Video, 1995.
The Professional. Dir. Luc Besson. Perf. Natalie Portman and Jean Reno. Columbia Pictures, 1994.
The Quick and the Dead. Dir. Sam Raimi. Perf. Sharon Stone. 1995. Videocassette. Columbia Tristar Home Video, 1995.
Rabinowitz, Paula. *Labor and Desire: Women's Revolutionary Fiction in Depression America.* Chapel Hill: University of North Carolina Press, 1991.
Rabkin, Eric S., Martin H. Greenberg, and Joseph D. Olander, eds. *The End of the World.* Carbondale: Southern Illinois University Press, 1983.
Radway, Janice A. *Reading the Romance: Women, Patriarchy, and Popular Literature.* Chapel Hill: University of North Carolina Press, 1984.
Rafferty, Terrence. "The Current Cinema: Moth and Flame." *New Yorker* 25 Feb. 1991: 87–89.
Rapping, Elayne. *Media-tions: Forays into the Culture and Gender Wars.* Boston: South End Press, 1994.
Red Sonja. Dir. Richard Fleischer. Perf. Arnold Schwarzenegger and Brigitte Nielsen. 1985. Videocassette. CBS/Fox Video, 1986.
Rehn, Rod. *The Bionic FAQ.* Internet. May 10, 1996.
Reidelbach, Maria. *Completely Mad: A History of the Comic Book and Magazine.* Boston: Little, Brown, 1991.
Rensin, David. "Lucy Lawless: The Woman Behind the Warrior." *TV Guide* 3 May 1997: 19+.
The Return of Superman. New York: D.C. Comics, 1993.
Rhodes, Molly Rae. "Doctoring Culture: Literary Intellectuals, Psychology and Mass Culture in the Twentieth-Century United States." Ph.D. diss., University of California, San Diego, 1997.
Rich, Adrienne. "Compulsory Heterosexuality and Lesbian Existence." *Adrienne Rich's Poetry and Prose.* Ed. Barbara C. Gelpi and Albert Gelpi. New York: Norton, 1993. 203–24.
Rich, B. Ruby. "Nobody's Handmaid." *Sight and Sound* 1.8 (1991): 6–10.
Richmond, Peter. "Mything Links." *TV Guide* 9 Nov. 1996: 35–39.
Roberts, Robin. "Adoptive Versus Biological Mothering in *Aliens.*" *Extrapolation* 30.4 (1989): 353–63.
——. *A New Species: Gender and Science in Science Fiction.* Urbana: University of Illinois Press, 1993.
Robbins, Trina. *The Great Women Super Heroes.* Northampton: Kitchen Sink Press, 1996.
Robinson, Douglas. *American Apocalypses: The Image of the End of the World in American Literature.* Baltimore: Johns Hopkins University Press, 1985.
Robinson, Lillian S. "Looking for Wonder Woman." *Artforum* 27.10 (1989): 100–103.
Rogers, Dave. *The Avengers.* London: ITV Books, 1983.

——. *The Avengers Anew.* London: Michael Joseph, 1985.
——. *The Complete Avengers.* New York: St. Martin's, 1989.
Romeo Is Bleeding. Dir. Peter Medak. Perf. Gary Oldman and Lena Olin. 1993. Videocassette. Polygram Video, 1994.
Romney, Jonathan. "Tanked Up on Attitude." *New Statesman and Society* 8.358 (23 June 1995): 35.
Rose, Lloyd. "Comic Books for Grown-Ups." *Atlantic Monthly* Aug. 1986: 77–80.
Ross, Andrew. *No Respect: Intellectuals and Popular Culture.* New York: Routledge, 1989.
Ross, Jonathan. "Talking with Aliens." *Sight and Sound* 5.6 (1995): 61.
"Runway." *Cosmopolitan* Sept. 1996: 213–25.
Rushing, Janice Hocker. "Evolution of 'The New Frontier' in *Alien* and *Aliens:* Patriarchal Co-optation of the Feminine Archetype." *Quarterly Journal of Speech* 75.1 (1989): 1–24.
Russ, Joanna. *The Female Man.* Boston: Beacon, 1975.
——. *To Write Like a Woman: Essays in Feminism and Science Fiction.* Bloomington: Indiana University Press, 1995.
Sabin, Roger. *Adult Comics: An Introduction.* London: Routledge, 1993.
Sackett, Susan. *Prime-Time Hits: Television's Most Popular Network Programs.* New York: Billboard Books, 1993.
Savage, William W., Jr. *Comic Books and America, 1945–1954.* Norman: University of Oklahoma Press, 1990.
Sawyer, Corinne Holt. "Men in Skirts and Women in Trousers, from Achilles to Victoria Grant: One Explanation of a Comedic Paradox." *Journal of Popular Culture* 21.2 (1987): 1–16.
Scanlon, Jennifer. *Inarticulate Longings: The Ladies' Home Journal, Gender, and the Promises of Consumer Culture.* New York: Routledge, 1995.
Schaefer, Jack. *Shane.* Boston: Houghton Mifflin, 1949.
Schindler, Rick, and Stephanie Williams. "An X-Files Encyclopedia from A to X." *TV Guide* 17 May 1997: 20+.
Schmetzer, Uli. "Dagger Lady: Tough as Steel, but Still a Lady." *Chicago Tribune* 3 May 1993: 6.
Schmitt, Ronald. "Deconstructive Comics." *Journal of Popular Culture* 25.4 (1992): 153–61.
Schneider, Karen S. "Xena-Phile." *People Weekly* 8 Apr. 1996: 93–94.
Schnurnberger, Lynn. "Should Angels Fear to Retread?" *Glamour* Sept. 1988: 61.
Schruers, Fred. "A Kind of Redemption." *Premiere* Mar. 1991: 50–57.
Scott, Melissa. *Dreamships.* New York: Doherty, 1992.
Scott, Tony. "Reviews: The X-Files." *Variety* 13 Sept. 1993: 36.
Scovell, Nell. "Leather Perfect." *Mademoiselle* Nov. 1993: 94–96.
See, Carolyn. " 'I'm Not the Difficult One.' " *TV Guide* 18–24 Feb. 1978: 26+.
Segell, Michael. "What's Driving Miss Jodie?" *Redbook* Nov. 1991: 76+.
Sennett, Richard. *Authority.* New York: Knopf, 1980.
Serial Mom. Dir. John Waters. Perf. Kathleen Turner, Sam Waterston, Ricki Lake, Matthew Lillard, and Mary Jo Catlett. 1994.
Shapiro, Laura. "Women Who Kill Too Much." *Newsweek* 17 June 1991: 63.
Sharrett, Christopher, ed. *Crisis Cinema: The Apocalyptic Idea in Postmodern Narrative Film.* Washington, D.C.: Maisonneuve Press, 1993.
Shattuc, Jane M. *The Talking Cure: TV Talk Shows and Women.* New York: Routledge, 1997.
Shaw, Peter. "The Tough Guy Intellectual." *Critical Quarterly* 3 (1966): 13–28.

Shindler, Merrill. "Short Takes: *Blood of Heroes.*" *Los Angeles Magazine* Apr. 1990: 183.
The Silence of the Lambs. Dir. Jonathan Demme. Perf. Jodie Foster and Anthony Hopkins. 1991. Videocassette. Orion Home Video, 1991.
Silverman, Kaja. "Fragments of a Fashionable Discourse." *Studies in Entertainment: Critical Approaches to Mass Culture.* Ed. Tania Modleski. Bloomington: Indiana University Press, 1986. 139–52.
Silverthorne, Jeanne. "The Cave." *Artforum* 29.7 (1991): 18–20.
Simon, John. "Horror, Domestic and Imported." *National Review* 29 Apr. 1991: 55–58.
Sinclair, Upton. *The Jungle.* 1906. Urbana: University of Illinois Press, 1988.
Skow, John. "Here's One Musher Who Is No Lazy Susan." *Sports Illustrated* 15 Feb. 1988: 14+.
Slattery, Dennis Patrick. "Demeter-Persephone and the *Alien*(s) Cultural Body." *New Orleans Review* 19.1 (1992): 30–35.
Slotkin, Richard. *Gunfighter Nation: The Myth of the Frontier in Twentieth-Century America.* New York: Atheneum, 1992.
Smedley, Agnes. *Daughter of Earth.* 1929. New York: Feminist, 1973.
Smith, David Alexander. *In the Cube: A Novel of Future Boston.* New York: Doherty, 1993.
Sobchack, Vivian. *Screening Space: The American Science Fiction Film.* New York: Ungar, 1986.
Space: Above and Beyond. Fox Television.
Sparks, Richard. "Masculinity and Heroism in the Hollywood 'Blockbuster': The Culture Industry and Contemporary Images of Crime and Law Enforcement." *British Journal of Criminology* 36.3 (1996): 348–60.
Spelling, Aaron. "On the Pitfalls of Creating Angels and the Threat of Dreams." *People Weekly* Summer 1989: 138–39.
Spiegelman, Art. *Maus.* 1971. New York: Pantheon Books, 1986.
——. *Maus II.* 1986. New York: Pantheon Books, 1991.
Spigel, Lynn. *Make Room for TV: Television and the Family Ideal in Postwar America.* Chicago: University of Chicago Press, 1992.
Spigel, Lynn, and Denise Mann, eds. *Private Screenings: Television and the Female Consumer.* Minneapolis: University of Minnesota Press, 1992.
Sochen, Jane. *Enduring Values: Women in Popular Culture.* New York: Praeger, 1987.
Solomon, Alisa. "Not Just a Passing Fancy: Notes on Butch." *Theater* 24.2 (1993): 35–46.
Staiger, Janet. "Taboos and Totems: Cultural Meanings of *The Silence of the Lambs.*" *Film Theory Goes to the Movies.* Ed. Jim Collins, Hilary Radner, and Ava Preacher Collins. New York: Routledge, 1993. 142–54.
"Stay Cool, Girl." *Mademoiselle* Mar. 1995: 158–65.
Steele, Valerie. "Clothing and Sexuality." *Men and Women: Dressing the Part.* Ed. Claudia Brush Kidwell and Valerie Steele. Washington, D.C.: Smithsonian Institution Press, 1989. 42–63.
Sterling, Bruce. *Heavy Weather.* New York: Bantam Books, 1994.
Stewart, Susan. "Xena vs. Hercules." *TV Guide* 20 Jan. 1996: 24–25.
Stockwell, Anne. "Flirting with Xena." *Advocate* 20 Aug. 1996: 81–83.
Street, Rita. "Hercules Lifts Genre." *Variety* 15 Jan. 1996: N16.
Strozier, Charles B. *Apocalypse: On the Psychology of Fundamentalism in America.* Boston: Beacon, 1994.
Sullivan, R. Lee. "Batman in a Bustier." *Forbes* 8 Apr. 1996: 37–38.

Sutton, Terri. "Media Kids: Terri Sutton on Bad-Girl Cartoonists." *Artforum* 30.2 (1991): 22–24.

Swallow, James. "X-aminations." *Starlog* Dec. 1995: 30+.

Swartz, Mimi. "Aaron Spelling." *Texas Monthly* Sept. 1994: 114+.

Szebin, Frederick C. "Lucy Lawless, Xena: Warrior Princess." *Femme Fatales* Jan. 1996: 46+.

Szirak, Candice. "An Intense Drive." *Women's Sports and Fitness* Mar. 1989: 66–67.

"Tailor Maid." *Vanity Fair* July 1984: 68–75.

Tank Girl. Dir. Rachel Talalay. Perf. Lori Petty. United Artists, 1995.

Taplin, Ian M. "Why We Need Heroes to Be Heroic." *Journal of Popular Culture* 22.2 (1988): 133–42.

Tasker, Yvonne. *Spectacular Bodies: Gender, Genre and the Action Cinema.* London: Routledge, 1993.

Taubin, Amy. "Invading Bodies: *Aliens 3* and the Trilogy." *Sight and Sound* 2.3 (1992): 8–10.

"Television's Top 25 Stars." *People Weekly* Summer 1989: 60–61.

Telotte, J. P. "*The Terminator, Terminator 2,* and the Exposed Body." *Journal of Popular Film and Television* 20.2 (1992): 26–34.

The Terminator. Dir. James A. Cameron. Perf. Linda Hamilton and Arnold Schwarzenegger. 1984. Videocassette. HBO Cannon Video, 1985.

Terminator 2: Judgment Day. Dir. James A. Cameron. Perf. Linda Hamilton and Arnold Schwarzenegger. 1991. Videocassette. Carolco Pictures, 1991.

Thelma & Louise. Dir. Ridley Scott. Perf. Geena Davis and Susan Sarandon. Metro-Goldwyn-Mayer, 1991.

Thomas, Karen. "Female Roles Are Packing a New Punch." *USA Today* 19 June 1992: D1–D2.

Thompson, Anne. "The Ten Most Powerful Women in Showbiz." *Glamour* Jan. 1995: 114–15.

Thrasher, Frederic M. "The Comics and Delinquency: Cause or Scapegoat?" *Journal of Educational Sociology* 23 (1949): 195–205.

Tiger, Virginia. "Alice and Charlie and Vida and Sophy—A Terrorist's Work Is Never Done." *New York Times Book Review* 10 Nov. 1985: 11.

Tobenkin, David. "Hercules Muscles in on Competition." *Broadcasting and Cable* 20 Feb. 1995: 15.

——. "MCA Hopes Xena Has Strength of Hercules." *Broadcasting and Cable* 8 May 1995: 54.

——. "MCA Muscles in on Action Hours." *Broadcasting and Cable* 21 Aug. 1995: 25–26.

To Be or Not To Be—Just Be Calvin Klein. Advertisement. *Vogue* (Sept. 1996): 220–28.

Toepfer, Susan. "Denise Crosby, Granddaughter of Bing, Beams Down from *Star Trek* for Some New Enterprise." *People Weekly* 2 May 1988: 57+.

"Tough." *Oxford English Dictionary.* 2nd ed. 1989.

Trebay, Guy. "A Voice of Her Own." *Harper's Bazaar* Jan. 1995: 126–29.

Trebbe, Ann. "Beauty and the Bicep." *USA Today* 5 July 1991: D1.

Turan, Kenneth. "He *Said* He'd Be Back." *Los Angeles Times* 3 July 1991: F1+.

"TV's Super Women." *Time* 22 Nov. 1976: 67–71.

Unsworth, Cathi. "Suave Central." *Melody Maker* 9 July 1994: 41.

Updike, Edith Hill. "'*X-Files*' Supernatural Hold on Japan." *Business Week* 27 Nov. 1995: 104.

Van de Walle, Mark. "Fear and Present Danger." *Artforum* 33.9 (1995): 18.

Van Zoonen, Liesbet. "Feminist Perspectives on the Media." *Mass Media and Society.* Ed. James Curran and Michael Gurevitch. New York: Arnold, 1991. 33–54.
Varley, John. *Titan.* New York: Berkley, 1979.
A View to a Kill. Dir. John Glen. Perf. Roger Moore, Tanya Roberts, Grace Jones. 1985. Videocassette. MGM/UA Home Video, 1992.
Wagar, W. Warren. *Terminal Visions: The Literature of Last Things.* Bloomington: Indiana University Press, 1982.
Wambsgans, Polly. "Tough Player Proves Football Is a Girl's Game." *Times-Picayune* 11 Oct. 1990: 1+.
Watts, Carol. "From Looking to Coveting: The 'American Girl' in *The Silence of the Lambs.*" *Women: A Cultural Review* 4.1 (1993): 63–77.
Weber, Bruce. "Sigourney Weaver in Alien Terrain . . . Yet Again." *New York Times* 17 May 1992, sec. 2: 15+.
Weinstein, Steve. "Forget 'Baywatch': The Action's With 'Hercules,' 'Xena.' " *Los Angeles Times* 17 Feb. 1996, sec. F: 1+.
Wertham, Fredric. *Seduction of the Innocent.* New York: Rinehart, 1954.
"What's New in Suits." *Essence* Sept. 1996: 114.
Wheeler, Edward L. *Deadwood Dick on Deck; or, Calamity Jane, the Heroine of Whoop-Up.* New York: Beadle's, 1885.
Wheelwright, Julie. *Amazons and Military Maids: Women Who Dressed as Men in the Pursuit of Life, Liberty, and Happiness.* London: Pandora, 1989.
"Where's Charlie?" *People Weekly* 19 June 1995: 68.
"White-Collar Cool." *Mademoiselle* Oct. 1988: 216–19.
White, Mimi. "Ideological Analysis and Television." In Allen, ed., *Channels of Discourse,* 134–71.
Whitney, Dwight. "Tigress or Pussycat?" *TV Guide* 18 Mar. 1978: 11+.
Wilcox, Rhonda V. "Shifting Roles and Synthetic Women in *Star Trek: The Next Generation.*" *Studies in Popular Culture* 13.2 (1991): 53–65.
Wild, David. "Television: 'X'-ploitation." *Rolling Stone* 30 Nov. 1995: 79.
Wilkinson, Rupert. *American Tough: The Tough-Guy Tradition and American Character.* Westport: Greenwood, 1984.
Williamson, Judith. *Consuming Passions: The Dynamics of Popular Culture.* London: Marion Boyars, 1986.
——. *Decoding Advertisements: Ideology and Meaning in Advertising.* London: Marion Boyars, 1978.
Willis, Susan. *A Primer for Daily Life.* New York: Routledge, 1991.
Winship, Janice. *Inside Women's Magazines.* London: Pandora, 1987.
Wister, Owen. *The Virginian.* New York: Grosset and Dunlap, 1902.
Wolf, Naomi. *The Beauty Myth: How Images of Beauty Are Used Against Women.* New York: Morrow, 1991.
Wolmark, Jenny. *Aliens and Others: Science Fiction: Feminism and Postmodernism.* Iowa City: University of Iowa Press, 1994.
Woods, Mark. "Youth TV Sizzles." *Variety* 6 Nov. 1995: 57+.
Wright, James. "Tiffany Moss Wants to Play in Urban Coalition." *Afro-American* 23 July 1994: A1–A2.
"Writers on the *Lamb.*" *Village Voice* 5 Mar. 1991: 49+.
Yezierska, Anzia. "Soap and Water." *How I Found America: Collected Stories of Anzia Yezierska.* New York: Persea Books, 1991. 71–77.
Young, Elizabeth. "*The Silence of the Lambs* and the Flaying of Feminist Theory." *Camera Obscura* 27 (Sept. 1991): 5–35.

Young, Thomas. "Are Comic Book Super-Heroes Sexist?" *Sociology and Social Research* 75.4 (1991): 218.

Young, Tracy. "*Vogue* Arts." *Vogue* Feb. 1991: 210+.

Zamora, Lois Parkinson. *Writing the Apocalypse: Historical Vision in Contemporary U.S. and Latin American Fiction.* New York: Cambridge University Press, 1989.

"Zip! The Motorcycle Jacket—Truly Cool Again." *Mademoiselle* Nov. 1988: 220–25.

Zwinger, Lynda. "Blood Relations: Feminist Theory Meets the Uncanny Alien Bug Mother." *Hypatia* 7.2 (1992): 74–90.

Acknowledgments

For a lengthy project such as this, there are always far more people to thank than one can mention in a brief acknowledgments section. I would, however, like to thank some people whose input has been central to the development of this book. Kathryn Burton, Ruth Ebelke, Faye Parker Flavin, Amy Mason, Michele Lloyd, and Diana Royer all read drafts of my entire book, or chapters of it, before its completion and provided insightful criticism that helped to enrich my thinking about the many forms that toughness can take for women. Faye and Michele's input deserves special acknowledgment, because they read the entire work and offered criticism that was perceptive and rigorous.

A number of scholars did not read my book before publication but helped to contribute to its theoretical underpinnings. Kathryn Shevelow deserves appreciation for her continued encouragement and advice for years after she was my dissertation advisor; her influence is felt throughout this book. My scholarship on the intersections between popular culture and the construction of gendered identities also has been influenced by such scholars as Susan Douglas, Stuart Ewen, John Fiske, Judith Halberstam, Dick Hebdige, George Lipsitz, Patricia Mellencamp, Tania Modleski, Andrea L. Press, Janice A. Radway, and Susan Willis—all of whom showed me the importance of thinking seriously about popular culture and how it shapes society.

I also wish to acknowledge the friends who offered me emotional support as I tracked down yet another obscure comic book or an episode of *Charlie's Angels:* Alice Adams, Martina Barash, Carolyn Butler Palmer, Jerry Griswold, Kate Johnson, Debra Mandel, Gillian O'Driscoll, Eric Palmer, Cindy Reuther, Judith Russo, and Wendy W. Walters. In addition, many more of my students than I can possibly name deserve my appreciation, but Samuel Gladden, Julie Hucke, Mary King, Andrew Niemann, Carrie Stevens, and Kellie Sucher should be singled out for their intellectual enthusiasm. A special thanks goes to my colleagues at Miami University, particularly Kathryn Burton, Barry Chabot, John Krafft, Sharon Krafft, Robert Martin, Allison McCormack, Diana Royer, and Dianne F. Sadoff, who have always been supportive about this project. I appreciate the unstinting efforts of the Miami University library staff, especially Christa Branson, Megan Schenk, and Rebecca Zartner, in tracking down the sources, often difficult to locate, that I required to write this book. In addition, Patricia Smith at the University of Pennsylvania Press could not be improved as a thoughtful and conscientious editor; I appreciate all her efforts and those of the others at the Press, including Noreen O'Connor and Susan Worley, who helped so much with this project. I especially would like to thank the two anonymous readers for the Press whose criticism of my book was astute and rigorous.

Finally, I would like to thank my twin sister, father, and especially my beloved mother, Ruth Ebelke (1920–1998), who died before this book could be published. Their support, as always, meant a great deal to me as I worked on *Tough Girls*. I can never sufficiently express my gratitude to them for all that they have done.

Index